NO JOURNEY'S END

A TRUE LOVE STORY

MY TRAGIC
ROMANCE WITH
EX-MANSON GIRL
LESLIE VAN HOUTEN

PETER CHIARAMONTE

PALE INK PRESS

TORONTO | MONTREAL

www.paleink.press

ISBN: 0986420204
ISBN-13: 978-0986420207

Produced by Publish Pros | www.publishpros.com

This is a true story based on actual persons and real events.
The names of some secondary characters have been changed, several of
whom are, in fact, composites.

DEDICATION

For my daughter, Mia Anna, and son,
Dylan Thomas,

and

For the memories of my mother, Anna Marie, and
son, Michael Gary

CONTENTS

PROLOGUE

Monrovia, California, Independence Day, 1978. We had been celebrating a revolutionary declaration of freedom and other noble causes. Complete with a modest, but earnest, fireworks display put on by friends and neighbors of her brother David Van Houten. Filled with red, white, and blue bursts of light against a night sky and the charred odor of gun smoke.

Leslie and I spent all day and half the night at a family picnic. We had a busy week planned, so we didn't stay late. Since Leslie's mother, Jane, was staying overnight at a neighbor's, we had her place in Monterey Park to ourselves for the rest of the night.

In front of the house on Sefton Avenue, Les stepped out of our old, teal-blue British MGB convertible and asked me, "Will we have time to stop by Judy's and pick up more of my things tomorrow?"

"We can get some of that on the way back from Glendale," I said. "Or we can grab it on Sunday. You and David can take the van to Isla Vista. I'll break the bike in on my own and follow you up there."

"Or you can lead the way," she said. "So, you've made up your mind, then?"

"That's what we'll do first thing tomorrow. You keep the MGB for now, and I'll buy a new motorcycle. Unless you and one of your beaus have made other plans for what to do with the money?"

"Don't be smart," Leslie said. "Just as long as it's something we *need*, not just something you want to play with. We have to be prudent, mister."

Placing a gentle kiss over her heart, I asked, "How prudent is that?"

* * *

The sun was already up when I opened my eyes. The air was warm and dry, and the skies were clear and unclouded. Except for the smog. Morning birds were making a racket. I could hear shower taps running and heard Leslie humming some old R&B song.

After we stepped out of the tub, I dried Leslie off first with one of her mom's thick cotton towels. Then used the same one on myself while she started to dress. Leslie put on a tight, bright, summer-print dress and canvas sneakers. I put on jeans and a long-sleeved sweatshirt. Laced up my old leather Pumas, no socks.

"If we do bring a bike home today, honey, you'll have to change into something rougher and tougher. Leather and spurs ought to do it."

"Most of my things are still at Judy's or in suitcases I left at Linda's.... What kind of spurs are we talkin' about, fella?"

Spinning her by the hips and wrapping both arms around her, I besieged the nape of her neck and shoulders with kisses. "This is how I want you to hold onto me when you're in the saddle behind me, okay?"

"Whatever you say," she said softly. "I'll make tea while you shave. Just *look* how chafed my chin is, you monster."

She covered all but her eyes and nose with her hands, asking no one in particular, "Where does my mom keep the cold cream?"

When we were done clearing up, I came outside to the patio, where Leslie was casually smoking a cigarette and reading about herself in an old *Los Angeles Times*.

"Time to get this show on the road," I said, clapping my hands.

Leslie locked up the house, and we drove straight through the heart of LA to Glendale. It took us nearly an hour in freeway traffic. Once we arrived at the motorcycle shop, Leslie put her hand on my forearm and tried one last time to appeal to my conscience.

"We don't need a lot of *things*, Peter. You know that."

"Bikes are cheaper to run," I said, sensing my bluff might be working.

Pointing over her shoulder at two rows of Italian motorcycles lined up in the showroom, I pleaded, "Come on, darlin', let's straddle one of those awful beasts and go for a surf on the highway."

"Not in this dress, I'm not," Leslie said. At least now she was smiling again.

Leslie needed to check in with Dante, her bondsman, every three to four hours during the jury's deliberations and asked the salesman if she could use his telephone.

The shop had one stunning gray and blue, brand-spanking-new Ducati 900 SuperSport on the floor. Exactly like my brother Mike's Desmo. But it was way out of our price range. There were, however, a few new and used Benellis and Guzzis all spiffed up and polished, just rarin' to go. Two were Moto Guzzi 850 Le Mans, one of which I thought we might afford with a loan. She was fire-engine red and had custom pearl-white trim on the fuel tank and fairing.

I climbed into the saddle of the red Le Mans, which felt quite unlike any motorbike I was used to. I couldn't wait to take her for a spin—anxious to feel how she handled at speed.

"Get off the phone, Leslie, will ya?" I said, impatient to start showing off.

The salesman kept smiling. Eager to help me push the bike out to the curb for a test ride. He could see I was a serious buyer. I was just about to switch on the engine when—looking ashen and pale—Leslie came striding toward us.

"We gotta go" was all she needed to say.

The verdict had finally been decided.

OTHER WORLDS

The morning this journey began, I'd woken up feeling guilty and sore. No doubt from the residual effects of some far-reaching intemperance gone wrong the night before. The human body has no reason to lie to itself. Whatever flesh of the devils I'd taken, it only seemed just that I suffer. Call it the price of tuition. Some drugs I took to escape; others I took to explore.

It was Christmas break, 1976, and winter was just getting started. The University of Toronto, where I worked while going to teachers' college, was closed for the holidays. Having graduated from St. Michael's College with a BA in philosophy two years earlier, I'd gone to work for the University of Toronto Track Club as an assistant to National Coach Andy Higgins.

Why philosophy? Lots of good reasons. Chief among them had to do with becoming whoever I choose. Not like law school— my poor second choice—where you're largely trained to become what somebody else expects you to be. I'd rather become who I want to be. Come hell or high tides, *amor fati*.

I figured, if all else failed, I could always go kicking and screaming into teaching school as a backup. A bad faith default strategy if ever there was one. For now, I was exploring the idea of coaching as a profession while at the same time working toward secondary school teaching certificates in English lit and physical education. Work on the family farm was no longer an option.

Truth is, my dream ever since I was fifteen was to have the letters "PhD" duly noted after my name. *With all the rights and privileges thereto pertaining.* More than anything else, I wanted to become a full-fledged academic. Dream on, dream on, Herr Doctor Professor. You can't just *rule* that into being.

In the meantime, I enjoyed being one of the gladiators who teaches the gladiators to become gladiators. Working with U of T's Head Athletics Coach Andy Higgins and School of Physical and Health Education Professor Bruce Kidd. Coaching high-caliber track and field athletes to compete at regional, national, and international events like the Olympics.

While I waited for my fate to unfold, I got by on a modest family allowance. Plus, the honorarium I scraped together as grad assistant to Andy and Bruce. I had thought I was pretty sure of what, where, and who I wanted to be. Only which path to take wasn't so obvious.

Andy said to meet him at his office in Hart House around 8:30 a.m. to discuss plans for the upcoming months' strength training protocols. We had obligations later that day to work with some of the sprinters and jumpers off-campus at the indoor track inside the Princes' Gates at the Canadian National Exhibition.

My apartment in the Annex on Madison Avenue was a mile north of the back campus. I drank a hot mug of Ovaltine, downed three aspirin, and jogged to the campus in less than six minutes. All without breaking a sweat.

Hart House is at the heart of the downtown University of Toronto St. George campus. It's the student activity center for music, theater arts, and athletics. The building itself is a gothic-collegiate structure built around an interior quadrangle, where some of us hippies played touch football in all weathers at odd hours.

Inside its stone, vaulted ceilings and stained-glass windows, there's a stunning art deco swimming pool and a suspended indoor running track, with banking as steep as the Autodromo Monza once was. Gorgeous but impractical for world-class athletes to train on.

The varsity coaches' offices were all on the second floor overlooking the back campus and Morrison Hall. My late start made me last. I could hear laughter and chatter coming from inside as I stepped out of the stairwell, stomping the slush off my Adidas.

There were three young gentlemen talking and drinking house coffee out of yesterday's Tim Hortons cups. I saluted my comrades and sat down at my lone cluttered desk in the corner. Andy Higgins pointed to which cup was mine, and I helped myself to half the remaining croissant.

With the exception of yours truly, everyone else in the room was an experienced Olympian. My other two friends were pole-vaulter Bruce Simpson and sprinter Jim "Buck" Buchanan. Bruce and I had been twin running backs for the Agincourt Lancers football team in the fall of 1968. The year before, Bruce went away on a full ride to vault for the UCLA Bruins, and I went off on a combined academic-athletic scholarship to study and play for The Ohio University Bobcats in 1969.

The men were discussing the previous spring training camp we'd held in Long Beach, California, two months prior to Bruce and Buck competing at the Games of the XXI Olympiad in Montreal. Andy was one of our national coaches, and I tagged along to assist him. Mostly I ran or tossed back the javelin and discus for decathlete Gordie Stewart and put the bar back up on the standards for Olympic high jump finalist Louise Walker whenever she knocked it down.

Our Canadian Olympic track and field training camp that year had been headquartered at the Cal State Long Beach Athletic Center the whole month of May. The place where we stayed was called the Golden Sails Hotel. On the surface, this sounded majestic.

"They named the area 'Palm Beach,' right?" Buck was asking. "I remember our balcony held a spectacular view of highways and parking lots."

"Beside an endless landscape of oil pumps and refineries," Andy added. Turning to me, he said, "We've been discussing plans for the spring."

"LA again maybe," Bruce said. "I don't think we want to go back to Long Beach, though. I'd prefer Malibu or Santa Barbara." I agreed, then wandered back into a daydream, recalling, not fondly, a severe ankle sprain I suffered the first week we were in Long Beach and cringing. But then, that gratefully triggered another extrasensory event that occurred six months earlier. Leading my mind back to an old girlfriend, Tricia, who drove down from Santa Monica to care for me while my ankle mended.

Patricia Woodbridge was a beautiful twenty-year-old woman when I first met her in the summer of 1971. It happened at UCLA at a comfy three-bedroom, second-floor walk-up near the corner of Ophir Drive, where I was visiting with mutual friends of Bruce Simpson. Looking for another roommate to start the new academic year, my friends posted ads on campus bulletin boards before they split to train and compete in Europe.

My knees buckled when I opened the door and saw her standing there. We both stood motionless while the pendulum slowed, approaching a state of provisional rest. The usual causal boy-girl relationship seemed suspended. Smiling back at me the way that she did—I guessed it was some random fluctuation in the cosmos that rendered me speechless.

"I'm here about the apartment," she said. I remained dumbfounded.

Trish had one green eye and one speckled brown. Her long, straight hair was strawberry-blonde, and her legs looked interminably long. What else can I tell you? We remained "casual agents" for years starting that summer night. Kind of an emblem for how, up to that point, I'd always felt about California girls in general.

Five years later, during the training camp in Long Beach in May '76—after I'd torn every unscarred blood vessel I still had left in my left ankle—Trish, who was a registered nurse, took time off work to help me recover. She prepared fresh fruit and healthy, yummy salads, for one thing. Bathed me in hot tubs of Epsom salts and brought me lots of good books and magazines to read while I tanned by the poolside.

In the evenings, at either her place in Santa Monica or my hotel, we got high on some excellent hash and sparkling wine, listened to the music of our times, and cuddled up under warm blankets where we purred like a couple of panthers.

The memory of this had led my mind's eye astray into a kind of tableau déja vu—when all of a sudden, everyone's laughter brought my free-floating consciousness back to Andy's office in real-time.

"I'd been going to UCLA for *four* months already," Bruce was saying. "One day, I look up and see the San Gabriel Mountains for the *first* time. I didn't know they were there." (*Laughter*). "The night before, a storm had come through the basin and blew all the smog out to sea. Suddenly, there were mountains!"

Everyone had another sad laugh over his tale of paradise smudged. Bruce and Andy switched subjects. I don't recall what about. What I do recall is Buck leaning in and asking, "Hey, Pete, whatever happened to that girlfriend of yours? The tall redhead in California?"

"What a coincidence. You must be clairvoyant. I was *just* thinking about her myself. You mean 'Trish,' Patricia Woodbridge."

"That's the one. The pretty nurse with the freckles. Heard from her lately?"

"Don't you love it when this sort of thing happens?" I asked him.

"When what sort of thing happens?" Buck grinned. "It's not really so strange. We were talking about the Golden Sails after all. You lucky dog."

I smiled at first, then, thinking things over, I felt my lips curl into a frown.

"Ah, Trish. I don't know. The way we left things wasn't so hot. She told me she felt we used her. You know. Private nurse and free taxi service. Then I dropped her."

"That wasn't polite. But don't let disgrace dampen your spirits. I'm sure you'll be forgiven. She liked you a lot."

"I know who you're talking about," Andy jumped in. "*We* didn't use her, Peter. You did. Speak for yourself. If she's the one I think you're talking about, she was a pest. She got in our way at the track and the hotel. We were there to work, remember?"

Buck intervened to lend me support.

"She did show us around LA," he chimed. "Peter's right. She was a good sport. I think we owe her respect."

"In fact," I added, "it was Trish who took us all to that book-shop you liked so much, Andy. The one in the Westminster Mall."

Andy shrugged and looked out the window. A light snow had started brushing down.

"The one where you were so happy you found a copy of Auden's *A Certain World*," I said. "I remember that clearly. It was the same day Trish gave me the gift of Vincent Bugliosi's book, *Helter Skelter*. About the Manson murders."

Andy looked decidedly bored.

Looking directly at Bruce and Buck, I asked them: "Do you remember when we kept Gord Stewart's rental after he went back to Vancouver? That near-quick Mustang convertible?"

"Right, I remember, of course," Buck said. "We went driving around Bel Air with the top down…to find the place where Sharon Tate was murdered. You had the maps in your book."

The other two were rolling their eyes.

"Let's change the subject," said Andy. You could tell he'd been patient enough.

"If it's blood you want to look at," he said, standing to gather his binders, "let me show you the sink where I cut myself shaving this morning. Gentlemen, I have a meeting to go to with Coach Mach. You all have work to do. I'll see you at the track after lunch."

Looking directly at me, he added, "You want to go with them or wait up so we can talk later?"

"Sure, I'll wait," I said, tossing the empty cups into the trash-can. "I'll be down at the end of the hall in the library. I'd rather work there."

I left with the others and took my schedules and notebooks to my favorite bay window enclave facing College Circle. Watching pedestrians dodge the gauntlet of traffic in the back of Queen's Park. There was a studious-looking coed sitting on one of the ox-blood leather library couches. When she got up to leave, she left pages of yesterday's *Toronto Star* scattered behind her. I gathered them up and tossed the business section and advertisements in the wastebasket.

Then went back to my cubbyhole and read over the rest of the paper.

The second I turned the page to A-13—Tuesday, December 28th, 1976—it felt like my breathing had stopped. Faint echoes of live piano ricocheted their way down the corridor toward me, calling me out. So what if it was just another random coincidence?

Printed above the caption head was: "Ex-Manson girl re-turns to court with new image." Then-and-now photographs of Leslie Van Houten suddenly captivated all but one aspect of my attention. The bass notes on the piano suddenly picked up their weight before ending abruptly.

The image on the left was of Leslie *then*, in 1971, with her head shaved and a scarred "X" freshly carved into her forehead for all the world to see. Pure madness. But the picture on the right was of the ex-Manson girl *now*. More than five years later.

Smartly dressed with dark bangs and hair that hung almost as far as to touch the top of her slender shoulders. Even though she looked understandably weary and worn, I found the picture of the *now* Leslie Van Houten alluring.

The six-paragraph column reported that Ms. Van Houten had entered a plea of "not guilty" for the August 9, 1969 slaying of Leno and Rosemary LaBianca. Her previous conviction for first-degree murder in 1971 had been overturned. The appeals court felt she should never have been tried alongside Charles Manson and his co-conspirators in the first place.

The California Court of Appeals ordered a new trial on the grounds that she hadn't been properly represented the first time. Since Ronald Hughes, her lawyer at the time of the first trial, had died while hiking alone during a flash flood in a desert canyon. During the original proceedings, his replacement Maxwell Keith didn't have adequate time in which to prepare a defense.

A new twist to the story.

I folded the page from the paper, tucked it away in my notebook, and wrote down the name of her lawyer, Maxwell Keith. Hours later, after track practice, Andy tried in vain to have a serious conversation with me about my career plans for coaching. He could see how distracted I was. Whatever he suspected the reasons for this were, I never revealed anything since, up to this time, I still didn't know myself.

I ducked into the Robarts Library on my way home to look up the mailing address of Maxwell S. Keith, attorney-at-law, in the City of Los Angeles Telephone Directory.

When I got back to Madison, I hurriedly brewed a full French press' worth of espresso to help me get started. Eager to dig right back into the copy of Vincent Bugliosi and Curt Gentry's *Helter Skelter: The True Story of the Manson Murders* that Tricia had gifted to me. It took me a couple of hours, three lattes, and four bowls of hashish to highlight and index all eighty-five pages with references to Leslie Van Houten.

Intuitively, I thought Mr. Bugliosi's depiction of her was inexplicably wrong. Plainly hers was a special case that should have been tried apart from the others. The DA never would have gotten a first-degree conviction against her had she stood alone. Yet the County of the City of LA's grand inquisitor went far out of his way to make use of the public fear he created. Painting each of the co-defendants with the same venomous blood as Charlie Manson.

What he had to say about Leslie didn't add up.

Images of what the *now* Leslie Van Houten might really be like raised in scenes I projected inside my head. Rather than wrestle and box with my blankets and pillows for another fifteen rounds, I finally gave in to the muse and stayed up half the night writing notes and questions.

I addressed the envelope c/o Mr. Maxwell S. Keith, Lawyer, Security Pacific Plaza, #2820 - 333 South Hope Street, Los Angeles, California 90071.

No sooner had I sealed the first letter when I immediately started another. I wasn't writing to the girl with the "X" on her forehead. I was writing to what I imagined to be "the real deal" as she existed today. Underneath the captured images lay the essence of what I imagined was a beautiful, intelligent, courageous young woman. I know what you're thinking.

Maybe because that's what I wanted her to be, that's all I could see. Athena with pouty lips and the kind of wide-eyed good looks that captured my sudden surprise and blew me away.

When I read about Leslie getting her second chance to be free of all that Manson madness the whole world had watched her submerged in a decade before, I felt bound to pursue direct contact. To inquire, and to let her in on my own values for freedom, fair play, and independence. Sure that she'd have one hell of a story to share if we ever had the opportunity of meeting once she was freed from prison.

Try as I might, I could not fall asleep. This was my second restless night in a row. When I did wake up late the next cloudy morning, the first thing I did was re-read the "Ex-Manson Girl Returns to Court with New Image" clipping.

At first, I'd had the distinct, hedonic sense that I was about to seduce somebody famous. From that moment on, there was never any question that we would meet rather sooner than later.

2

"IT COULD HAVE BEEN ME"

Krrrack—an' *kapow!* You've got to love being awakened by sonic booms that rattle the windowpanes—with flashes of light hotter than the sun's surface. It's been suggested that if you awaken slowly, you will have a better chance of recalling your dreams than if you are awakened by alarm clocks or explosions.

Monday morning, the second week of 1977, I awoke to a phenomenon meteorologists call "thunder snow." Temperature and turbulence pelted gobs of wet snow at wind gusts up to ninety kilometers an hour. Positive and negative electrical charges divorced, and lightning bolts evened out the difference.

I was already practiced at writing my dreams down and could sometimes recall three or four events at a time. In my last dream that morning, I started out with a female stranger for a companion. Then she became the familiar image, more or less, of my steady girlfriend, Gabrielle Adler.

In this dream, Gabe and I started out house-hunting late at night. Every place we looked at resembled a bombed-out ruin, like the set for a production of Samuel Beckett's *Endgame*. Wrecked cats and stray dogs, plus a few unsavory primates, inhabited the neighborhood abyss we were lost in. Lightning struck and the rest—whatever it might have been or become— never happened.

Dream traces fade quickly, don't they? That's why I scribbled mine down in a diary. I had to force myself to scratch them out right away upon waking, before they evaporated back into the ether they came from. I finished my notes and turned to CHUM-FM on the radio. They were playing Fleetwood Mac's "Dreams." Giving notice to the fact that love affairs are sure to blow up at one point or another.

Only, deep down at the core, most dreams are romantic. I'd soon have to face up to the cold fact of that deep imperfection.

My apartment on Madison Avenue in the heart of Toronto was on the second floor of an old, red-brick mansion with two great stone arches out front. It was still very early. I smoked a joint on the porch and quickly finished my latté. *Brrrr...*it was cold. The wind, the sleet, and the snow changed my mind about going for a morning run.

Instead, I went back inside to continue my newfound enticement with Leslie Van Houten—marking up pages of *Helter Skelter* with a highlighter and making notes in the margins with my pencils.

Hated having to put her aside and ready myself for work. This was the second week of my "practice teaching" assignments that term. (One of the requisite hoops one had to jump through to obtain an English teaching certificate in the province of Ontario.) This stint was at the Stephen Leacock Collegiate

Institute in Scarborough. I'd already spent the first week of this impractical duty "observing" my supervising "associate" demonstrate how teaching was done in this jurisdiction.

The class I had been assigned to this morning was on contemporary Canadian poets. It was so-so. My associate chose the poets; not my favorites. After class, I had nearly two hours to spare for lunch, so I grabbed a bowl of chili and crackers in the teachers' lounge, put my feet up, and tried to forget all about how Leonard Cohen's "Portrait of a Girl" was received by the class overall.

Fooling myself into believing I wanted to be alone, I picked a table in the farthest corner of the teachers' lounge—away from the cigarette smokers and those I assumed to be cheating at cards. I continued reading prosecutor Vincent Bugliosi's book and taking notes about Leslie Van Houten to get my mind off the energy of manufacturing obedient employees.

Bells rang and students mechanically moved to their next stations. The factory model for manufacturing new employees.

It wasn't too long before another student-teacher doing time at Leacock Collegiate—a cool-looking guy I'd seen around the faculty of education building downtown on campus—asked to sit down and join me. His name was Jean Cousineau, and he offered me one of the honey crullers he had in a box. He said they were fresh.

Jean had dark, wavy hair pulled back tight in a ponytail and a classic Frenchman's nose that reminded me of a young Yves Montand. He was wearing an open white shirt with denim Levis and had on one of those awful Harris Tweed blazers you often saw teachers wear in situational comedies. He said he was practicing teaching French language and literature all term. I asked him how it was going.

"This place is more or less the same as the others," he said with a shrug. Then he asked, "How do you like it here?"

I frowned at first and kept my book open. "Not exactly having the time of my life," I said. "I more or less hate living in such bad faith as this."

Right away, Jean recognized what I was reading and asked me, "What's your interest in Charles Manson?"

"Not Manson so much. Rather Leslie Van Houten. She's more interesting than Manson or Bugliosi and much better looking." I felt myself smiling for the first time since class ended.

"Van Houten. The cheerleader... The pretty one, right? No. Not the cheerleader...the homecoming *princess*. That's right. What's your interest in her?"

I pursed my lips and frowned. I don't know why I didn't mention her retrial. I suddenly felt a tinge wary and defensive, thinking he might know as much or more about Leslie than I did.

He asked instead, "What's your take on Charlie Manson? A creep, eh?" An easy presumption.

"Yes, I guess so."

"They should've executed that goof with a maul and punch hammer," he said very matter-of-factly. I put the book down and invited Jean to keep talking.

We seemed to hit it off well enough. It felt good to make contact. We discussed everything at a rate of a hundred miles an hour—The Beatles, Sharon Tate, LSD, *Rosemary's Baby*, sodium pentothal, deep hypnosis, Albert Camus, and Aleister Crowley. It turned out Jean knew more about Manson than I did. But I had him beat on The Beatles and Roman Polanski.

"You know," Jean said, "all the Manson Family was primarily was a sex and drugs cult. My take is, he perverted their minds with acid and orgies to the point that they no longer had any will of their own. Gave themselves completely. He knew what he was doing. He's one ugly monster."

I wish I knew enough at that juncture to disagree with all that but let Jean carry on.

"I have a buddy...a writer," he said. "Knows a lot about the whole gory fiasco. He told me something.... What was it? I didn't realize at the time. He might have been talking about the retrial of Leslie Van Houten. Something about the judge upholding the ruling against the others' appeals? All except hers."

"Yes, I've read that, too, in the papers. From what Bugliosi acknowledged the first time, Leslie had been no more than a 'mindless robot.' So how could she plot first-degree murder? It never made sense to try her alongside the others. She didn't personally kill anyone."

"Did you know she's going to be getting married? Yeah. Some ex-con who publishes books by other convicts. 'Prose From Prison' or something like that."

I cringed when I heard this news of a rival but tried not to show it. After another pause, Jean continued.

"She wasn't there the first night at the Tate house, was she? Just the LaBiancas."

"If she'd testified against Manson, she'd have gotten the same deal they gave to Kasabian. She'd have gotten off. Why'd she turn that down, I wonder?"

"I'll ask her," I said, showing off. Feeling careless in general, I went on to blurt out, "I've written her a letter care of her lawyer, in fact. I'll write another and ask her."

"Really? Has she written back?"

"Only just sent it."

"What did you write her about, if you don't mind me asking?"

After a pause, I admitted, "What I said was that I thought what happened to her could have happened to me...or just about anyone else at that time under similar circumstances."

Jean said he had to leave right away to meet with his "associate." Either way, both he and I had afternoon classes to teach, so after he finished the last of his coffee, he got up to leave. We promised to meet up again soon. I'd see him around campus.

Since I still had a little more time left to myself before my next class, I drifted back to Vincent Bugliosi's opening statement from the Manson trial. Something about it wasn't right by a long shot. That's when I started taking more extensive notes of his theories as I plowed and plodded along. Not so much in order by page or by chapter as by finding my own way around using the index.

* * *

"On behalf of the people of the state of California..." Deputy District Attorney Vincent Bugliosi stated in open court, Charles Manson was the dictatorial leader of the Manson Family; everyone was slavishly obedient to him; he always had other members do his bidding for him; and he ordered his followers to commit the Tate-LaBianca murders on command.

In his opening statement in 1970, the Deputy DA is quoted as saying, "Manson's total domination over the family will be offered as circumstantial evidence that on the two nights in question it was he and he alone who ordered these seven murders." *He and he alone.* Then why so insistent on executing all the others, including Leslie?

Vincent Bugliosi portrayed Leslie Van Houten as an indoctrinated robot driven savagely out of her mind by the Devil incarnate. And, at the same time, he depicted her as a free-willed individual, acting with the cruelest cunning imaginable. Double-bind or double-blind? I was cross-eyed by the Deputy DA's circular logic. The jury may have been duped, but not others. (Bugliosi ran for Los Angeles district attorney in 1972 and 1976 and lost both times.)

On February 18th, 1972, the California Supreme Court voted six to one to abolish the death penalty. The Manson murderers' sentences were reduced to life in prison *with* the possibility of parole. That's what the law said. Something about cruel and unusual punishment. I wondered what the law had to say about institutionalized psychosis and premeditation.

With so much evidence to support Manson's domination over the others, I didn't understand how the prosecution could find Leslie responsible to the degree she was charged. One of the DA's expert witnesses testified that the easiest way to program someone to murder is to use fear. Convince them that "others" are threats that must be stopped, or else they'll eat your babies.

Mr. Bugliosi discussed the ways Manson used fear to make his followers' sense of themselves disappear, so he could replace their will with his own. In fact, the deputy DA admitted in open court, "Whether he [Manson] perfected this technique in prison or later is not known, but it was one of his most effective tools for controlling others."

I recall asking myself, if Manson had such complete control over his followers, as Bugliosi seems to have reasonably claimed, how was it that Leslie's lesser involvement warranted the death penalty inside the state-sanctioned gas chamber at San Quentin? Mr. Bugliosi seemed to be using fear, sensationalism, and careful omissions with the jury in much the same way he described the techniques Charles Manson used with his followers.

Now it seems even weirder how such strange bedfellows as Misters Manson and Bugliosi conjured up similar stories somehow. Each one played into the hands of the other's colorful allusions well enough for their combined audience to imagine an imminent revolution brewing.

Apparently, Charlie's primary objective was to instill righteous purpose, especially among his female followers, whom he had indoctrinated into being submissive vessels for their masculine foremen. Vincent Bugliosi's gallant self-portrait. Presenting a fearful appeal to the jurors by portraying himself as the public protector from such nightmares. "The man who took down the dangerous Manson clan." Quite a fantasy headline.

These were obviously just a handful of ragged, vagabond kids. Hardly an elite cadre of revolutionary guards. With flowers in their long hair—plus a handful of buck knives and more six-string guitars than they had guns. And yet, Vincent Bugliosi had everyone believing the Manson Family marauders were just aching to make blood sacrifices of society's children and fight for their lives to the end.

From the moment I first opened Bugliosi and Gentry's book—while tanning beside the pool at the Golden Sails in Long Beach in May '76—I remember thinking that this was one of the best opening lines I'd read in some time: "It was so quiet, one of the killers would later say, you could almost hear the sound of ice rattling in cocktail shakers in the homes way down the canyon."

I recall being so locked into Bugliosi's Helter Skelter account for the first day or two, I came away deeply entranced, and terribly sunburnt.

Here is a precis of Deputy DA Vincent Bugliosi's emergent theory of the motives in this case—in my terms, not his—beginning with how the prosecutor presented things to the jury in the first trial in 1970:

When he finally got out of prison at Terminal Island in San Pedro in '67, Charlie Manson landed at Berkeley amid the Free Speech Movement. Seeing for the first time what was going on among a generation half his age. It must have felt to him like the conversion of Paul the Apostle as he neared Damascus and the brushfire of Zeus flashed all around him.

Charlie hadn't even a vague notion or interest in the Civil Rights Movement or the conflicts in Korea and Vietnam. He was in shop class making license plates and learning to weld bedframes. Studying Scientology in his spare time rather than real physical science or refereed social studies.

At Berkeley, Charlie took note of the student activists—some black, some white. Some working together to clothe the homeless, feed hungry kids, or carry groceries for single mothers beset with their offspring in tow. And then there were the Black Panthers. He'd seen them before in the prisons but not like this. Not acting out openly. Free on the streets in their dark, menacing militant regalia and armed with more than a placard. It must have frightened the racist, paranoid tar clear out of him.

From the ragtag hipsters in the parks, he could see it was all right to dress as you pleased. Freely taking on different personae on a whim or sometimes with more pronounced intentions. Your call.

It didn't take Manson long to read the writing on their clothes and faces. College towns would not be his department. People who had been taught Symbolic Logic 101 were largely immune to his charms.

Since sex was generally free just for the asking, Charlie couldn't make enough just by pimping the girls out. Students had ready access to one another and places to go and lie down alone with each other, or not. He would need a new program to deploy in order to survive as a professional con artist in this environment.

Everywhere he looked, there were faux-guru types standing on misshapen soapboxes. An uncomfortably pitiful pew to preach from. Quite a scene. Ragged clusters of recruits seated in circles under trees burning incense, sharing cheap wine, and smoking joints of pot and hashish. Groups of four to forty—chanting, singing, and listening to all stripes of sermonizers preaching old and new faiths. Charlie would listen to each of these "guiding lights" and watch what it took to enchant their disciples: How to live, how to think, how to make love with one another. All would become one in the end, and you know who that one was.

Manson went from park to park and corner to corner—listening to every other spiritual sideshow barker spout their stuff. Charlie wasn't much of a writer, so he memorized and repeated their best lines and cobbled together his own script with bits he cribbed from the Bible and The Beatles' Revelations and Revolution. What nonpareils he skimmed from Scientology and Dale Carnegie might have even shown up in the lyrics to some of his adlibbed songs. With his perverse charm, he soon gathered a following.

Those were the days he used to hone his own oral litany— a manifesto of sorts. Like some of the lyrics from his frivolous, sophomoric songbook: *Look at your game girl—let go your ego— love everyone—surrender to love—there is no right or wrong—the more you surrender, the more you got to give.* So, the girls let go of their egos, unshackled their inhibitions, and some felt both blessed as well as compelled to have sex with Charlie to prove their love.

Once he had a few "chosen" devotees like Mary Brenner, Susan Atkins, and Lynette Fromme on the roster, Charlie could send them out to recruit others. They likened their cult leader to a new incarnation of Jesus Christ. Which is easier to promote or imagine on LSD.

Scruffy messiahs like Manson did all have one thing in common—besides beards, sermons, and gullible disciples—they all started their tribes from the ragtag lees of society. Castaway children somehow at odds with their parents and hitchhiking far from home in search of "transcendental consciousness" or otherwise figurative expressions of warmer spaces they could call home.

Charlie could take one look at you and reach back into his playbook. Drop-outs and runaway hitchhikers were ready targets he could easily control with sex, drugs, and a spectrum of hedonic bliss at one end; paranoid duress and ritualistic re-education ceremonies at the other.

* * *

When time was up and class let out that day at Stephen Leacock Collegiate, I noticed a scrum of three or four of the girls gathering in the hall outside the classroom. My supervisor, Ms. Kressler, had already vanished with two other students in tow. This gaggle stood away from the door where everyone else was passing. Finally, one student stepped forward, clearing her throat. Her name was Donna Reed. The only word I understood at first was that I was "wrong."

"I'm often 'wrong' about many things, Ms. Reed," I said. Then gave a smile over her shoulder to the group that had gathered around. "What is it this time?"

"Just wrong!" she resounded. After a pause, she added, "And I'm not coming to class if you're going to keep reading poems like you...like the things you said. Poems like that."

This last bit came out all at once but still sounded fractured. "Poems like what?" I taunted. "Which ones offend your fine sensibilities?" My tone wasn't polite or very professional, however that sounds. I kept hoping she'd get quiet and back down, only she didn't.

Donna suddenly wasn't so shaken as she was only moments before. She glanced around at the others who stood staring from nearby their lockers. Then she spoke very clearly, looking me straight in the eye.

"Leonard Cohen, Mordecai Richler, and Irving Layton. They all used women and then bragged about it," she protested. "Their poems are sick, filthy, and vulgar. Bragging about...about wanting sex with fifteen-year-old girls. It's disgusting! We've complained to Ms. Kressler. Just want to warn you. I'm telling my parents when I get home."

It seemed Donna was becoming accustomed to the adrenaline in her bloodstream. Feeling outmatched and exposed, I waited as long as I could before firing back. Nothing but bitterness burned at the edge of my tongue. It's fair to say I was naïve and in deep over my head.

Tangled up with a frustrated temper, I said, "I'm sorry you didn't like the poems. But these are well-respected poets. The poems are legit and that's how I presented them.

"Tell you what, though, Donna. Why not take a spare next time I'm teaching and save both of us from wasting our time?" Right as I said this, I wished that I hadn't. But I kept on talking anyway. It must have come out worse than I thought. Ms. Donna

Reed broke into tears, and then she and her mob shuffled away among echoes of crying.

Acting calm, though I wasn't, I walked out the nearest door like Michael Corleone leaving the restaurant from where he'd just shot Sollozzo and headed straight for my car. The MGB started right up, and I drove away without warming the engine. That's not like me at all. I needed to think more clearly but didn't know where I might gainfully start. Now wasn't the time for strategic thinking.

Traffic was stacked up as usual, until I turned off at Bayview. The road was bumpy and wet. I got the car a bit bent out of shape braking late at the entry to Rosedale Valley Road. A twitch left and then right around slowpokes let me expend some defensive aggression. I still hadn't quite settled down, narrowly missing some oncoming traffic racing through two miles of blind, winding corners. It only seemed right to take chances.

I parked in the lot across from Varsity Stadium beside St. Hilda's College. From there, I jogged the rest of the way to Hart House looking for Andy Higgins. He wasn't at the track office, in the weight room, or by the lockers. I searched each face in the Arbor Room. All without luck.

"Absence haunts the café," said Jean-Paul Sartre.

I was just about to give up and go find a couch in the library to crash on when I spotted Andy coming out of the archway of University College. He stopped and waited as I sauntered up.

3

THE DIABLOS CAFÉ

The Diablos Café used to lie hidden beneath a labyrinth of corridors and stone spiral stairwells, deep inside the main quadrangle of University College. Andy suggested we go inside to stay warm.

When I was a kid living less than a mile away on Yonge Street, I used to sneak off and go there alone. Under floodlights at night, with its pointed arches and flying buttresses, UC looked just like a Disneyland castle, only for real.

Legend has it that during its construction in the 1850s, a Russian stonemason named Ivan Reznikoff was courting a beddable debutante with family ties to the city. The young lady was also seeing another of the masons, a Greek immigrant named Paul Diablos. According to Toronto folklore, Mr. Diablos carved one of two of the gargoyles adorning the college in the image of Reznikoff. The other was of himself, laughing behind poor Ivan's back.

When Reznikoff uncovered proof of his girlfriend's infidelity, he confronted his rival near the construction site with an axe. Reznikoff chased Diablos through the unfinished tower, leaving a scar on the door that remains visible to this day. Afterward, both of the men and the young lady mysteriously vanished from Toronto.

Decades later, after a fire in 1890 severely damaged the college library, the corpse of a man was unearthed in the debris. Although these sorry remains were never identified, the gargoyle hasn't stopped laughing.

So, it was into the dark but illustrious confines of the Diablos Café that Andy and I descended. We each ordered coffee, and he sat down while I waited in line. He'd chosen a point far from the madding crowd in the corner of the large, open room where I joined him.

Cradling a pint of hot coffee, Andy asked, "So what's this about?" I held up my hand, shook my head, and remained silent a moment while I swallowed.

"Tell me what hap-pen-ed," he said, in the curious way he had of emphasizing certain words by elongating their syllables.

"I had a complaint from a student today who got defensive and lost it," I said.

Pinching my shoulder firmly with his palm, Andy spoke softly, "Lost it how? Was this about teaching or something else?"

"After class. I was trying to do something different with an intro to Canadian poets. I'd planned a lesson on Irving Layton's notion of 'poetry as the fine art of pugilism.' I wanted students to connect with something current in place of E.J. Pratt and Bliss Carman. But some of the girls were offended by the sexual satire expressed by these younger poets."

"What did your supervisor have to say about sexual satire?"

"I don't know. I split in a hurry. Never hung around long enough to find out. That's one of the things I wanted to talk to you about. More than ever, I'm convinced teaching high school isn't for me. Do I stop wasting my time or fake it for a few weeks longer 'til I get the certificate stamped?"

Andy leaned back. "You know what they say? First, you have to be part of the system before you can start trying to change things."

I moaned when he said it. I'd heard that so often, it was all I could do not to shake my head and yawn. No wonder nothing ever gets done.

"Everyone says that, don't they? I'm not trying to change things, Andy. There's no room for anything even *remotely* current in this stale, wearied curriculum putting everyone's feet to sleep."

"It's not meant to be cutting-edge," Andy explained. "They expect you to teach what's well-established. That's all. You have to prove you can do that before you go off on an inventive tangent."

"From what I've seen in the system so far, they only teach what they've been taught. There's nothing new or self-taught about it. If teachers were force-fed *To Kill a Mockingbird* in grade nine, then that's what, *and how*, they teach when it's their turn."

Andy asked, "What were the *students* complaining about?"

"Some of the poems I chose. Probing and poking some fun at uptight sexual moirés and prudish behavior..."

"Which poems are we talking about?"

"I read them some tongue-in-cheek stuff by Leonard Cohen like: 'the 15-year-old girls I wanted when I was 15.' Honestly, Andy, I thought that was the *perfect* poem to read to fifteen-year-olds. Only it seems that has gotten some girls' skirts in a twist."

Andy said nothing at first but frowned at *my* smiling.

"That will sure enhance your credibility with the administration," he quipped before breaking a smile of his own.

"I considered it a 'teachable moment,'" I defended. We relaxed after that and moved on to other matters.

"I had another meeting with Gerard Mach today, and one of the things we discussed was you. He has agreed to have you work with his group of elite sprinters and coaches this summer. It's up to you. But if you want to continue to coach at this level, then this is the next step."

"That's not exactly a part-time job," I said, reaching to put my cup on the table.

"Could be a once-in-a-lifetime chance to work with a *master* athletics coach. Just think about that for a moment." Andy put down his coffee and reached out to massage my shoulder.

"It's what you make it."

Gerard Mach had been an Olympic sprinter prior to becoming Poland's national coach. He became the first "professional" track coach in Canada in 1972 and, by 1976, had coached all four of our national relay teams to the Olympic finals in Montreal.

One reason I held back my enthusiasm for what Andy was suggesting had to do with the fact that he had me working with another legendary coach before. In those days, we called it the *generation gap*, but that phrase didn't quite capture the deep divide between me and Mr. Fred Foot, another of Andy's truly great coaching mentors.

Andy and I talked some more about teaching and coaching as complementary professions. Rather than treat them both as separate endeavors, he suggested I think of more creative ways of putting them both together.

Since it was nearly half past four and soon would be time for us to head up to the gym to work with a dozen athletes, I decided on another coffee for myself. Andy shook his head "no thanks" just as someone he knew stopped over to have a chat. I got up and ordered myself a double shot of espresso.

While standing in line at the counter, I was surprised by who walked up from behind.

"Hey, Peter," he said.

I turned around and smiled broadly, sincerely happy to see Jean Cousineau again on the same day that we had met.

"Small world," I said.

"No, not really. It's a big world, Pierre. It's a small café. The odds were good I'd run into you someplace like this."

"I see what you mean," I whispered while glancing around, unsure at first of what I meant. When I thought a little bit more about it, I wondered if maybe I'd seen him in here before we met. In those days, you needed an initiation (almost) to find your way to the Diablos Café. Many believed the place wasn't as real as the metaphor.

"I'm headed off to the gym right now. Just waiting, having one last shot of expresso. Care to join me? Faculty of Ed. building at Huron and Washington Park."

"I'm going that way myself," Jean said. "Only, I'm late for a meeting with my advisor already."

"Can you wait a few more minutes? I'd like you to meet someone. Then we can jog up together."

"Not unless you can leave this very second. I was just running out the door when I saw you," he said.

"Why not hang around afterward and meet up with me later? Seven o'clock. If you want, we can take a pizza back to my place.

I live up the street from the Faculty on Madison Ave. How does that sound?

"You can tell me some more about Charles Manson and Leslie Van Houten."

"Pizza sounds cool. See you past seven then. Which gym?" Jean asked, walking backward.

"Northwest corner, ground floor," I called back, just as Jean disappeared through the archway.

Just after seven, we were completing our final sets of cooldowns and stretches that evening—after an intense ninety minutes of hopping and bounding and medicine ball exercises with long-, high-, and triple-jumpers and pole vaulters—when I spotted Jean Cousineau peeking into the gym.

I introduced him quickly to Buck and a few of the guys just as we were leaving. Having decided to stay warm in fresh sweats while Jean and I waited across the street in Poppa's Pizza near Spadina. An extra-large Italian with anchovies to go. We sat on stools while we waited, watching the traffic and sidewalk passersby trudging their way through the slush.

Before we were too settled in back at my place, I called Ms. Cynthia Kressler on her home phone. The call was cordial. In fact, to my relief, it was over inside of ten minutes. I apologized for my rudeness that day with Ms. Reed and made excuses for leaving early. She said she'd spoken with some of the students, who told her that Donna Reed and the others may have "overreacted." But that didn't let me off the hook.

Kressler was stern about one or two things in particular—the outcome of which was my promise to discuss my lesson plans in advance from now on. It was an accommodation—meaning more to her and next to nothing to me, so I told her I'd do whatever she wanted.

After the phone call, Jean and I talked some more about school and the many compromising frustrations we'd been having with practice teaching. After side one of the *Plastic Ono Band*, I put on side two of Neil Young's *Zuma*, easing the needle down gently in the groove right before "Cortez the Killer." Then rolled a couple more joints from the ounce I had left in a Jamaican cigar box. I had nothing on hand to drink except milk, water, and coffee. That seemed to surprise and disappoint Monsieur Cousineau.

I made us both lattes, and we sat slouched on hand-me-down pillows that I had tossed on the rug.

"You're pretty serious about track, are you?" he asked.

"Less, lately. I was always into track and field in school. Right up until now. Is French your only teaching subject?"

"General elementary. And your second subject?"

"English lit is my primary; phys. ed., a far second. I'm only discovering this now. I think I prefer English. Not so much to teach it as learn it better myself. Then again, my coach keeps telling me the best way to learn something is to try teaching it to others.

"I wished I'd played more sports in school," Jean said, reaching to pass back the burning joint back to me. I waved him off and sparked up another one of my own.

"You look very fit, Peter," Jean commented. "Do you still race to compete?"

"Nah. Still play competitive hockey, though. I hope to keep that up. But I've run my last race on track—except against a stopwatch. Or a subway train," I added. Jean laughed at that. After which we somehow got around to talking about high school, risk-taking on motorcycles, and fast cars we'd driven or owned. It was dark, so I pointed out the window to my MGB parked out back.

Jean asked me, "What's the biggest risk you've taken recently?"

"For some reason, don't ask me why, one chill-wet night months back, my buddy Mike Flynn and I were taking the subway home to our parents' homes in the suburbs. My car was in the shop, and Mike's sister had to borrow his, or something. We'd *just* missed a late car heading east from Yonge Street Station. We stood on the platform staring as the train and its screeching faded away into the dark-lit tunnel.

"'Meet me at the next station,' I shouted at Mike back over my shoulder. His reaction came late. Before I gave him any chance to talk me out of it—not knowing for sure how far it was, or how long it would take me to get to Sherbourne Station—I ran to the edge of the platform, jumped down between the tracks, and started running. Focused on staying right of center between the tracks, I was sure to keep away from the third rail. Where all that ungodly 'juice'—six-hundred-volts worth—hummed beside me.

"It's not a straight tunnel the whole way, though pretty level. It turns right near the end, which was when I could hear the echoes of the next train coming. Flynn looked relieved when he saw me climb back up on the platform. I was a little bit out of breath but otherwise no worse for wear and feeling pleased with myself."

Jean shook his head in disbelief. "What do you attribute it to?" he asked. "A sudden abundance of youthful exuberance?" To which, all I could do was shrug.

"That's as good a guess as any," I said, and left it at that.

Picking my book up off the wooden chest I used for a table, he noted, "Still reading *Helter Skelter*, I see. *And* taking notes. Preparing another letter for Ms. Van Houten?"

I didn't mind him flipping through pages of *Helter Skelter*, but I picked up my notebook and closed it. Jean put the book down and told me about other books and sources concerning the Manson Family that he'd come across in *Rolling Stone* and a few other magazines I'd never heard of. One of the things we discussed was how we might have reacted—ourselves—if these crimes had happened to our friends or family. Jean said something about twisting and tearing Manson's balls off with a pair of sizzling-hot pliers. This image seemed to amuse him.

Combining what facts we knew from things we'd read, we reviewed the ghastly scene the LaBianca children first encountered—the day after the news of the slaying of Hollywood actress Sharon Tate Polanski and four others.

* * *

August 10th, 1969. The LaBianca children, Frank and Susan, together with Susan's boyfriend, Joe Dorgan, were the first to discover the crime scene. They called the police to their parents' moneyed home at 3301 Waverly Drive, near the famous observatory in Griffith Park. Upon entering the house, what the LAPD officers saw in the living room caused them to call for immediate backup. There were splashes of blood on the walls and the floor.

In addition to the pillowcase wrapped over Mr. LaBianca's head, there was a cord attached to a heavy lamp knotted around his neck, and his hands were tied behind his back with leather thongs. There was an ivory-handled, twin-tined carving fork embedded in his stomach, and, on his abdomen near several deep stab wounds, the letters "WAR" were engraved into his flesh. A small, sharp kitchen knife had been thrust into his throat and just left there.

A sergeant from the backup unit was the first to discover Rosemary LaBianca's body in the master bedroom—but only after the first responders had already taken her husband away in a body bag. Mrs. LaBianca was found lying face down on the bedroom floor in a pool of blood. Like her husband, she had a pillowcase wrapped over her head, which was secured around her neck with a lamp cord.

Leno LaBianca had been the forty-four-year-old president and chief stockholder of the State Wholesale Grocery Company, which operated Gateway Markets. It was rumored that Mr. LaBianca also had horse racing and property interests in California and Nevada. He died as a result of twelve knife wounds and fourteen punctures made by the carving fork that was left protruding from his stomach. In the living room beside the front door, there was writing—"Death To Pigs" and "RISE"—in the victim's blood. As well, on the refrigerator door, one of the intruders had misprinted the phrase, "HEALTER SKELTER."

Mrs. LaBianca, an independent businesswoman who owned her own boutique, had been stabbed a total of forty-one times. Six of the punctures could have, in and of themselves, been fatal. Some of the wounds perforated her stomach and lung. She also had lacerations of the cervical spinal cord and spleen. The most murderous wound was to the posterior of the neck, just slightly left of the midline. This single wound in itself was savage enough to be fatal. In addition, more than a dozen "superficial" cuts had been inflicted post-mortem.

The coroner Dr. Thomas Noguchi established there were perhaps as many as sixteen superficial, evidently post-mortem, lacerations to Mrs. LaBianca's lower back. These injuries, he said, were readily distinguishable from the others. The coroner's report also stated these wounds to the lower back did not show any significant hemorrhage into any of the surrounding tissues.

* * *

What explains this? Judging from crime scene photography, the prosecution would have us believe Leslie Van Houten acted like some wild animal, whom they imagine stabbed Rosemary LaBianca dozens of times—even after the woman was dead. What was it Marshall McLuhan taught us about the peculiar characteristics of photography? For one thing, it abolishes time. To say the camera cannot lie "is merely to underline the multiple deceits that are now practiced in its name."

As far as I could tell from reading *Helter Skelter* this time around, there was nothing there that was incongruent with Leslie being in an altered state of mind, if indeed she did what she was accused of. What if she had been mentally impaired or brainwashed at the time? Would that make any difference? Assistant DA Vincent Bugliosi wanted it both ways. And Manson did, too, for that matter. They wanted us, their audience and jury, to see Leslie both as a crazed Sgt. Shaw in *The Manchurian Candidate* and as a Manson co-conspirator working alongside him and the others. All with one mad motive in mind and one common purpose to serve.

I wasn't buying either of them either way.

"So, what really went on here and why?" I asked Jean if he knew. He admitted he didn't.

"I wouldn't believe anything the DA said—not about who, why, or wherefore. Only the people who were there know for certain."

We kept talking until a quarter past one. Then Jean called a cab to take him home to his flat near the corner of Bathurst and Bloor. He told me he lived on the same side of the block as Honest Ed's Department Store.

I thought it safe to say we had a good time indulging our morbid fascination with the Manson murders and the brutal events surrounding Leslie Van Houten. Despite his definitive portrait, Jean and I agreed there had to be more to the story than Bugliosi unveiled or uncovered. Perhaps Leslie's retrial would clear up more of the mystery. What if "Helter Skelter" wasn't the true motive? And to what *degree* were the co-defendants equally guilty of first-degree murder?

I stayed up another hour or so scribbling more notes. Though my body was aching and begging for sleep, I had a hard time shutting my mind off. Finally dozed off for a spell—only to be startled awake by nightmarish cityscape scenes of people on fire being chased by armored marauders.

After scratching that down in my notebook, I returned to the very same dream I'd already come out of. After tossing and turning and trying for hours to stay asleep, I finally dozed off until dawn. When I stopped dreaming and opened my eyes, I did not want to wake up.

4

RAZOR'S EDGE REDUX

That winter—outside of track practice and regular hockey games with some of the old St. Mike's gang at Varsity Arena twice a week after midnight—I spent one, sometimes two nights a week with my off- and on-again girlfriend, Gabrielle Adler. I also made time to hang out on a regular basis with Jean Cousineau.

Monday, January 17, 1977, was the date of my 26th birthday. There was a note in my mailbox at Leacock Collegiate from Ms. Kressler asking me to come see her before class that day. When I stepped into her office, I could see from the way her hands were clasped together, there was no mistaking her smile as friendliness. Then she commenced:

"This morning, Mrs. Reed, Donna's mother, called me. As you well know, we still have a problem." (I didn't know.) "So, to simplify matters at this time, you are not to speak to Donna if you see her. She won't be attending English class until after you've finished your time here and have left the school. Do we have an understanding?"

"Perfectly clear." I nodded in agreement and immediately turned to leave.

Before I had time to close the door behind me, she added, "Oh, and one other thing. Do remember to *not* start your class until you've taken the roll call. Is that understood?"

"Of course," I nodded, smiling. My teacher evaluation wasn't likely to suffer much more inconsequential nonsense no matter what I did at this point.

Finishing nearly all that day's lesson plan in the staff room, I walked into the classroom, put the unopened text down, and stared pensively at the class assembly. "Have you ever had some *really* difficult times in your lives? Tough times, dark times? Sleep-disturbing times?" I asked no one in particular.

That got their attention. I slowed down to allow them time to reflect.

"Can you think of a poem, a song, or a line from a movie that helped you, inspired you, soothed you during hard times? A line or a scene that made you smile or cry?" Students closed their texts and slowly some began raising their hands and volunteering their favorite songs.

A few glanced apprehensively at Mrs. Kressler. One kid reported that his cousin really liked Bob Dylan's song "Hurricane," and so did he. When someone asked him what it was that he liked so much about the story of professional boxer Rubin "Hurricane" Carter, this led to a discussion about social justice that engaged and excited the class more than I'd ever seen them before.

The students that day continued their discussion while I gathered my gear to move on before Donna Reed made her appearance. Mrs. Kressler was waiting for me outside the class-room and immediately summoned me to her office.

I entered to find yet again a frowning, disgruntled young woman I was beginning to have real sympathy for.

"You know, Peter, you have a rather specific job to do here. One which is clearly delineated by the department's approved curriculum. I don't see what today's 'entertainment' contributes to the students' ability to satisfy these learning objectives."

To myself, I repeated the line from *Hamlet*, "There are more things in heaven and Earth, Horatio, than are dreamt of in your philosophy."

Out loud, what I said was "My objective was for them to consider more than just abstract textbook concepts. In my view, their positive response accomplished that."

"How so?" she demanded.

"By helping them see how important concepts like art, jus-tice, and equal rights can help us to enjoy, reflect, and ultimately pull through the best and worst of times in our lives. How poetry and the arts of singing and writing are a daily part of their lives and deserve paying attention to—"

Clearly unmoved and impatient, Mrs. Kressler interrupted, "And…?"

"And…just being able to recognize how poetry is *meaning-ful*. Aesthetic experiences can be used as touchstones that carry a greater significance."

No response to my quest for meaningful experiences, and no surprise either. A terse, "Thank you, Peter, for your enthusiasm. You are young and fresh, but you have a very clear curriculum to cover so let's just get back to work, shall we?"

To myself, I was making my mind up not to pursue this charade much longer. Teaching high school seemed too soul-crushing an endeavor for me to seriously consider wasting any more of my precious time pursuing.

That evening at Jean's Bathurst Street apartment, we four friends—including Gabrielle and her best friend, Karen—gathered to celebrate my birthday.

Just as it started to snow on the way over to Jean's place, the girls and I stopped at places up and down Nassau Street for coffee, milk, butter, eggs, and two boxes of Betty Crocker brownie mix. Everything in Jean's refrigerator except the bottles of beer was spoiled and had to be thrown out when we got there.

Jean also invited his friend and houseguest Martin to celebrate with us. Those two went out to the Liquor Control Board of Ontario (LCBO) outlet on Spadina Avenue to pick up beer, three bottles of Henkel, and one marvelous four-liter jug of red Portuguese wine. In the meantime, the girls had ordered Chinese take-out from The Palace Garden that we picked up and carried back in separate tubs of rice, stinky tofu, and crispy, baked octopus.

Martin Bijaux was an old friend of Jean's from McGill University. He was spending a few nights in town on his way back to work in Los Angeles. He told us he worked as a freelance journalist for the "underground press," which I thought sounded very cool. He seemed a *bona fide* member of the literati, for which I felt some envy, but mostly, I was curious to know more.

"To make a living at freelance writing, I imagine you have to be pretty darn good," I ventured. "Anything you've written I might have seen?"

"Not much in Canada. Only pamphlets I wrote when I was a kid. I live in LA now. I did write something last year that was picked up by *Georgia Straight* on a bounce. But mostly, I write for offbeat sheets like *The Barb*. Still learning the ropes, you know, makin' the rounds."

"Working on anything interesting at the moment?" Karen asked him.

"Right now, I'm delving into a story on museums of death in California." That turned everyone's head and spurred plenty of further questions. Quite a good start to the night. I was feeling engaged. Making my birthday celebration a happy gathering.

I noticed how Jean kept following the girls out of the room and into the kitchen. He'd shuttle back and forth every now and then to listen in on how Martin and I were getting along. The scent of cannabis-infused brownies, sounds of plastic corks popping, and sudden bursts of laughter accompanied the music of The Doors' early albums.

Martin looked about five years older and grittier than the rest of us. To me, he resembled the thirty-something Hell's Angels' leader, Maurice "Mom" Boucher, but without the brush cut. Heavy set. Long, straight, light-brown hair to his shoulders. Once we got high, Martin really started to open up. Quickly downing three or more bottles of the dozen Molson Brador we had, he pulled out a hash pipe, which he offered to share.

At one point, when Martin mentioned a close friend of his who had once interviewed Roman Polanski in Paris, our collective curiosity was aroused. That particular reference led me directly to ask him what he knew about the Manson Family and the Tate–LaBianca killings. (The mere mention of which caused Gabrielle and Karen to moan loudly, then disappear back into the kitchen.) I was unmoved by their annoyed indifference. It turned out Martin knew quite a lot more about the Manson saga than I had expected.

Reaching over the side of the couch he was sitting on, Martin picked up a sack and took out a couple of plastic-wrapped *Rolling Stone* magazines.

"Before I left Montreal, I dug these out of a box I had stashed at my brother Guy's," Martin explained. "Jean told me you were interested in Manson when we spoke on the phone. So, I brought these with me knowing it was your birthday."

"I appreciate that. It's a real treat, Martin. Thanks very much. I'll read them with interest." Actually, I was anxious to start flipping through them right away, itching to find some mention of Leslie.

Martin flipped one of them open to show me the page beginning with, "The Year of the Fork, Night of the Hunter." An interview that journalists David Felton and David Dalton conducted with Manson in prison. The other article, simply titled "Manson," was written by a Hollywood talent scout who went by the pseudonym Lance Fairweather. His real name, Martin explained, was Gregg Jakobson—and he was friends with Beach Boys' drummer Dennis Wilson, Columbia Records producer Terry Melcher, and Charlie Manson.

"It was Jakobson and Wilson who introduced Manson to Terry Melcher," Martin said. "It was no accident that Terry lived at the scene of the crime—10050 Cielo Drive in Benedict Canyon—just six months before the Polanskis moved in. Both Tex and Charlie already knew the layout, having been there with Dennis a few times looking for Terry."

I asked Martin what he thought of Polanski's film *Rosemary's Baby*.

"Some people are fixated on the ending," he said, "but the sequence that really got me was the one in which Rosemary discovers her husband is in cahoots with their elderly neighbors—then finds herself helplessly paralyzed and pinned naked to a bed, with a grotesquely bare-naked clique of devil worshipers surrounding her...."

"I remember that!" Jean interrupted as he re-entered the room. "Some were chanting spooky, ritualistic hymns while others painted her breasts with occult symbols in blood." Everyone seemed to stop and picture the scene for themselves.

Gabe and Karen suddenly reappeared in the room, and that's when Martin asked, "Have any of you ever seen Ingmar Bergman's *The Devil's Wanton* or *The Hour of the Wolf*?"

"I have. Both," I said.

"I audited a film course once," Karen announced. "*The Silence of God* with Father Whatshisface—who was crazy about Bergman, so we got to see all his films one semester. Though there's no devil figure in *Hour of the Wolf* that I can remember."

"There's an interview where Bergman explains that 'Hell is created by humans,'" Martin started. "We carry around these destructive tendencies. That's what's in that film. You might want to have another look at it."

He didn't say it to be rude, or so I thought. Karen and Gabrielle may have thought differently.

"I've read *Bergman on Bergman*," I stated with confidence. "I still have the copy I picked up traveling through Stockholm two winters ago. He gives an example of two little girls taking a younger boy of two for a walk together. The girls put their skipping rope around the boy's neck, tie the ends to a tree branch, and just walk away.

"What causes two kids to agree to do such a thing, no one knows for sure."

Everyone silently bowed and shook their heads from side to side.

"While Bergman's point of view in *The Virgin Spring* takes a very serious look at questions of rape and revenge," I said.

"Polanski seems to have a rather disturbing detachment toward rape in his film."

Jean smiled and said, "Polanski makes movies for art and money, Peter. Everybody wants to see something wicked sometime."

"Not everybody," Gabe ventured. She and Karen returned to the kitchen, quietly plotting among themselves, I imagined. I glanced at Gabe just as she turned and smiled.

Gabe had a beautiful swimmer's body. Broad shoulders; dark hair; big, brown, almond-shaped eyes; and a wonderfully soft, pale complexion with freckles. She was serious and sincere about family matters. I liked most things about Gabe. Except that she wasn't keen on literature, nor was she any more emotionally available to me than I was to her.

Feeling in need of fresh air, I rolled a joint and stepped outside on Jean's fire escape to do some thinking and hit it alone.

Honestly, I wasn't a very good boyfriend. Even sex between Gabrielle and me was awkward and most often hesitant for both of us. Lately, we'd started begging off spending consecutive nights together. No doubt we each had our own reasons why, but we never discussed them. It was 1977, and we were still culturally lingering in the shadow of the "free love" customs we exercised en masse in the sixties. Whatever suspicions I held about Gabrielle still seeing her old boyfriend, I really didn't care all that much anymore.

Back inside, it seemed like hours later when someone cut the lights. There were twenty-seven birthday candles (one for good luck) on a Harbord Bakery cake, with a blue maple leaf number "26" in the icing. Everyone gave me a book or record album with cards attached as presents. Everyone except Jean, who was already so stoned he couldn't find his gift. Gabrielle gave me W.

Somerset Maugham's *The Razor's Edge* and Carl Gustav Jung's *Memories, Dreams, Reflections.* Karen gave me the latest records by Steely Dan and the Electric Light Orchestra.

Someone had taken The Doors album off the turntable and replaced it with David Bowie's *Diamond Dogs.* With its notable reference to a shop on the corner "selling papier mache, making bullet-proof faces—*Charlie Manson, Cassius Clay.*" Listening carefully, this was the first time I realized I'd misunderstood that line and had heard it as "Charlie Manson *catch a plane,*" which, it turned out, I liked even better.

After a brief interlude, Jean came groovin' back into the living room with a woman on each arm. They were waving joints around like fireworks sparklers. With his free hand, Jean handed me a hastily wrapped (in tinfoil) copy of *The Garbage People* by John Gilmore. Then immediately went spinning back toward the others, and all of them went back into the kitchen. That left Monsieur Bijaux and me alone.

"Peter, you know how Van Houten met Manson, don't you?" Martin asked me. I admitted I knew very little about that part of her story. Except, I knew it was through Leslie's boyfriend at the time.

"Bobby Beausoleil—the guy who killed Gary Hinman—introduced them," I said.

"That's right. Bobby's nickname was 'Cupid,' on account of his pretty-boy looks. Leslie met him and another Manson zealot Catherine Share. Called herself 'Gypsy.' They met in San Francisco a year before the murders. Gypsy and Bobby were crazy with stories about this amazing 'magical prophet,' Charlie Manson. A 'genius' who left the Bay area and moved his Family to LA. Presumably, to be closer to the music business."

"*That* was their pitch? That worked?" I squinted incredulously. "I would have thought that Leslie might have been pretty skeptical of any myths like the one about Manson. More so than most other girls, I imagine."

"I think it was really Beausoleil who convinced her to go along to meet Charlie. She would do anything he wanted. She told him she thought he was the most beautiful man she had ever seen in the world. It's all in the book Jean just gave you, *The Garbage People*. Named for the supermarket dumpster-diving the Family did to find food."

"Could be a metaphor for a generation."

"What was I just saying?" Martin questioned himself. "Oh, yeah, Beausoleil told a reporter friend of mine that the first time he had sex with Van Houten, they were both tripping on acid."

"The heart has its reasons," I said, hoping he'd leave it alone.

"Yes, well, to each his own. Both Beausoleil and Manson had a thing for putting on kinky get-ups and acting out sexual fantasies with all the girls. There's another thing they held in common. They thought Melcher and Wilson were gonna make them into big rock stars—like the next David Crosby and Roger McGuinn of The Byrds.

"Beausoleil always had lots of girls because of his looks," Martin continued. "I think all Charlie had or needed was his repertoire of steady con jobs. Smart enough to see he could use a guy like Bobby to lure more girls to his cult. The girls in turn would lure more men. Manson was paranoid about needing the men for protection."

"How do you mean? Protection from what?" I asked.

"Among other things, Charlie was mostly afraid of the Black Panthers. After he and Tex Watson ripped off a drug dealer, Bernard Crowe, less than two weeks before what they did at Tate–LaBianca. They had conned Crowe out of $2,500. That's when things first started to unravel. Crowe naturally demanded his money back.

"Claimed he was connected with the Black Panthers; Bernard scared the paranoid-racist shit out of Charlie. Being a career criminal, Manson decided to end Crowe's threats by shooting him. He ended up shooting him in the stomach and believed he'd killed him. Only he hadn't. But Charlie didn't know that.

"Crowe never reported the shooting to the cops," Martin said, then paused to open another bottle of Brador, which he then passed to me.

Grateful for whatever fates had brought us together—regardless of what the others were up to—Martin was the only person to thoroughly capture my interest that evening. Predominantly, on account of how much more he knew about the circumstances surrounding the Manson cult than anyone else I'd yet read about or spoken to. His information made me hunger for more.

And much more is what I got. Another surprise birthday present.

Everyone at my birthday celebration was beginning to get off on the high-octane chocolate brownies kicking in. Martin was taking me on a fantastic trip I could not have expected.

The next stint of this evening's journey involved him telling me details about the tragic fate of UCLA chemistry student Gary Hinman. This brought a whole new perspective I had not come across. With Neil Young's "Everybody Knows This Is Nowhere" playing in the background (a song about moving to Los Angeles and missing home), I asked to borrow a pen and pad from Jean's desk.

I wanted to take down the gist of what Martin had to say about the killing of Gary Hinman, "starting the whole month of 'Manson murders' and mayhem off."

* * *

49

Bernard Crowe liked people to think he had close ties to the Black Panthers. He didn't. According to testimony during the first trial, Tex and Charlie promised him twenty kilos of marijuana for $2,500—cash upfront—then stiffed him for all the money. Crowe put some serious, threatening heat on Tex, so Charlie ended up shooting Crowe in the gut with a .22-calibre handgun to shut him up. Thinking he'd actually killed him.

Crowe survived and never reported the assault to the police. Now Charlie was terrified the Black Panthers would come and burn the ranch down. After, of course, they would crush all of Charlie's bones one at a time from the bottom up as a sign of revenge.

Martin explained it was Bobby Beausoleil who—after Tex screwed things up with the Bernard Crowe fiasco—came up with yet another lame-brain drug scheme for getting Charlie the security and money he desperately needed to protect himself from the Black Panthers.

After Bobby heard from some of the girls that the Venice Chapter of the Straight Satans motorcycle gang was planning to throw a wild, trippin' orgy—he went to Charlie with the idea of selling the bikers one thousand tabs of synthetic mescaline for $1,000. Bobby's friend Gary Hinman would make the drugs at his place in nearby Topanga Canyon.

Manson would get the bikers to front him the money. Beausoleil gave the cash to Gary for the supplies and the equipment he needed to manufacture a jar of one thousand mescaline tablets. Each about the size of a B-12 vitamin tab.

The day after Bobby delivered the drugs to the party, some of the gang rode up to Spahn Ranch on their Harleys—complaining to Bobby and Charlie that the drugs they sold them were tainted and made everyone sick. The bikers wanted their money back immediately or else threatened to kill them both.

Charlie sent Bobby, Mary Brunner, and Susan Atkins over to Hinman's to get the front money back. In spite of the young ladies' alluring charms, Gary claimed he had already spent the cash Bobby had given to him.

A fight broke out, and the 9-mm revolver Bobby brought with him went off. No one was hit. But just for making the attempt to break free, Beausoleil issued his friend Gary a terrible beating. Gary kept insisting he didn't have any money, so the trio took turns beating him silly. After things settled down, Hinman finally relented and signed over the Department of Motor Vehicles (DMV) registrations for the vehicles he had parked outside—a Volkswagen bus and a Fiat station wagon. The papers were signed, and calm was restored.

One of the girls must have already called Manson from the house while Bobby and Gary were still fighting and alerted him to the fact that Gary wasn't going to cough up the dough. So, when Charlie and Bruce Davis plunged through the door just as Gary unlocked it. Without warning or hesitation, Manson slashed Hinman across the face with the sharp-edged sword he brought with him and damn near severed his ear off.

Panic set in. Manson told Susan and Mary to sew up Hinman's wounds and clean up the blood. As he and Bruce were leaving, Charlie left instructions for Bobby to keep up the program of torture and pain until Hinman fully succumbed.

The torment finally ended, although not abruptly, on Sunday, July 27th. After Bobby called Charlie one last time to say the torture tactics weren't working, Manson told him, "You know what to do. He knows too much." Gary Hinman would not be the last person Charlie Manson would condemn for that reason.

Bobby Beausoleil stabbed Gary Hinman five times in the chest. His tormentors watched for hours as he slipped into a coma, chanting a Buddhist mantra. Then Bobby had Mary and Sadie take turns holding a pillow over Gary's face until his breathing stopped. After which, they kept checking his pulse until his heart finally stopped beating.

Beausoleil staged the scene to look like the Black Panthers stabbed and smothered Gary Hinman. Bobby wrote, "POLITICAL PIGGY" on the wall in Hinman's blood—smudged a paw print with claws to make it look like an official manifest of the Panthers. His plan was to give the Straight Satans one of Hinman's cars as payback for the "tainted" drugs and keep the other for himself.

Bobby had the girls drive Gary's Volkswagen bus back to the ranch for Charlie to give the bikers. Then Bobby drove off into the sunset in Gary's Fiat. But why did he take the murder weapon—wrapped in a bloodstained rag tucked inside a tire well in the trunk—with him? Neither Martin nor I had any good guesses.

When Gary's friends hadn't heard from him for a week, two of them went up to his house in Topanga Canyon. The first thing they noticed were bustling torrents of flying insects swarming in and out of the windows. Both cars were gone.

Inside, they discovered the walls and floors splashed with blood and imprinted with gory inscriptions. The whole house was thick with whirling storm clouds of red-eyed flesh flies. What was left of Mr. Hinman's corpse was shrouded in blankets of chomping maggots.

Bobby Beausoleil was found days later, asleep by the side of the road where Hinman's Fiat had broken down. The California Highway patrolmen naturally ran a check of the vehicle's registration. An APB had been issued in connection with a murder. When they searched the car, police found the bloody knife in the tire well, which tests later revealed had Hinman's blood on it.

Then they dutifully arrested and charged the handsome, dark-souled cherub with murder.

Bobby Beausoleil was tried for the murder of Gary Hinman in November 1969. Despite Beausoleil's bloody palm print being identified by the forensics team of the LA Sheriff's Department, and the blood on the knife belonging to the late Gary Hinman, the trial ended in a hung jury. During his retrial in 1970—in return for testifying to Beausoleil's and Atkins's roles in the torture and killing of Hinman—Mary Brunner was granted immunity for her testimony.

This time, the jury found Beausoleil guilty of first-degree murder and sentenced him to the death chamber.

His sentence was later commuted to life in prison, along with all the other Manson Family members who were later convicted in 1971, including Leslie Van Houten. In a separate trial in 1971, after his Tate–LaBianca convictions, Manson was also found guilty of the murders of Gary Hinman and Donald "Shorty" Shea. These were the two bookends of Manson's entire murderous campaign.

* * *

"So, from July 27th to August 28th, 1969," Martin Bijaux began summing up, "there were, all told, nine victims in the Charles Manson murder spree lasting thirty-one days. Gary Hinman was the first to be killed—to keep his mouth shut about all the criminal enterprises Manson was involved in."

"What about Manson's motives for killing those innocent people at Cielo Drive two weeks later? Where's the connection?" I asked.

"Don't forget the LaBiancas," Martin said, "and don't forget about Donald Shea a few weeks after the Tate–LaBianca murders. That was about Donald keeping his mouth shut and also to settle a grudge Charlie held against him." This made perfect sense to me. All that Bugliosi BS about Helter Skelter was a distraction. All the mythos about Manson was somehow still missing the point.

"I'd completely forgotten about Shea," I confessed. "So, with Bobby Beausoleil jailed in July 1969, Charlie was afraid he'd talk?"

"Charlie thought he could get Beausoleil out of prison if he could pin Gary's murder on the Panthers. So, the Tate–LaBianca murders were his ploy to get the police to go after the Panthers," Martin added.

"What grudge was so terrible that Manson killed Donald Shea?" I asked.

"Same thing he feared from Hinman, basically. Shea ratted him out to the cops and ranch owner George Spahn over all the drug dealing and car theft. It seems these killings were all connected. I'm still not entirely sure how," he shrugged.

"Couldn't be something so common as revenge or as mundane as settling grudges, could it?" I shrugged back.

"I wish I had all the answers. I don't," Martin confessed.

"I don't think any of this had anything at all to do with instigating a race war, do you? I know that's what the girls were led to believe at the time, but they were also led to believe that Charlie was Jesus Christ."

Martin tilted his head back and widened his eyes. "Why don't we ask Bugliosi?" he grinned at last.

The whole time Martin and I were having this conversation, Jean was the only one who had occasionally shown any interest at all in what Martin and I had been talking about. The party ended not with a whimper, nor with a bang as things turned out. I called for a taxi.

After lifting Gabrielle out of the taxi and helping her up the stairs, I dropped her into my bed and covered her up with her clothes on. She quickly passed out. Just as well, I thought. That, too, was becoming another puzzle without all the pieces.

Right as this new year was starting its swing from the point in the earth's orbit when the planet is actually at its *closest* to the sun, I started my new year's diary—as I always did—on the date of my birthday.

Thus, it was at the celestial crux of a snowy, overcast night, I tumbled into my twenty-seventh lap 'round the heavens. The same as the first one. More or less sleepless and naked. The same way I'm bound to check out.

As I laid next to Gabrielle breathing lightly in a sound sleep, I stared wide-eyed at the ceiling wondering about Leslie Van Houten. Wondering what she was doing. If she had gotten my letter. *Not* wondering if she would write back.

That much I felt sure of right from the start. I glanced at Gabe's birthday gift of Maugham's book, *The Razor's Edge*. I'd read it before. When I lived with Jackson Tovell and his family. Quite appropriate. The road to enlightenment is a narrow path. One slip to either side, and you can cut yourself to ribbons.

5

INSPECTED, LOS ANGELES COUNTY JAIL

Friday, February 11th, 1977, the day of the annual Star-Maple Leaf Gardens Indoor Track Meet. The competitive indoor track and field season had begun.

Up until the Montreal Olympiad six months earlier, I only knew Olympic athletics coach Fred Foot by reputation. Then I had the opportunity to work with Coach Foot at the University of Toronto Track Club. At the time, I was also Professor Bruce Kidd's graduate assistant at the School of Physical and Health Education and liaison with the Olympic Artists-Athletes Coalition. Naively, I had assumed that since Coach Foot had inspired the likes of Higgins and Kidd, he would have the same effect with me.

Fred Foot was a *bona fide* legend in Canadian track and field. Since the fifties, he had successfully coached a steady stream of athletes to the Olympic Games as well as all other major trials in which Canadians were eligible to compete. He had coached Bill Crothers and Bruce Kidd into their respected international status as distance runners. Foot trained and motivated Canada's best track and field athletes to compete on a world stage and reach its podiums. Under Foot's tutelage, long-distance runner Bruce Kidd won eleven Canadian championships, five USA National titles, and one in the United Kingdom.

Bruce was only twenty-one years old when he competed at the 1964 Tokyo Olympics. Both Kidd and Foot had been instrumental in getting the *Toronto Star* involved in sponsoring what became the annual Toronto Star-Maple Leaf Gardens Indoor Track Meet. A premier athletic event having several internationally ranked athletes competing each year.

The year before, my friend Bruce Simpson won the pole vault with a clearance of 5.38 meters—more than seventeen and a half feet—ranking Bruce among the top five in the world. He still had another foot or two in him, so we anticipated this evening's events to be memorable. I secured tickets for Gabrielle, Karen, and Jean, getting them seats close to the action.

One of Coach Foot's athletes decided to pass on her sixty-meter heat to be fresh for her two-hundred heat later. Unfortunately, it ended up too late in the day for her to pass without being disqualified from running in the two-hundred later. Her better event. I saw how concerned she was, so I advised her to pull up "with a strain" a few strides after the gun.

Three strides out, she pulled up and began faking a limp but made it look terribly obvious. The whole scene gave me a very bad feeling. Someone complained to the marshals, and I readied myself for the expected verbal rap on the knuckles for that mix-up. Coach Foot saw it differently. Angry, Fred chewed me out for what seemed an eternity in front of a crowd of athletes, spectators, coaches, and snack vendors. Anyone within general earshot, which included my friends in the stands.

Discredited, I could feel my face brightly blushing before it started burning. Finally, the esteemed coach stormed away dismissively in one direction. I silently crawled away in the opposite direction.

Thankfully, Andy had defended my actions, and any additional humiliation was avoided as my friends and I engaged in chatty table talk instead of whining about it. After the meet ended that day, Gabrielle, Karen, Jean, and I shared a pitcher of draft, maybe two, and a basket of wings somewhere on Yonge Street. I appreciated their kindness as I had made that prestigious meet memorable for all the wrong reasons.

Neither Gabe nor I was much in the mood for clumsy lovemaking that night either. So, we kissed goodnight at the Wellesley subway station, and I walked the rest of the way home through Queen's Park feeling rather downbeat and abandoned.

Dragging myself in the front door—as a matter of course— the first thing I did was to check for mail in the front hall. On top of the radiator, beside a pile of junk mail and electricity bills, I saw a letter addressed to me stamped with US postage. The return address in the upper left corner read:

NAME: L. VAN HOUTEN
BOOKING NO. 4186-613 BKS. NO. 5001
P.O. BOX 54320 TERMINAL ANNEX
LOS ANGELES, CALIFORNIA 90054

Twice on the back—with the utmost surety—was stamped: INSPECTED LOS ANGELES COUNTY JAIL. How reassuring that was. At first, I simply weighed the envelope in my hand. It was lighter and thinner than the letter I'd sent her six weeks before. That was expected. I tossed the envelope on my desk, switched on the lamp, and put water on to boil. They were playing Paul McCartney's "Silly Love Songs" on CHUM-FM while I rolled a joint and Black China tea steeped in my favorite mug. It didn't take long for me to feel, I could not wait any longer. I ripped the corner of the envelope off with my teeth without daring to imagine what fate lay inside.

The letter was written in pencil on both sides of three pages of yellow, legal-sized foolscap. Leslie thanked me for taking the time to write a "long and thoughtful" letter. She had a wonderful, light, easy rhythm to her handwriting. Her penmanship reminded me of my mum's.

She mentioned that her lawyer Maxwell Keith had passed it along as soon as he got it. She also wrote a few things about her transfer from the California Institution for Women in Frontera to the Sybil Brand County Jail in Los Angeles for the new trial. She'd spent time there before, she said, when on trial with Manson in 1970—71.

"Not much has changed," she wrote. Sybil Brand was a short distance from her mother Jane's house, somewhere called Monterey Park. Her mom was a teacher. Her stepbrother David and stepsister Betsy lived in and around LA as well and could visit her more often than before at the California Institution for Women at Frontera. Her brother Paul Jr. lived with his wife in San Francisco, and her dad was working up north somewhere in Washington state. Pretty tame stuff for the most part. Still, I thought it was a pretty good start.

Leslie then turned to asking questions about me. Her questioning struck me as an invitation to write back. Would we

become friends or pen pals? It seemed certain. Certain I was beginning to see her for who she really was. It's hard to describe the
undertow of feelings after having crossed some sort of bound-
ary. Speaking to one another directly, creating mental pictures of
growing up in our families, and asking about each other's current
lives. I read her letter once again before falling asleep.

I woke early. It was Saturday morning, and I had nowhere
special to be. I went for a run after taking a glance at Leslie's letter again. The weather was crisp and clear that morning, and the
sun shone through curls of high, whirling clouds. I headed west
along Davenport Road, up the Baldwin Steps two at a time, and
jogged past Casa Loma to recover energy and store some for the
rest of the way home. Whereby my dusky subconscious could
break free to roam alongside the rest of me.

Gabrielle called soon after I'd stepped out of the shower and
asked if she could come over. She promised to bring a half-dozen
warm, chewy Montreal-style bagels with cream cheese. She was
true to her word. As she made us both coffee I sat and watched.

We seemed to be becoming good friends and, in the end, that
would be all. When she asked what I was up to, I told her, somewhat guardedly, "I got a letter from Leslie Van Houten."

Abruptly, Gabe turned to look directly at me." Really? From
prison?" I nodded. "Well, Peter, that really changes things, don't
you think?"

"What do you mean?" I'm sure my face had some sort of per-
plexity on it. It wasn't deliberate.

"This Manson obsession of yours is no longer just a pile of
books and articles, is it? What did she have to say, if it's not too
private?"

"She thanked me for writing and wishing her good luck in
her upcoming trial. She said that very little goes on in county jail

life, but she was happy to be closer to her mother and family during the trial. So, they visit her regularly. She's optimistic. That's about it." Gabe knew it wasn't.

She just stared, then calmly started, "Let's talk about you and me. Romantically, at least, things have been over between us for quite a while now, wouldn't you agree?" I confessed she was right.

"Now what?" I asked. With her usual clarity, Gabe started, "We need some space apart. You need... If I may? For one thing, you need to figure out how to play the adult game and not be so radical when it comes to condemning the 'system,' if you want a good teaching job.

"I wouldn't mention your pen pal in job interviews either."

I shook my head at first and stared straight through the floor until Gabe turned away and helped herself to a second cup of coffee. "You want me to fix you another?"

"I've decided not to go on with teaching high school," I announced.

"Oh?

"I'm not surprised. Not really. So, you've decided to go for coaching?"

"Probably. In one form or another. I'm waiting to hear back from the Higher Education Group about getting into their MA program this summer. If they say 'no,' I'll decide something later about coaching. Professor Sheffield, Head at HEG, requested that Andy and Bruce forward letters of recommendation directly to his office. I think I may stand a chance."

"So, coaching is, or isn't, still a part of your plan?"

"I might do both at the same time. My instincts are pushing me to the research program in the history, philosophy, and governance of universities. I'd love to be part of that," I said, surprising even myself at how certain I sounded.

"Why are you smiling?" I asked, sensing a bit of warmth coming my way from her.

"Peter, to be honest, that sounds just right for you." Then, looking straight at me with a smile, she added, "You'll be moving on soon one way or another, that's obvious.

"I need to move on too."

Stepping toward me, Gabe turned my face toward hers gently with her hand under my chin. "Can I just be honest?" She hesitated, then asked, "Isn't your interest in Van Houten just an infatuation with somebody famous?"

"Is that what you think?" I'd started to flinch.

"There are plenty more famous people besides those convicted of murder to be infatuated with, don't you think?

"You've been unhappy with a lot of things lately, including me. I know you have a soft spot for all sorts of rebellion and rebels, and I'm not particularly rebellious. Leslie is dark rebellion. It's not a preoccupation with her legal problems that's driving you."

We didn't talk again right away for a while. Much later on, after she'd gone, I wrote of this moment, thinking how much of what people perceive of one another is a projection of all sorts, shapes, and shading. My impressions of Gabrielle, like hers of me, were largely shortcuts and stereotypes we use for convenience.

Gabe began gathering up her things. "I need to go, Peter. You are a really smart, nice guy. Try not to get burned."

Before stepping out the door, Gabe kissed me twice on the lips and once on the forehead. That finishing touch felt like the uncertain beginning of one thing and the definite end of another. "Let me know what you think about Maugham's *Razor's Edge*. Take care."

Then she turned and closed the door behind her. Once she was gone, it hit me how empty a familiar room can be when someone who had been a relatively significant part of your life suddenly leaves it.

I let out a deep sigh and put on Todd Rundgren's side one of *Runt*. Wandering around my apartment and sorting things out on my desk, I reread Leslie's letter and scribbled my responses to what she wrote. Each time I looked over the notes, I'd tear a few of them up and start over. Shortly, there was a minefield of scattered, crumpled papers on my desk and all over the floor.

Since Leslie had not written much about her upcoming trial, I asked about that. Starting with what recent bits I'd read about the trial—*never* about anything to do with the cult or the murders. She'd been polite in asking me about my family and where I went to high school. I started again rather anxiously. I told her about summers growing up on our family farm thirty miles north of Toronto. Spending each school year, until I was eight, in the heart of downtown TO. A tale of two separate realities.

I described how I was expelled after my first year and a half at a private boys' school for breaking the terms of my scholarship. I was recruited to play football, hockey, and track for the Neil McNeil Maroons, though I quit to play hockey full-time for the Toronto Bruins.

After transferring to public school and failing grade ten twice, I wrote how the principal at Victoria Park Collegiate, Mr. Jackson Tovell—who knew me from the school's football and track teams—had a look at my grades and said he was puzzled. He called me into his office and had me sit for the Dominion of Canada IQ exam. He said he needed to know whether I was "truly a moron."

When I was sixteen, I left home to live with Mr. Tovell, his wife, and their two young kids, Lisa and Craig—at Jack's invitation. We lived in a nice suburban house near Windfields Park in

York Mills. It was a big break for me—a very real turning point in my life—that happened right after an exceptionally hard-hearted beating, not the first in a lifetime full of them, I'd taken from my father Frank.

Living with the Tovell family showed me a family that really loved one another and supported each other completely. While I missed my mum and brother Mike, I finished high school living with the Tovells and then, amazingly, was offered an academic/athletic scholarship to The Ohio University in Athens, a small college town near the West Virginia border with an exceptional university for its size. Authors Walter Tevis and Daniel Keyes, with whom I studied, taught there. As did existentialist philosopher Algis Mickunas, still my lifelong favorite professor.

My major subject was philosophy, so after two years at Ohio University, I transferred to the University of Toronto and graduated with a BA in philosophy from St. Michael's College. Presently, I told her about working with Andy Higgins, our national "multiple events" coach for the Canadian National Athletics Program.

Lastly, I wrote about Southern California and the many times I'd spent there. At that point. I simply signed the letter, *Yr. Mst. Obt. Friend @ Srvt., Peterx*, and included the photo she requested. Asking if she would send me a photo of herself. I pressed a Canadian dime into the sealing wax on the back of the envelope and placed it upright on my desk to admire the imprint.

I spent the rest of the day and well into the evening reading more about how Leslie had met Bobby Beausoleil, along with her history of boyfriends in general. What Martin had said about her dedication to Bobby still bothered me. Gabe's remark about my infatuation with Leslie Van Houten also lingered annoyingly.

Growing increasingly tired as the night grew old, I was ready to call quits to this day of track meets, break ups, and letter writing. Smoking a joint, having decided to mail my letter first thing in the morning, I slid a video into the Betamax. *Casablanca,* I think. Sometime later, I woke up on the couch, then dragged myself to bed, feeling as though I was covered in the gray-blue smoke of Humphrey Bogart's and Claude Rains' packs of cigarettes clinging to my pajamas.

* * *

That winter's end, while expecting to hear back from Leslie, I started reading the first edition of Ed Sanders' *The Family,* which I found in The Fifth Kingdom bookshop on Harbord Street. What a cool find that was! Sanders was a prominent counterculture activist, musician, and author I'd come across before. He had covered Leslie's first trial for the *Los Angeles Free Press* and had interviewed members of the Family and the Straight Satans at Spahn Ranch.

His style of writing was hip, energetic, and filled with material witness testimony and direct correspondence with Manson himself. Sanders' book had Bugliosi's beat.

Now, I was beginning to see where Martin Bijaux had gotten a lot of his information. Putting this and other additional sources into perspective, I started to track basic points about Leslie's upbringing.

Leslie Van Houten was twice voted "homecoming princess" at Monrovia High School, named after the small town twenty-five miles from downtown LA. She grew up in a middle-class neighborhood with an older brother Paul and two younger siblings. David and Betsy Van Houten were Korean war orphans her parents had adopted. When Leslie was just fourteen, she was shaken by her parents' divorce, which came as a frightening surprise. Her first experience with a deep feeling of abandonment.

Very pretty, smart, and popular at school, Leslie was adored by her younger siblings. But then, after her parents split up, Leslie started spending less time at home. She and her first serious boyfriend started experimenting with sex and drugs, which was also a part of the new "counterculture" generation people of age were experiencing in the sixties.

By the time Leslie was seventeen, it had become something of a habit to skip school and explore her sexuality with her boyfriend. They started experimenting with a powerful, new life-altering drug, LSD. It was the time for "Tuning In, Turning On, and Dropping Out," as Professor Timothy Leary preached from his podium at Harvard over national airwaves.

Soon after, Leslie dropped out of high school and ran away from home to San Francisco with the same boyfriend. Like many other "baby boomers," she was headed to Frisco Bay with flowers in her hair and a song in her heart. Then, shortly after their arrival, her boyfriend left her.

Once more feeling abandoned, she was completely cut off from home with no money in her purse or friends to protect her.

For those not part of those times of cultural upheaval—with war protests, civil rights protests, political assassinations, cities burning, *et cetera*—it may or may not be hard to imagine what it was like for teens and young adults in the sixties.

Unguarded sex and subsequent pregnancies were not uncommon. Neither was legal abortion common. It wasn't long before a pregnant, destitute Leslie returned to her family in Monrovia. She wanted to have her baby, but both her parents agreed she would not. They arranged for Leslie to have the abortion conducted privately at home.

Reading about this teenage stretch in Leslie's life really played on my mind. As far back as I can remember, I was always recovering from and/or dreading another beating from my dad. So, when I left home, I felt relief, not abandonment.

I couldn't imagine what it would have been like for Leslie to have her divorced parents take control of her life yet again. She was bound to leave home again. Why not? She was already alone.

After the abortion, Leslie returned to high school. After graduation, she attended business college briefly before dropping out. And sure enough, Leslie left home again. Needing to be a young, free spirit in charge of her own destiny. This time, she would not be alone for very long.

For those who remember this time in the late sixties, hitch-hiking was a pervasive means of transportation. It was a deeply embraced hippie code at the time that you never passed up a fellow traveler if you had room. And sometimes, even when you didn't. Just put your thumb out, and within a short period of time, you were more than likely to be picked up by a gaily painted VW van with other free spirits on board.

Somewhere near Mendocino, Leslie joined a camp of kindred souls pursuing a New Wave of music, mysticism, drugs, and relationships. That's where she met the handsome Bobby Beausoleil, already a purported Manson cult recruiter. Bobby, whose nickname was "Cupid," had another young companion with him who called herself "Gypsy," aka Catherine Share, another devotee of this guy "Charlie" they never stopped talking about.

Leslie was quite smitten with Bobby. Reportedly, when she offered to go "anywhere" with him, he asked if she would go "as far as Hell?" He claimed, she answered, "Take me."

It wasn't long after, nor that unusual an occurrence, when Leslie discovered she was expected to share "Cupid" with a gaggle of other girls. Bobby traded his old, beat-up school bus for an old, beat-up truck that he and his gypsy ducklings used as a camper. Eventually, Leslie, Bobby, and Gypsy ran off for LA together, leaving the others behind.

Gypsy assured Leslie they had friends there with a swell place to crash and swore to Leslie that her life was going to be "changed forever" after she met Charlie Manson. It was Gypsy, more than Cupid, who convinced Leslie to drop out of society and join their "journey of peace and love in the here and now" in Charlie's cult of a New Age.

After meandering down the coast, stopping in public rest areas, and parking overnight in a series of vacant lots—the trio eventually settled at the Manson Family encampment near Chatsworth.

The Spahn Ranch was the site of an old dilapidated Western movie set owned by a near-blind cowboy named George Spahn. There were a few hired hands around to look after the "Rent-a-Pony" horses they still had for hire. In exchange for having a few of the girls look after him personally, Mr. Spahn let this small group of Manson followers bunk in the tatty old trailers and derelict buildings scattered about the property.

When Manson first met the new, pretty brunette Beausoleil had brought with him, Charlie dropped what he was doing to approach Leslie. He studied her closely like he might examine a car or a gun.

He'd had plenty of experience handling runaway teenage girls like Leslie before. First, he would imply that he possessed insight into all her lonely disaffections. Second, and without any acting classes, Charlie would instinctively use a common theatrical device to mirror someone's moods, thereby making that person awkwardly self-conscious. By mimicking each changing expression or gesture Leslie made, Charlie was showing her how well he knew what she was thinking and feeling.

Charlie's impersonations were always short-lived as they had nothing more to them than his need to manipulate and control. Leslie may have been vulnerable on the streets with people she barely knew, but at least now she wasn't left to feel alone anymore. She was now in the company of other young females who were bonded amongst themselves with a new sense of family.

Leslie was, for the moment, not having to sleep in a trashy van or constantly tired and hungry from life on the open road. Who wouldn't prefer the presence of children, gardens, horses, and open spaces?

Danny DeCarlo, a member of the Straight Satans motorcycle club who was also camped out at the ranch, shared a dusty bunkhouse with Bobby, Gypsy, and Leslie. According to DeCarlo, Leslie seemed more independent and smarter than the other girls. She was comfortable around Charlie but seemed skeptical of his antics at first.

Once Leslie and Bobby split up, Leslie got closer to Charlie. Despite the closeness, Charlie told Danny he would "set Leslie straight, and damn quick at that." The words DeCarlo used to describe Charlie's process were, "Leslie was going to fit in like she was being *locked down.*"

Charlie was a heartless misogynist. In another culture, he would have had women walk at least five steps behind him. Women held limited value to Charlie. Though he used everyone he met equally, women were always "intended for a man's use," Charlie quoted from Scripture. Profiting from this primitive notion just like other good folks who parrot its excerpts.

* * *

It was bitter cold every night during the first week of March in Toronto. It was now a bit over three weeks since I'd sent my first letter to Leslie. I'd kept writing letters to her anyway and sent at least one or two every week. Mostly condensations of my diaries mixed with imaginative riffs and tangents. I was spending a fair amount of time studying Nietzsche's series of lectures, *On the Future of Our Educational Institutions,* published under the title *Anti-Education* and playing pick-up hockey at Varsity Arena.

Reading about Leslie and the Manson saga continued to occupy rare hours of downtime. I was also growing disdainful of so many characters I read about in the Manson Family. A real pack of thieves I had nothing in common with. Except, maybe a tiny bit with Charles Watson. Tex had played football and sprinted in high school. He was also Leslie's boyfriend for a time.

Watson was also the prime murderer at the Tate–LaBianca residences. Killing all but one of the nine people Charles Manson ordered killed that month. All except for Gary Hinman, who was killed by Bobby Beausoleil, Susan Atkins, and Mary Brunner. Susan Atkins helped to kill Sharon Tate, and Patricia Krenwinkel helped kill Abigail Folger. Although it was really Tex who finished both the pregnant actress and young heiress off.

Watson also killed ranch hand Donald "Shorty'" Shea, along with Charlie, Bruce Davis, and Steve Grogan each taking part. Charlie made each of them complicit so they wouldn't rat him out.

Eventually, after his own trial for the murders and his appeals based on "diminished capacity" were exhausted, Charles Watson eventually confessed. Tex's obvious guilt aside, I wondered, could his failed defense of "diminished capacity" have been a sound defense all along? Maybe Leslie's lawyer Maxwell Keith could argue that she never "murdered" anyone. What was Leslie Van Houten actually responsible for?

That end of winter in 1977 was mostly a detention of sorts for me and an anguishing waiting game.

Waiting for more daylight hours. Waiting to be forever finished with teacher's college. Waiting to hear if I would be accepted into the grad program with the Higher Ed. Group at OISE (Ontario Institute for Studies in Education). Waiting to see if I would get another letter from Leslie Van Houten. What I was not waiting for that cold night in March was to hear my phone ringing so late. Answering, I heard Jean Cousineau sounding substantively drunk and incoherent.

What I gleaned from what he was saying was that he was calling from a payphone outside of a convenience store and that he and Gabrielle would like to come over. Would that be okay?

6

WAITING FOR THE SIREN'S CALL

Naturally, I welcomed Jean and Gabe over. I was curious—even if it was obvious what they had to announce—to hear what they had to say about "going out" together. I put the water on to boil, lit a scented candle, and took a quick inventory of how I was feeling inside. Even though I could hear gusts of a cold, timorous wind rustling the branches outside, I was obliged to open the window to clear the air before they arrived.

When I opened the door, the rush of cold poured past me down the steps. I could see that Jean was too drunk to talk. He quickly confirmed I was right when he stumbled in, holding one hand to his mouth, brushing me back with the other.

"Where's Gabrielle?" I asked, stepping back inside, only to hear Jean flushing the toilet. I put a roll of paper towels and a trash bag beside the door to the bathroom and left him to his privacy. When he dragged himself out two minutes later, he asked for a glass of water. I had one ready with ice cubes and handed it off to him as he staggered to the futon and nearly fell down.

"How...*rar yu?* Have you aspirin...or anythin' stronger?" he moaned, rolling over into the cushions. I went ahead and found him something better.

"What are they?"

"Sixty milligrams of codeine sulfate. One is a good dose to take this side of a hangover. More than that would be negligent. Be sure to drink plenty of water," I said, pouring him a second glassful. "*Rx* in peace." I shut off the light.

Jean slept in his clothes under the sleeping bag I'd thrown on top of him. In the morning, I could see he was awake when I came back from my run. He'd made himself coffee. It took us a while to get around to talking about Gabrielle.

As he explained it, "She's more confused than upset, which is why she'd rather not talk right now. So, I thought I'd come over alone."

"Hey man, listen, I'm cool with all of it. I'm happy you two are dating. This way, we can still all be friends. It's so...*modern.*" Up until then, I hadn't been *too* possessive or jealous around girlfriends. Maybe a few times during my teens. But none meant more to me than I was prepared to let go of when the time came. There's no escaping the inevitable disappointments.

"What did she say?" I asked. "Anything more about my burning interest in the Van Houten case?"

"She said, she thinks you need to find something you feel has been missing from life. Something 'closer to the edge,' I guess. Fair enough?" He shrugged. I nodded.

"She said, she thinks there's 'something self-destructive' about you. That's all. Personally, I think you should take it as a compliment." Neither of us said much more about Gabrielle that morning.

Jean listened to the radio while I showered. What we spoke about afterward was his hope of finding a job teaching French lit and my chances of getting into the OISE that summer. I'd already told him about my plans to visit California at some point.

"To friendship and daring!" We clanked coffee mugs. Jean left soon after that, and I went back to reading some more. Thinking to myself that I'd just dodged a bullet.

Jean called the next day to say, "Thanks again for the tablets." He'd talked to Gabrielle, and she said everything was "hunky dory" when it came to her and me. Sounded worn but was welcome news all the same. Since it came without recriminations. I promised to call her but didn't speak to her again until I ran into her by chance weeks later at school.

Jean told me Gabe and Karen were going up north that upcoming weekend. Jean said he was free Friday night and asked if I wanted to join him for "something special cooking at the El Mocambo." Guy Bijaux, Martin's younger brother, was coming through town for a few days on his way back to Montreal.

"He's staying at the Park Plaza and would like to meet you," Jean said. "He's offered to treat us to a night on the town. Martin told him all about you. Guy's promised to bring along some surprises. What do you say? Jus' don't come dressed in a sweat suit."

"*This* Friday night? I don't know. There's a big track meet the next day. What kind of surprises? It's the Ontario Intercollegiate Indoor Finals at the Canadian National Exhibition track on Saturday. I was planning to get up early and help Higgins set up." First, silence at both ends. Then, on a sudden impulse, I blurted out, "Sure, okay, why not? What time do you want to head out?"

"Guy said to come by the hotel about nine. He has business 'til then. I can meet you beforehand and we can head over together. I'll introduce everyone." I agreed with his plan.

The temperature outside that morning was just above freezing. There was a light wind and rain in the forecast. I treated myself to another long, slow-distance jog in the gray, swollen fog. I ran for a few miles east along Davenport Road and turned south at Church Street. In my mind's eye, I imagined myself talking to Leslie, telling her about where in our previous lives she and I might have met along the Highway 1 coastline.

Cooling down, I ducked inside Hart House to finish my workout, eventually settling into the hot tub for half an hour before a cold shower. It felt cozy to change into the fresh cotton sweats and clean socks that I kept in my locker. I would write her about silly stuff like that, too, to help get her mind miles outside of her cell block. Knowing that she wasn't alone. Somewhere, someone was thinking of her.

Andy Higgins was nowhere on campus I could find him. Was this even a good time to talk? I did run into Jim Buchanan coming out of the northwest corner of Hart House, though. He told me he'd skipped lunch with Higgins also.

"Where're you headed next?" Buck asked. I pointed north. He said he was meeting someone that way at the Colonnade and asked, "Want to walk up together?" Of course, I did. It was always good to spend time with Jim Buchanan.

Buck was a dependently upbeat and positive person. Popular with everyone. Modest for someone as accomplished as he was. A remarkable, natural athlete with a gentlemanly competitive spirit and a real flair for entertainment. For instance, in May—the day we were checking into the Golden Sails in Long Beach—Jim spontaneously, without warning, came bounding across the lobby doing a series of backflips and handsprings.

Those of us watching, including the hairstylists looking out from the salon, cheered and applauded.

Now, as we crossed Hoskin Avenue and passed through the hallowed gates at the south end of "Philosopher's Walk"—I reminded him of that Golden Sails check-in event, and we had another good laugh recalling all that again. We also talked about my reaching out in support of Leslie, so it wasn't long before I baited him into asking, "How's that Van Houten trial going? Still writing her letters?"

"Her trial starts at the end of the month. I'm expecting another letter any day now." I should have said, "hoping for."

"You really think she stands a chance of ever being released?"

I'd heard that question a lot, so I took my time searching for a novel response or evasion. Jim and I had always supported one another. We respected each other. I know he defended me to others who thought it was "stupid" of me to bother getting involved with an "ex-Manson girl."

"The woman I'm trying to get to know deserves a fair trial," I told him. "It's clear she didn't have one the first time. Maybe they should just let her go."

"Good luck with all that! What makes you think she's any more likely to get a fair trial *this* time? I still don't get it, Pete. You say she didn't kill anyone. But she was there, right? She got into the car. She knew that those she was with were going to kill some people. I couldn't do it. Neither could you."

"*She* didn't kill anyone or plan to. She was delusionary. From her point of view at the time, it's obvious to me she was practically volunteering to die. Manson was taking advantage of her courage to fight.

"Exactly why, I still haven't figured out."

"What's your guess? You have to see it for what it is, Peter."

I didn't say so at the time, but by now, I was convinced that Leslie had been coerced into stabbing the deceased Mrs. LaBianca's body. For one thing—perhaps in order to save herself from the same fate. After he'd taken his seventh life in twenty-four hours, Tex Watson confessed to putting his knife in Leslie's hand and then commanded her to "Do *something!*"

"Look, Jim. I'm as sickened by what she took part in as I imagine you are. And so is she, I bet. Then, as now. The terror she must have seen in those innocent people would have traumatized anyone. It's horrible what she did."

"And what she must live with. She was originally sentenced to the gas chamber, wasn't she?" he asked.

"She was only twenty years old. I believe that made her the youngest woman in the history of California to be sentenced to the death chamber at San Quentin."

"How can that even be possible?" Jim asked. Recoiling from the thought of it. Shaking that off, he assured us both, "It can't happen here in Canada, though, can it? Not since the feds abolished the death penalty last year."

"Capital punishment in California has been abolished *for now*," I assumed. "But here, the Tories can always bring it back when it's their stint to turn the screws. I'm pretty sure the Canadian Armed Forces always retain their 'right' to put us in front of a firing squad."

I noticed Jim checking his watch. Without saying a word, we stopped walking the path and sat on a park bench under the trees outside the Royal Conservatory of Music. Jim took a notebook from his bag to check his day diary. Somewhere, someone above in one of the practice rooms was playing Chopin's "Nocturne" for violin with its window partly open. Turns out, Chopin was something else Jim had learned about in school.

Picking up from where I thought we'd left off about Leslie, I said, "I don't think she claims, or believes, she's innocent of participating in a terrible killing. She didn't plan *any* of it. She couldn't. Not given the state of her cognitive-affective health at the time."

"An insanity defense may seem kind of cliché to a jury," he replied. Which was a poignant remark that pricked my defenses.

"I'd say, Leslie Van Houten was guilty of 'involuntary man-slaughter,'" I told him. "But that's not enough for the DA. It's not the checkmark in the win column he's counting on. He *could* just let her go."

We got up again and walked into the Colonnade on Bloor Street. Jim was digging inside his shoulder bag again, so I held the door open for him, and we went straight up the escalator to the mezzanine. We sat down at a table in front of Mauk's Sandwich Shop, drank milk, and split a cheese and mustard sandwich. Gossiping about some of the personal relationships within our club.

Inevitably, when I must have appeared to have lost interest in all that, Jim asked me what I was thinking about. I couldn't say right away. I was lost.

"Never mind, Pete. I don't need to know anything about it really. But now I'm curious. How did her retrial come about any-way? I thought she was in for life. An', how come that other guy… not Manson…?"

"Charles Watson."

"Yes, why wasn't he tried alongside the others?"

"Watson ran back home to hide in Texas when the others were arrested. His family's lawyers fought his extradition back to

California for nine months. Somewhere near the end of October '71, Bugliosi convicted him too. Taking full credit for an easy 'slam dunk.' Chalked up another death sentence to be proud of.

"On appeal in 1976, Maxwell Keith argued that, because he hadn't been given adequate time to prepare a proper defense in 1970—after Leslie's original attorney Ronald Hughes' mysterious disappearance during the first trial—Judge Charles Older should have severed Leslie's case from Manson and the other defendants.

"The appeals court agreed and overturned her conviction."

Jim didn't say anything. Neither did I. I just finished my milk and ordered us lattes.

"All I know," I said at last, "is that, as of this moment, she's not been proven guilty of anything. And personally, I do not think that 'murder' is a proper indictment.

"I get the sense I'll know for sure if and when I get to meet her in person. I hope very soon," I winked.

"Interesting," he said, looking at me sideways. "So, you think you'll know for certain. People *were* murdered, man. Come on." He said it politely, but no less wholeheartedly. Momentarily, I was stumped for an answer.

"There are *degrees* of culpability, Jim. Outside of that horrific hour she spent inside the LaBianca home, she's never been party to any serious crimes or misbehavior reported anywhere. Before or after time spent in prison.

"Assuming the obvious, if Leslie Van Houten was effectively brainwashed at the time, she would be incapable of planning such violence beforehand, wouldn't she?"

Right as I was waiting for him to respond, Jim's rendezvous appeared at the top of the escalator and came walking toward us. We both stood up to greet her. He introduced us, but I regret I've since forgotten her name. Despite meeting her again several weeks later. That ended our talk for now. But at least Jim had listened. We split up soon after his girlfriend arrived. I'd see him Saturday morning at Maple Leaf Gardens' indoor track meet.

Instead of turning for home right away, I backtracked to the Robarts Library as I had previously planned to do before I ran into Jim. There was a recent edition of the *Los Angeles Times* (as recent as February 17th) with a report by staff writer Bill Farr about Leslie. I copied parts of the paper and read it in the periodicals room. Some of what I read kicked my heart rate up a notch.

In her response to reporters' questions, Leslie admitted she was "still haunted by nightmares for my role in the killing of Mr. and Mrs. LaBianca. I know that I did something horrible. I don't expect people to forgive me, but I hope eventually they will give me a chance."

She went on to say she looked forward to telling the truth about what really happened. She told the reporters that at the first trial, she could only say what Manson wanted her to say. Same as he orchestrated the exact scripts for each of the others to play in front of the media cameras and spectators.

The *LA Times* interview with Leslie suggested that Manson's motives for instigating massacres at the homes of the Polanskis and the LaBiancas—complete with allusions to The Beatles' lyrics printed in blood on the walls—were "deliberately staged to mislead the authorities."

Manson was worried that, after his arrest, Bobby Beausoleil would implicate him for the murder of Gary Hinman. So, in order to show Bobby how far he would go to help him in his defense, Charlie had innocent people slaughtered at 10050 Cielo Drive, and the next night, the LaBiancas. His way of assuring Bobby that he had his back. Designed to look like the real killers were still out there roaming wild.

From all of my reading thus far, it was becoming clearer to me how Manson used brainwashing, criminal culpability, sex, and threats of violence to get what he wanted. Absolute power over others' survival. The scores of acid trips Leslie took with the Manson Family I saw as part of Charlie's indoctrination program of mind control. At first, its sudden and profound effectiveness for brainwashing control must have surprised him.

Apparently, things changed dramatically from that summer in 1968 to the next. Former cult members explained how Manson staged things. For example, whenever a new girl would show up, the whole Family would come out to welcome her by name. Making her feel welcome. There were horse rides, children playing in gardens, and pot parties during the day. Psychedelic campfires, dune buggy rides, and frantic orgies by night.

Midway through '69, all the "peace, love, and family" glow had been replaced by an abundance of darker, hardcore drugs; guns; paranoia; and bikers who called themselves the "Straight Satans." Then there was Charlie. Ringmaster at the center of the cult circus. Preaching about an impending Apocalyptic war, "Helter Skelter." A war Manson conjured out of his own paranoid hallucinations and infectious delusions. Claiming to his followers that The Beatles had written in special messages they were sending to him in the lyrics of their songs.

The court testimony of several former Family witnesses showed that "everything was done at Charlie's direction." Paul Watkins described the orgies that took place usually once or twice a week. Saying they would always start out with a peyote or a ritual LSD sacrament.

Charlie would dispense doses of drugs like a priest laying the Holy Host of Sacred Communion on everyone's tongue—all according to how much he wanted each person to take. The same as with everything else, he kept the women on much tighter reins than the men. The men were his confidantes, the girls his disciples.

When asked how Manson would usually go about "programming" someone, former Family member Brooks Poston testified, "With a girl, it would usually start out with sex." Charlie might persuade a plain-featured girl that she was beautiful. Or, if she had a father fixation, have her imagine that he was her father.

When a man first joined the group, Manson would take him on an acid trip, ostensibly "to open his mind up." Then, while he was in such a highly credulous state, Charlie would talk to the dope about how he had to "surrender to love."

If a guy or girl was looking for a leader, he might imply that he was the second coming of Christ. A teenage Brooks Poston testified at the first trial that Manson's "claim to divine status wasn't so much stated as implied."

Charlie claimed to have lived two thousand years before and often referred to himself as both "God" and "the Devil." Charlie could be whatever you or he wanted him to be. He often repeated, "I am just a reflection of you."

He would put on any guise you wanted to see. A father, friend, brother, the "fifth Beatle," or your worst nightmare. Especially if the right Beatles record happened to be playing "Helter Skelter," just as you were peaking on some sullied acid he laid on you.

Leslie told *Times'* reporter Bill Farr how, after years of rehab and extensive prison counseling, she finally came to recognize the truth. Which had nothing to do with triggering a race war or a real revolution. Although that's what she was once completely duped into believing. That was a big part of the tragedy right there. *Indiscreet faith in idealism leads to a chamber of horrors.*

* * *

Weeks had gone by with me working hard and writing more un-requited letters to California. Then it *happened.* Twice as thick this time, the second letter both uplifted and unsettled my day-dreams when I read it the first time.

One thing she said got me thinking about how wrong I had been in making certain assumptions based on the reading I'd done. I presumed she'd been a politically disaffected middle-class teenage hippie just like me. With an impossible home life. Not so.

Leslie told me the reason she left home wasn't because of any intense alienation from her family. The real reason she went "on the road" was due to a healthy curiosity about spirituality and communal living. And to be with a boy she'd fallen madly in love with.

Another thing she had me thinking about more precisely was just how unlikely paralleled that "summer of love" in 1969 had been for me. That summer before Leslie went off to jail and I went off to college. I shivered to think how easily we might have traded places.

She said she was writing quickly, hoping the "Officer" would take the letter before the weekend. In part, this is some of what she had to say:

Hi Peter,

… Got two letters from you. From now on I'm puttin' numbers on the letters. Please tell me how long it takes you to get them. Your letter took weeks to get here. Is that normal?

I love your letters, so full of surprises. They are so scat-tered you made me smile. Boy—you're going to have a terrible time w/me and surprises. I confess, I speak every chance I get. I can't help it. Just happens. So it's a warning, OK?

This place has been hell. Today a "tour" by a bunch of creepy people from some part of the Sheriff's Dept. came around and the Sgt. giving the tour starts hashing over what she thinks she knows about me and they keep craning their necks to stare.

I think we are both going through some weird sort of scene in our late twenties or something. The big evaluation. I think we're premature. I think the late '30s ought to be our time to search and see where we are. When I feel like giving up, I know I can't. Like you, I have to have dreams to fight for and that's where we're at. I think part of the scene is that our painful youths have ended, and now we know who we are and what we want and any wait seems absolutely forever.

I wonder what you're doing. It's 9 o'clock. Spending time wondering what fills your life these days. Reading? Writing to me, perhaps. Do you have a swell girlfriend? Probably. Thank you for the picture. I'm too embarrassed to send the ones I have here. I'm going to ask my friend Linda to send you one a photographer from the Christian Science Monitor took of me recently.

Please send my love to all of your family. I'm so pleased they dig what you told them about me. Please tell them how important that is to me. Tomorrow I'm going to tell you a story. Dad and Mom are all right. Thanks for asking. Bets and David too. Betsy really likes your picture too. Everyone's hopeful. I'm going to try and mail this now and hope it gets on its way soon. This is #2 but let's call it #1, okay?

Yours, Me!
Leslie-Lou

P.S. You asked about how my family and friends took it when they first heard the news I was in trouble. The worst part for me was the pain that I caused them. They thought what happened to me had been their fault somehow, and that wasn't the case at all. I didn't run away from them. I was just searching for my real self. You know. Still searching. Xxo

"PLEASE TELL ME YOU'VE MISSED ME"

The Park Plaza Hotel was a grand hotel at the northwest corner of Bloor and Avenue Road, across from the Royal Ontario Museum. Jean called up to the room, and Martin Bijaux's brother Guy came down to the lobby to greet us. Guy was more fair-haired than his older brother Martin and more boyish-looking, with a thin frame and straight blond hair halfway to his shoulders. I guessed he was in his early twenties, but he may have been slightly older.

Guy invited us up to his suite where he said he'd left a friend of his waiting. When we entered the room, he introduced us to his buddy Mike Pomer. The room had a spectacular view of the cityscape lights facing south toward the lakefront and Toronto Island Airport. All four of us stood at the window staring out at the citadels of corporate banks, which reminded me of giant crystals all at odds with each another.

"When I was a kid growing up here in the fifties," I told our hosts, "the tallest buildings in the city were its church steeples. Serving a spiritual function, I suppose." I pointed out the direction of the Cathedral Church of St. James, which, "When it was completed in the 1870s, its spire was the tallest structure in Canada. Nearly three hundred feet and remained so until the end of the nineteenth century."

We soon got to drinking and talking much about nothing worth remembering. Other than how quickly a row of 50-ml bottles of various liquors and soda cans disappeared from the minibar. Scattered empty on the floor like kids' abandoned toys. Before anyone said what the plan was on offer, Guy opened the clothes closet to take a cardboard shoebox out of a duffle bag.

"Here it is," he said as he lifted the lid and found what he was looking for. Guy took out an engine-turned container with, I'm sincerely sad to say, a polished plate of pink and blue ivory adorning the top.

"Elegant," I couldn't help saying. Despite the likely cruel circumstances of its origins, it really was something precious to admire.

"*What's* inside?" Jean asked.

"Blotter acid," Guy's friend Mike said as he leaned forward from the edge of the bed to have a closer look. "Pure LSD-25."

"Who wants a hit or two on the house?" Guy smiled, looking around at each of our faces. He pulled out a strip less than an inch long with measured doses lined in rows on one side of the paper.

"This comes with the room service, does it?" Jean asked.

Guy laughed. Mike smiled, and I said, "I really shouldn't be dropping anything this late in the evening. Not tonight. I'm supposed to be somewhere tomorrow."

"It's up to you," Guy responded as he carefully cut eight 4-mm squares with a pair of barber's shears and lined them up in a row on the table. Each one had the image of a ripe strawberry on it, the notice of which made each of us smile after Mike pointed this out.

"Thanks, no. Really, I shouldn't," I said, holding my hand up to tap my heart. "I'm grateful for the kind offer, though."

"Don't be a wuss," Jean said. I waved him off, so Guy put the rest of the blotters back in the jar.

"Mike works at the El Mocambo," Guy said, changing the subject. "Word is Keith Richards may be there tonight, maybe playing with a band calling themselves the Cockroaches."

"I can get us all in for the show," Mike proudly added. "That's where we're planning to go." Jean looked enthusiastic.

Then, turning back to me, he said, "You'll get enough sleep before dawn, Peter. Where's your nerve for adventure? This is an *event,* my friend. Let's make a night of it!"

All three of them swallowed a whole blotter each, and Jean borrowed the scissors to cut his piece in half. Suddenly, I changed my mind and let my good conscience go. On a sudden whim, I licked my finger, pressed it onto one of the halves, then washed it down with the last swigs of Mike Pomer's Smirnoff and tonic.

Whatever satisfaction or regrets I might have later, I'd already crossed the Rubicon.

An hour or so later, we four psychonauts were headed out the doors of the plaza on foot, although it felt to me as though I was floating on a paddle boat at times. Wading our way down

Philosopher's Walk, I asked Mike, "Isn't Keith Richards supposed to be under house arrest at his hotel?"

"Not exactly," he said, going on to explain to us all that the police had detained The Rolling Stones guitarist in February. "When he was charged with possession of twenty-odd grams of smack. That's a lot. Keith and his girlfriend Anita Pallenberg and their three kids have been kept in their suites at the Harbour Castle ever since without their passports."

"Mike heard tonight, he's plannin' a kind of comin'-out party," Guy said. "Who knows who else might show up?"

"Something I'd like to see," Jean announced. Turning to me, he asked, "Are you feeling anything yet?" Seconds later, as if by auto-suggestion, I started to notice far-away objects seeming a bit closer and faraway echoes sounding louder with each new horizon that tumbled into our view. I could feel positive or negative magnetic waves of vibration whenever a passerby came close to our party.

The El Mocambo, or "El Mo" as it was known, was housed in a building first used as a safe house for American slaves escaping on the Underground Railroad. It's been a bar and music venue for more than a century since. The place stands on a property south of College Street on the west side of Spadina Road. Very near campus. The El Mo was considered a stronghold of rock 'n rhythm and blues by savvy fans of the genre.

The club at first seemed to me to be lightly attended. But I couldn't be sure of too much abstraction by now. Music seemed to pour down the steps in a torrent. Mike's friends at the door let us right in and one escorted us upstairs in no time at all.

The place seemed to shrink with more people, but the room wasn't bustling with too much charge or excitement just yet. Must be between sets. I hadn't noticed the band yet for some reason;

my mind was stirring with something else just as the music, and I along with it, really began to get off.

The stage on which the band stood to play was set just a foot off the floor and a yard from the edge of crowded tables. There was no place for us to sit right away, so we leaned against the wall near the piano. Behind the stage, against the wall, there was a sunset mural with palm trees that began bristling and spinning as if driven by the solid sounds of multicolored vibrations coming from each of the walls as if they were all speakers.

Not as big a Stones fan as I once was, I could still see why their groupies adored them.

I'd always liked the quiet detachment in the way Charlie Watts beat out his signature rhythms. None of us recognized the bassist that night. It wasn't Bill Wyman playing behind guitarists Ronnie Wood and Keith Richards, who were up front having a blast. Whiskey bottles adorned the tops of their amplifiers. Mick Jagger was singing and prancing between them in a white, zippered jumpsuit done up so tight it looked like his "jag" might bust out of its socket.

The room itself came alive with vibrant, colliding electrons, and a bright firestorm seemed at times to surround and embrace me. Other times, people's faces seemed covered in layers of peeling paint, which caused me to wonder about my own appearance. I touched my own face just to check if it was still intact.

Multi-costumed bipeds skipped in flames; all the while, the walls and ceilings never stopped billowing. And then, crackling and swelling with a pure energy, Mick and the band started belting out that old bluesman Bobby Troup's travel advisory— telling me to "go take that California trip" on *Route 66*. They seemed to be talking to me, so I had to take them seriously, right, Charlie?

Sometime later, I recall having the distinctive sense of plateauing. Feeling as though I were watching the whole scene from a perch in one of the painted palm trees on the wall behind the band. There were moments I felt I was entering into a strange realm of shadows and fog. At other times, I sensed myself being lifted off the ground by the music toward the ceiling, which was cracked and would occasionally open up to reveal the night skies above.

Then I'd look again moments later and find the ceilings had closed but were cracking again just like before.

After another song I thought I'd heard on the *Aftermath* LP, I began to feel a tinge claustrophobic, and my skin started to crawl. Just a tingle at first, then I noticed myself involuntarily starting to yawn. My brain needed more oxygen. Some way of regaining my equilibrium. Everyone in our quartet kept smiling and looked happy enough.

Though nothing was certain.

Not even how I found myself standing alone in front of a mirror in what I found out later was the women's washroom. There were sure to be other people around, but all I could see were the whites of my eyes inside the head of a wolf in the room behind the mirrors.

The rest of the room fell into starless, purring pitch-black darkness. The he- or she-wolf seemed as curious about me as I was about him or her. I couldn't tell its sex from its fangs or its snarls. I did remember marveling at the effects I was getting. Evoking ever-changing beasts beneath fearsome masks with my steady white eyes showing through the sockets.

Still makes the hair on my forearms stand up like quills on the back of a porcupine.

When I got back to my posse by the piano, I signaled that I had to be leaving right as the band started belting out "Let's Spend the Night Together." I had no idea how the others couldn't be tripping blazes like I was. Jean did try to say something I couldn't comprehend—even if he had gotten all his words out. I gestured and mouthed something to signal I'd be sure and give him a call. I waved goodbye to Guy and Mike and tried to say, "Thanks again for taking us out." Only my tongue was numb and too dry to help out.

When I turned down the stairs and brushed up against someone, I thought I recognized her to be a Hindu goddess on tour. I think she gave me a nudge on the shoulder to turn me in the right direction.

As I writhed my way down the stairs, a dark-haired woman's face came close to mine, and I noticed something odd but strangely familiar about her. When I looked back, I could see diamond-crusted dragonflies chasing each other around her eyes where there should have been lashes.

The radiators moaned all night and the house shivered like a dog asleep dreaming. I toughed it out and kept rolling along into dawn. At first, the daylight made every object—including myself—appear out-of-rest and in continuous motion. Then I'd close my eyes for an instant. When I opened them again, everything ground to a halt. I kept trying in vain to remember all of the last night's ineffable, dazzling bright moments. Wrote down what little I could make sense of or recall in a letter to Leslie, *sans* the acid.

* * *

For the next couple of weeks, I remained busy with my studies and more practice teaching that would soon be over. Then what? If I got into summer school at OISE, I'd still have some time to get hip to Mick Jagger's tip and take that California trip? Or at least engineer a reconnaissance mission regarding the interior frontier of that desert paradise wilderness.

Jean and Gabrielle stopped by Varsity Arena the next Tuesday night near the end of a scrimmage. We three grabbed a bite to eat, got high, and went to a movie. We went to see *Bound for Glory* and stayed up half the night talking about each other's personal sufferings and life's hesitations.

Predictably, I made a connection between Woody Guthrie's yearnings for fame with Roman Polanski's saying he believed the *real motive* for his wife's ill-starred murder was Charlie Manson's bitter envy toward those like Polanski. Those with the kinds of talent, wealth, and recognition that were denied him.

"A pretty astute take on the case, if you ask me," I recall Gabrielle saying. Thinking how much more attention I paid now that she was seeing someone else.

"I'd always thought Vincent Bugliosi was far less swift than Mr. Polanski from the get-go," I added.

A few days after that, the news broke out of LA that Roman Polanski had been arrested and charged with raping a thirteen-year-old girl at the home of his friend and actor, Jack Nicholson.

The young teenage model was Samantha Gailey—who Polanski had been commissioned to photograph for *Vogue* magazine. News agencies around the world listed a broad spectrum of charges, such as: rape using drugs, furnishing a controlled substance, and performing lascivious acts with a minor. Quite a headline.

I'd also been reading how Charlie and Bobby Beausoleil had moved to Los Angeles with the same dreams and ambitions in mind as those with the kinds of real talent that earned them wealth and recognition. They each imagined making names for themselves on the rock scene, believing they had all the talent they needed. All they believed that they lacked were contacts inside the recording industry.

Then along comes The Beach Boys' dreamboat drummer Dennis Wilson, driving his silver GT 250 Ferrari.

Wilson stopped to pick up Patricia Krenwinkel and another Manson girl, Ella Bailey, called "Yeller," whom he spotted out on the Sunset Strip with their thumbs out. Reading all about how the girls went with Dennis back to his place for a full-on sexual frolic reminded me of the threesome in *A Clockwork Orange* when I thought about it. The scene Stanley Kubrick set to the rhythm of the "William Tell Overture" in fast forward.

The Manson girls didn't really know who Dennis Wilson was—but when they told Charlie about the encounter, he knew right away what that meant. He insisted the girls take him and the rest of the Family back to Wilson's house at 14400 Sunset Boulevard—a beautiful log cabin estate near Pacific Palisades. It was similar, in fact, to the French country-style house Wilson's friend, Columbia Records producer Terry Melcher rented at the end of a cul-de-sac high in the clouds above Benedict Canyon.

After that chance encounter with the two "Manson girls," the next night, when coming home late from the recording studio, Dennis pulled into his driveway and could hear loud Beatles' music playing from inside the house. Wilson noticed a party going on inside, with a dozen people—mostly girls—running around the place naked.

When he opened the door, there stood all five feet, two-and-a-half inches of Charles Manson. Manson dropped to his knees to pay homage to the famous rock and roll legend. First, by kissing his feet, then offering the famous Beach Boy drugs and whatever, or whomever, however he wanted. Dennis Wilson was welcomed to have all the drugs and girls one at a time or in countless, staggered formations.

Since the girls reliably proved themselves willing to engage in whatever drug-induced sexual fantasies Dennis desired, The Beach Boys drummer consented to having Charlie and these nubile groupies stay at his house. Eating his food, driving his cars, and peeing in his pool if they had to.

Not known for his brains, style, or good sense, Dennis thought Charlie was some kind of deep thinker. More than that, of course, he was seduced by the orgies that Manson set up for him and his friends, who fancied chasing sexy, naked sprites and fairies around the pool and gardens 24/7. Someone should have thought to invite Roman Polanski.

Dennis was fascinated with Manson and pitched him to many of his famous friends as an "amazing singer-songwriter" hippie guru with whom he collaborated. Charlie also thought he had a pre-existing agreement with Dennis that he would be paid five thousand dollars for the song he wrote, "Cease to Exist," if The Beach Boys recorded it.

In the meantime, before what was left of Dennis Wilson's milk of human kindness had completely run dry, Manson put the bite on every celebrity who showed up at Dennis's door, looking for a party. Besides Wilson's famous brother, Beach Boys composer Brian, Charlie was introduced to another *bona fide* singer-songwriter rock 'n roll legend who spent time at the house, Neil Young.

One time, when Mr. Young came by, he tried to improvise a few chords on the guitar to go with the lyrics that Charlie made up on the spot. Young referred to Charlie's music as that of a "song-spewer" as opposed to a "songwriter."

In 1968, during that time of drug-induced, philosophical vaudevillian discussions—between bouts of singing, ceaseless guitar strumming, and plenty of free-wheelin', spontaneous sex—also among the many celebrities who came carousing to the never-ending frolics was The Byrds record producer Terry Melcher. Son of famous Hollywood actress Doris Day.

Melcher had produced more than eighty top-selling hits for Columbia Records. He and his girlfriend, actress Candice Bergen, rented the house at 10050 Cielo Drive up until a few months before the pregnant Tate-Polanski couple moved in.

In due course—sick of all the theft, destruction, and lies visited upon him by Charlie and his band of squatters—Dennis Wilson cut his losses and defaulted on his lease. That left the Manson sect on their own to await the sheriff's eviction.

All tallied—what with all the stolen items, dental treatments, and serious damage to an uninsured Mercedes-Benz—Dennis Wilson was out hundreds of thousands of dollars. The medical bills alone had been staggering, especially after the girls all suffered a virulent outbreak of gonorrhea.

Coincidentally, Terry Melcher had just hired Dennis Wilson's friend Gregg Jakobson to find him new talent. Jakobson knew Charlie from the Sunset Estate parties and promised Manson he could convince Terry to come up to Spahn Ranch to hear Charlie sing some more.

Dennis and Gregg finally succeeded in dragging the music producer to Spahn Ranch to give Charlie Manson a listen. Manson must have felt sure a recording contract would soon follow once Melcher heard him play, and he told the girls what they must do to help make this happen.

"You're good," Terry reportedly said, shining Charlie on, "but I wouldn't know what to do with you." Melcher never returned any of Manson's phone calls, hoping that he'd get the message. He got it, all right, but it wouldn't suffice a pathological narcissist. Not by a long shot.

Terry Melcher *did* return once again to the ranch to hear Charlie audition. Not so much because he'd changed his mind about Manson's singing, but because he was partial to having sex with a cutely precocious teen named Ruth Ann Moorehouse.

Melcher promised to return to hear Manson again in exchange for another romp. Somehow, Candice Bergen caught on and put the nix on that. She knew what was going on with Terry, even if Charlie didn't.

However groovy Charlie's songs may have sounded to fanatics ripped on mesc and meth at the ranch, Manson's songs made little impact on a veteran critic like Melcher. When Melcher didn't show up next time as planned, some of the girls said Manson went "completely ballistic." Maybe he should have listened more closely to the title of one of his own songs. "Ego is a Too Much Thing," after all.

Presumed to be perpetually intoxicated, Dennis Wilson had thought he saw something in Charlie's song about getting a girl to submit herself and let go of her ego to the point that she would "Cease to Exist." In Wilson's version, the singer is asking the girl to "cease to *resist*"—a control method more to his liking. That's quite a premise.

Beach Boy Dennis Wilson retitled the song "Never Learn Not to Love" and recorded it on The Beach Boys' own Brother Records label *without* Charlie's permission or participation.

Thinking about what the Manson Family's occupation had cost him, Dennis listed himself as sole composer, cutting Charlie out. When Wilson told him he had recorded his song with The Beach Boys, Charlie at first was elated. He expected "Cease to Exist" to appear on the next Beach Boys' album that winter. Instead, The Beach Boys released "Never Learn Not to Love" as the "B-side" of their new single, "Bluebirds over the Mountain." There was no mention of Charles Manson.

To Charlie, this represented an unforgivable act of disloyalty in the long saga of persecution he'd claimed to have suffered for thousands of years. There was sure to be hellfire and fury whipped upon the backsides of those rich and famous brats who dared dick around with the Devil. Charlie handed Gregg Jacobson a .44-caliber slug to pass along to Wilson for him. "Tell Dennis I got one more for him."

By most Family members' accounts, matters soon got even more crazy and violent back at the ranch.

One sign of the changes taking place at the end of the summer of '69 was how obsessively Manson kept The Beatles' *White Album* with the song "Helter Skelter" playing repeatedly. And with everyone tripping like mad whores on acid, Charlie continued to program his malleable, dutiful sect with endless mantras and repetitions.

"Can you hear it? Can you hear it? Can you hear it? They're speaking to me. They're speaking to me. They're speaking to me...." Crap upon piles of crap like that *ad infinitum*.

There were plenty of things I was reading and taking note of that I never wrote about in my letters but kept in my diaries. Right then, I was more focused on coming to grips with the circumstances surrounding Leslie's exact role in the killings themselves and what led up to it. I still had a long way to go.

Charlie Manson must have certainly felt the heat closing in throughout the second half of 1969.

Ranch owner George Spahn had started asking hired hands like "Shorty" Shea to run an increasingly violent and megalomaniacal Charles Manson and his Family off his property.

Since the recording arrangements Charlie was counting on never ensued, things overall weren't looking so rosy. Manson became evermore paranoid as his troubles wore on. Right from the start, he never forgave Tex for fouling up his deal with Lotsapoppa. Or Bobby for his dumb pact with the Satans that accelerated the unraveling with his arrest for the murder of Gary Hinman, for Christ's sake! It was all too much to stop the entire Family madness from spiraling totally out of control.

On Thursday, August 7th, 1969, the day before Manson sent Tex and the girls to kill everyone who was there at what they still believed was Terry Melcher's address. Charlie had sent word to Bobby that he had a sure-fire plan underway for throwing a spanner into the case the police had against him. Less than twenty-four hours after Beausoleil's first court appearance, when he and Manson were both being held in the same county jail, Charlie got a message to Bobby to keep his mouth shut. Charlie had a plan to make the detectives think they had the wrong man in custody.

It was clear Charlie Manson held a bitter grudge against Terry Melcher. Not just for turning him down as a recording artist after hearing him sing and play. Also, for going along with his friend Dennis Wilson in promising to pay him for any songs of his they recorded.

So, Charlie came up with the brilliant idea of getting Bobby out of jail by having Tex go to Terry's house and kill him and whomever else happened to be there with him. Making it look like the same people who killed Gary Hinman were responsible. Tex "owed him," Charlie said, for buggering up the Bernard Crowe shambles that started all the Manson Family unraveling that ensued. This was his penance.

Leslie's retrial was well underway in the spring of 1977. Sometimes, news in the *LA Times* was delayed in getting to me, as were so many of Leslie's letters. I read how Deputy District Attorney Stephen Kay, who assisted Vincent Bugliosi during the first trial, was now in charge of her second prosecution. Leslie wrote to say she could see right from the start that Kay "thinks it's all right to play dirty." In his eyes, she was still a "Manson girl," after all.

Kay requested that the testimony she had given in the penalty phase of the first trial be read again to the new jury. Maxwell Keith objected, saying his client's earlier testimony in 1971 was *deliberately* "false and misleading." It had been established by then that Leslie was coerced into "a pathetic attempt to exonerate Manson and immolate herself," Keith protested. I could imagine Mr. Kay smirking, but he stuck to his guns.

Leslie testified she lied on the stand because that's what Manson told her to do. At one point, she said Charlie leaned over the counsel table and told her to say she'd been at Gary Hinman's house the day he was murdered. Manson told her to get the story straight from Susan Atkins. But now (in 1977), she said the reason she lied six years before about what really happened at the LaBiancas was to help Charlie and Tex get off.

Manson had impressed upon her and the others for over a year how essential it was for him to remain free at all costs to save the Revolution.

The trial continued through April, and sometimes letters from Leslie would arrive two and three at a time. I wrote her back almost every other day with as many questions as I had news. She wanted to know when I was planning to travel to LA to meet her. *Now that was a thought.* I would have more than a month off before the OISE summer session got started—assuming I was admitted. I had my fingers crossed on both fronts.

Leslie wrote quite a lot about her old friends from high school—certainly more than she did about the lawyers, journalists, and famous psychiatrists who presently crowded their way in to see her.

During April, it felt like the tail end of winter had bitten back hard with a blizzard. I didn't mind. I knew that spring would take over soon, and I'd be back in the open more often. On morning runs, it felt good to breathe the sour-sweet scent of snowmelt still caught in the evergreen branches.

There was a good-luck new moon still rising on Wednesday, April 20th when I got the news from the registrar's office at OISE. I'd been accepted into the master of arts program in the History and Philosophy of Higher Education. *Woo hoo!* I could begin in the summer.

The first person with whom I wanted to share this news flash was Leslie. So, on my way to Hart House that morning to tell Andy, I stopped in the campus book room to shop for some new stationery. Then, after training, I was anxious to get back home and write Leslie a long letter, which I signed off by saying, "I'm coming to see you next month! Please tell your friend Linda I'll call when I get there. You know I'm a fool for you, girl." Then, I taped a tiny magazine photo of Marlon Brando from *The Wild One* to the outside of the envelope.

On Monday, May 16th, I'd posted another letter to Leslie, which began, "I'll be there to see you in person before you even receive this..." Then another letter from her arrived the same day, which included a reminder of her friend Linda's address on Victory Boulevard in Woodland Hills and Leslie's sister Betsy's telephone number in Hermosa Beach.

That same day, I took fifteen hundred dollars out of the Canadian Imperial Bank of Commerce in US dollars (enough, I hoped, to get me through a month or more in LA on my own). Lastly, I booked an open return ticket with an Air Canada agent in the same mall as my bank.

One week later, the day after high jumper Carl Georgevski's wedding at Saint Clement's Church—and the last time I would ever see Carl, Andy, Bruce, David, Louise, Mike MacVarish, and Buck Buchanan all together again—I took a limousine out to the US customs terminal at Pearson Airport.

It went from gray, overcast skies when I left that afternoon in Toronto to a rare morning shower when I landed at LAX before noon. That famous Los Angeles sunshine was on hold until after my arrival, it seemed. As we taxied to the Air Canada terminal, I caught a glimpse of that old control tower that looks like a tacky spaceship yet never failed to excite me.

Stepping outside the cabin, I felt the difference of two thousand miles, three time zones, and more than twenty degrees Fahrenheit.

There she was. Dressed in a pale-yellow blouse with a powder-blue skirt and braided blue leather sandals, smiling brightly. I could see her long, lanky arm waving as she approached from a distance. We began with a rock-solid kiss and embrace. Then, pressing her entire body as close to mine as epoxy, a beaming Tricia Woodbridge said, "It's been a year, Peter. *Please tell me you've missed me.*"

8

LOS ANGELES TIMES

The City of Los Angeles was the second or third largest metropolis on the continent, with the City of Toronto closing fast. Although landing at major airports makes most modern cities look the same.

This vast mountain basin of desert hills on the Pacific coast only averages a foot or so of annual precipitation with little overcast skies from November to April. The rest of the time, the sun shines, so even brief storms and showers like this late one in May were fairly uncommon.

Tricia and I were soon out of the wet inside the parking lot across from Terminal One, kissing against the side of her car, when I stopped to take in the whole, long, tall strawberry blonde.

"I love what you've done with your hair." She'd cut it by ten inches or more since last year but kept a few flyaway ringlets and tangles. Proudly possessed with a wonderful smile that instantly provoked the remark: "Look how beautiful you are." All that aside, we had been close friends and occasional, casual partners off and on for years. Free to be with other people when we needed to be. Without recrimination.

Trish tossed the keys to her Mustang II, climbed in on the pilot's side, lifted her hips and legs over the console, and strapped herself in on the passenger side. I stared at her the whole time before climbing in behind the wheel. Laughing, she said, "I'll navigate, you drive. Just don't be a madman as usual."

The engine was still warm, so we pulled out into airport traffic straight away without warming her up. The brakes were soft and long, and the suspension felt mushy. All the millions of poorly sealed oil pans dripping onto the roadways made the water bead up, and the tires aquaplaned on the pavement. Whenever I tried putting the spurs to her lackluster 105 horses, there was no torque in response. Even in the dry, the Ford Mustang II handled about as well as a sofa on coasters.

The rain let up. A windy, gray day for LA but warm and comfy just the same. During the days I remembered, even the ugly parts of Los Angeles had palm trees and yuccas enhancing its endless rows of stucco dwellings. They weren't all glamorous, though many were nicely adorned with red Spanish tile. For now, it was easy to ignore any unsightliness. It was midday in LA, and I was focused less on the road than on the radiant young woman seated beside me. While we sat idle in northbound traffic on Lincoln for half an hour, at least we got to hold hands and catch up on recent events.

Trish told me where to turn, and we found a spot to park near her favorite delicatessen. Somewhere close to the beach at Santa Monica and Ocean Avenue.

Seated in the booth next to ours were two supersized fellows with thick German accents and necks as swollen as the trunks of well-nurtured oaks. Tricia recognized one of the men and whispered to me that he was "Mr. Olympia." Apparently, the man having the beef dip on rye was a bodybuilder who'd appeared in a couple of movies I'd never heard of.

"His name is Arnold Schwarzenegger," Trish said in a low tone close to my ear. "Or something like that.

"What are you staring at? Did the color of my eyes change again or somethin'?" she asked, acting shy and embarrassed by my gaze.

"No. Well, maybe. I was thinking back to a year ago when…"

"Let's not," she interrupted.

"Okay. Whatever you say. Where do you want to go next? Hit the beach?"

"Oh, do we have to? The beach on an overcast day sounds good to you?" She faked a frown. "Not today. I haven't had time to shop. I'll need to pick up a few things."

"Where would you like to start?"

"I don't work until tomorrow. How about we go shopping first?"

"The UCLA bookstore!" I was enthusiastic.

Westwood was one of my favorite places. So that's where we headed for Trish to get what she needed from the pharmacy, dry cleaning, and sundry store. I shopped for tube socks, shampoo, razor blades, size-8 Puma trainers, and a medium-soft toothbrush that, in those days, you had to use manually.

Eventually, as always, I led the discussion around to my interest in the Van Houten story. I did that with just about everyone, but with Trish, the Manson murders were something we'd been talking about for a year. Ever since she made me the gift of Bugliosi's book. She wasn't surprised that was one reason I'd come to LA when I'd told her straight-up over the phone that I had plans to meet Leslie Van Houten in person.

Tricia said, "I've been reading about her new trial in the *Los Angeles Times*. I've kept copies. You can have a look whenever you like."

"You're a good friend," I told her.

It went deeper than that, but neither of us ever seemed to know how far to take things. We'd known each other for five years already, ever since she came to Bruce Simpson's door asking about the room for rent. At times, we might have pursued our friendship further, only now, in a sense, I knew to leave enough space in my heart just in case.

Despite not yet having met Leslie in person, she wasn't entirely unimagined in that moment. It was all in my head, of course, but what isn't? That's where some things begin to give some other things their scale.

After running errands that evening, we drove back to the flat on South Sepulveda Boulevard that Trish shared with her roommate Joanne. During the night, under LA lights, everything in this desert metropolis looked entirely different. For instance, right as night was falling, the lights from behind the bars on people's windows cast shadows like they do in film noir prisons. While sirens pierced the night air with shock waves near and far away.

Trish, Joanne, and I shared two bottles of sparkling rosé and smoked a cube of hashish outside on the balcony listening to Fleetwood Mac. Predictably, Tricia and I stayed up late and made out like a couple of wildcats. It almost felt as though I was cheating on Leslie.

Soon after going to bed, I recall, one of us whispered, "It's been a long time for me too." It hardly mattered which one of us said it first.

"Some things bear repeating."

We didn't sleep in. We couldn't. My body was still on Toronto time, and Trish had an early shift to get to. I dropped her off at Cedars after a quick stop for coffee and newspapers, then ran a couple of laps around Mar Vista Park before finding a payphone to call Leslie's girlfriend, Linda Grippi. No answer. I tried making a long-distance call to Toronto. There was no reply there either. I was hoping Jean might have Martin Bijaux's telephone number or street address in LA. I'd try again later.

After a drive to the beach, I took advantage of what was left of the firm sand at low tide to run sets of fifty-meter accelerations along the shoreline. I stopped at another payphone at Venice and Tuller— right across from Madame Paulyn's Mystic Temple. This time, I was put through to Linda's staff room switchboard at Calabasas High.

We agreed to meet on Wednesday. She said something about my needing to have the county sheriff's approval before I could get on Leslie's visitor list. Was I one step closer to seeing the face of my far-away dreams or just hours away from a terrible disappointment? No way to know. That evening, I didn't tell Trish anything about it just yet.

Wednesday, May 25th. Linda Grippi picked me up where I asked her to, in front of the Century Wilshire Hotel. She drove a BMW—not exactly the 630CSi—but what the hell? It sure beat Trish's gelded Mustang for power to weight.

Linda Grippi was the first in a gauntlet of gatekeepers who kept watch over Leslie. She was about my age—twenty-six or twenty-seven, tops. I could see she was protective of Leslie and rightly wary of me. I thought it a sensible stance for her to take under the circumstances.

We drove east along Highway 10 to near where it intersects with the 710. On top of the hill where City Terrace Drive turns into Sheriff Road stood the Sybil Brand Institute/Los Angeles County Jail for Women. Where inmates from the California Institution for Women sixty miles away in Frontera were housed whenever summoned to appear in Superior Court.

From a distance, I thought the site resembled Bergen-Belsen without all the smokestacks. Close up, it resembled a large, fanciful high school fortress with razor wire coiled on top of the fences. Given the way it was fenced-in and guarded by men and women trained and ready to kill if they wanted, just the thought of the place made me shiver.

Linda and I sat parked in her car talking until it was time to line up with the other ten or so visitors. She explained how the earliest I could get in to see Leslie might be the next day, on Thursday. But first, I had to fill out a battery of forms, have my picture and fingerprints taken, and promise to abide by the rules of which there were many.

Before leaving me for her own visit with Leslie that day, Linda said she would tell her I was there and that I'd be back tomorrow. Then a male deputy took me into a sparsely kept room to be captured on film shot with a cheap Polaroid camera. Meanwhile, I assumed Linda and Leslie would have an additional twenty minutes to chat while I waited out by the car writing notes in my diary.

On the way back to the Century Wilshire, Linda and I talked some more about Leslie. "Do you mind if I ask you something, Peter?"

"Of course."

"What are you expecting to get out of this?" The way she asked wasn't harsh, but she was unexpectedly direct. Which put me off-balance.

Feeling nervous, I said something trite like, "I jus' want to show my support. No more than that." How lame is that? There was more to it than that, of course—more than I understood or could say—but already I could see her frustration at the way her amiable interrogation was going.

"How do you see this whole Charlie Manson business, if you don't mind me asking?"

"I think the whole 'Helter Skelter' myth was a scam. Invented for reasons I'm still trying to figure out. The district attorney's explanations seem bogus. The defense's arguments make better sense. Leslie was almost as much a victim as were the LaBiancas," I mumbled, awkwardly bumping into myself coming and going. Linda laughed politely and that put me at ease.

"And what about Leslie?" she asked at the stoplight.

"Despite all she's been through...I'm sure you feel the same way: I think, judging by her letters, she's been sincere and honest with me. It's clear she's very smart and funny, and when she writes, her spirits are high and that raises mine also."

Linda said nothing to that but smiled as she nodded and drove on ahead.

"You asked me what I expect," I continued. "I guess I expect I'll get to know Leslie and friends like you better. That's all. I want to hearten her spirits if I can. I believe that I have. And I want to continue if she wants to."

"Yes, well...I do know she's been looking forward to meeting you too," Linda said reassuringly.

"You've known Leslie since school and during the time when all of this craziness happened. Does she seem much different to you now than before?

"I'm sorry, Linda, I know this is none of my business," I added.

"I can tell you this much. She wasn't herself at the time this whole crazy Manson business came about. It was like waking up from a bad dream for everyone, especially her family. It took a lot of hard work, but she's back with us now. It hasn't been easy."

Worthwhile things seldom are, I thought to myself.

Pulling her car up in front of the hotel, Linda and I had a few minutes to discuss arrangements concerning my visits to Superior Court.

"What's going on at the moment?"

"Last week, Dr. Ditman, a psychiatrist Max called to testify in Leslie's defense, said the combined effect of LSD and cult beliefs were prime factors in what happened to her. Leslie really believed Manson *was* Jesus Christ, you know? Ditman also said how incredibly strong and healthy Leslie is now. You can see for yourself tomorrow."

That evening, Tricia called a friend from work to trade for a shift later the next day on Thursday. We wandered near the beach in Santa Monica and found a nice outdoor place where we sat breaking bread, drinking wine, and sharing a pot of steamed mussels.

After that, we rolled a few joints to take with us to walk in the surf. I still recall how good it felt to be getting my feet wet. At some point, we talked about my going out with Linda again the next day to meet Leslie in jail.

When we got back to her apartment, I used Tricia's phone to try calling Jean (in Toronto) again for Martin's number. Still no luck. But I did manage to get Linda at home, and we agreed to meet the next day at the same spot in front of the Century Wilshire.

"Who was that on the phone?" Tricia asked, carrying clean clothes from the laundry room.

"I just called Leslie's friend Linda again to firm up a time to meet tomorrow."

"Okay, want to tell me about it? I've been reading about her trial in the *Times*, you know."

"I give her a lot of credit," Trish continued. "For owning up to the truth about what she did. Not acting crazy like the last time. Remember that? Of course, you do. To be honest, I hope she gets out.

"I just don't understand what any of this has to do with you."

Picking the *Times* up off the floor, I said, "It has to do with this curious sense of identification I seem to have with her in some way. Or my image of her. I'm trying to figure it out.

"But I think you're right. She's not pretending she's guiltless. All she's asking for is to prove herself deserving of a second chance. Surely the jury will see that."

"Will they?" Tricia asked, looking down at the newspaper in my hand. "Although I'm confused by what it says in there about Judge Heinz…*Hinz*, is it? Who ordered her testimony be given *without* the jury present? What's that about? What am I missing, or have I got it all backward?"

I gave Trish a rough summary of what Bill Farr had to say in a series of columns he wrote in the *Los Angeles Times* in May 1977 ("Miss Van Houten Tells Role in Slaying," May 13; "LSD Influence on Miss Van Houten Told," May 20; and "Miss Van Houten Believed Only Duty Was to Manson, Expert Says," May 25).

Farr reported the reason Maxwell Keith called Leslie to retestify about what she told the court at her first trial was to block Assistant District Attorney Stephen Kay from using the false testimony she gave in the previous trial against her.

In 1971, during the penalty phase, Leslie told the jury she planned all the murders herself. She said at the time that she intended to massacre innocent people, including Gary Hinman.

Of course, she was only saying what Manson ordered her to say. Now, in 1977, Judge Edward A. Hinz, Jr. rejected Maxwell Keith's contention that Leslie's prior statement not be read to this jury. Instead, the judge ruled the prosecution could proceed to read the entirety of Leslie's earlier testimony from the trial almost seven years before.

Here is a summary of what I wrote and remember telling Tricia that evening in their apartment.

After driving from Big Sur to San Diego on August 6th, 1969, less than three days before the Tate and LaBianca slayings, Charles Manson took his new teenage conscript Stephanie Schram home to pick up some clothes from her sister's. They'd dropped LSD together, and Charlie went through his tried-and-true sex and "surrender your ego to love" routine. Soon, she was spreadeagled under Manson's trance like so many others before her.

While Ms. Schram packed her things, Manson played The Beatles *White Album* over and over. He warned Stephanie's sister, also a big Beatles fan, that John, Paul, Ringo, and George were the four angels prophesized in the *Book of Revelation*. He intimated they were writing their songs as coded messages to him *personally*.

Manson explained how the message he got from the song "Helter Skelter" announced the black race was about to overthrow the white wealthy classes in a bloody and violent Armageddon. It was comin' down fast. "Can you hear it...? Can you hear it...?" Charlie told the sisters, "People are going to be slaughtered. They'll be laying on their lawns dead."

Just a few days later, Manson's presage proved true. Even if it wasn't what The Beatles had in mind when they wrote that album of songs from separate rooms at the Maharishi's Ashram. "Helter Skelter" is, in fact, according to the songwriters, a deliberately discordant parade of electronic-musical overkill. Its composers have said the song was meant as a send-up of the sexually charged guitar riffs of Pete Townsend and Jimi Hendrix.

So, where did Manson get his twisted message from?

He made it up. Manson preached that he was the "fifth angel" in the *Book of Revelation*, the keeper with the keys to the "Bottomless Pit." Where, presumably, the Family would be safe until the raging battles burning the cities above ground were over.

The other four angels were supposed to be The Beatles writing their songs as messages to him. Communiqués instructing the "fifth angel" to take his family to the desert—where they'd be protected from the impending *Revolution*—came from no less authority than The Beatles and the Bible. Who could doubt it?

On Sunday, August 10th, shortly after 9:15 a.m., Mrs. Chapman accompanied West Los Angeles Police Department officers onto the property at 10050 Cielo Drive in Benedict Canyon. Although the police didn't yet know any of the victims' identities, the first body they found was actually that of a red-haired high school kid from El Monte, Steven Parent. Steven was slumped over the front seat of his Rambler sedan. His plaid shirt and blue jeans were soddened with blood. Young Mr. Parent had been slashed in the arm and shot four times at close range in the face and head with a small caliber revolver. He bled to death in his car.

The officers slowly proceeded past the black Porsche parked beside the garage. No sign of any activity there. Then they spotted two more bodies sprawled out on the lawn in front of the house. Cautious, the killer, or killers, might still be lurking around, Mrs. Chapman was kept back while police searched the rest of the premises.

Out by the guesthouse, officers heard dogs barking and someone yelling for them to stop. They kicked in the door and immediately handcuffed and arrested the lone occupant, who turned out to be a friend of the dead boy they found in his car. Police dragged the young caretaker, William Garretson, out to look at the bodies. It wasn't until much later that the police figured out he had nothing to do with the murders.

After a thorough search of the buildings and automobiles, the officers went back to the front of the house to have a closer look at the body of a man who turned out to be Roman Polanski's friend from Poland, "Voytek" Frykowski. As police came nearer the corpse, they could see from his torn, swollen face and head just how brutally he had been bludgeoned to death.

Mr. Frykowski was found on his side, with one hand clutching blades of grass in his palm. Fifty-one stab wounds and gashes had punctured his body and limbs. He had also been shot twice with a revolver and clobbered over the head with a blunt object more than a dozen times. Hard.

Also on the lawn underneath a fir tree in front of the shimmering blue pool laid the remains of coffee fortune heiress and Radcliffe grad, Abigail Folger. Ms. Folger had been just twenty-five years old when she bled to death from twenty-eight stab wounds. Both she and her boyfriend, Voytek, were later found to have psychedelic-entactogenic drugs (THC and MDA) in their bloodstreams. Just enough to make them acutely aware and hypersensitive to the terror of those final moments before drowning in pools of everlasting unconsciousness.

One of the officers was standing beside the front porch when he noticed the word "PIG" smeared in blood on the door. Inside the house, near the fireplace on the far side of a bloodstained couch, lay the vanquished bodies of another man and a pregnant young woman. Splashes and smears of gore were on all the walls and floors. A nylon rope was slung over the rafters above the bodies and tied at each end around the necks of the victims.

Jay Sebring had been shot once and stabbed no less than seven times. The gunshot alone, as well as each of the three stab wounds, would have in and of themselves been enough to end his life. Mr. Sebring, like the others, died of exsanguination. His heart pumped all the blood out of his body. Four feet away at the other end of the rope lay the remains of a blonde and strikingly beautiful Hollywood actress. Someone had draped a bloodstained American flag over the sofa beside where she lay on the floor in a fetal position.

Sharon Tate Polanski had been eight months pregnant at the time of her death. She died of hemorrhaging from sixteen stab wounds, some of which penetrated deep into her lungs and heart cavity. Five wounds were in and of themselves lethal. She was wearing a colorfully patterned bikini, now soaked with the last of her blood. In death, at last, actress Sharon Tate was about to reach true celebrity status. That's how awful this world had become.

The next morning, the mood at Spahn Ranch was perversely ecstatic. Each of the previous night's marauders—Charles "Tex" Watson, Susan "Sadie" Atkins, Patricia "Katie" Krenwinkel, and "Lyin'" Linda Kasabian—stopped by the trailer next to George Spahn's house to watch the breaking news on TV. Newspaper headlines read:

STAR, HEIRESS, 3 MEN SLAIN IN L.A. SUBURB; ACTRESS AMONG 5 SLAIN AT HOME IN BEVERLY HILLS

Hearing the victims' identities revealed for the first time, Tex got excited and ran to let Charlie know who they had butchered twelve hours before as well as how rich and famous some of the victims had been. Some other Family members were shocked to learn that the kid in the car was still in high school and that the Hollywood actress had been eight months pregnant. I surmised that even Manson was unsettled by this news. But for very different reasons.

Charlie had been expecting to hear that Tex had ripped open the bodies of his adversaries—Terry Melcher and Dennis Wilson—and made the scene look like the same mess Bobby left at Gary Hinman's two weeks before. Those were Charlie's instructions. The murder of a beautiful movie starlet married to a noteworthy film director with rich, gorgeous friends made this indelible tragedy international news.

Though grimly ironic, this was disturbing news for Charles Manson. On top of all the other grenades he had to juggle already, it was what Charlie *didn't* hear that tied his jock in a knot and alarmed him.

There was *no* mention of the bloody "PIG" markings on the door at 10050 Cielo Drive resembling the "POLITICAL PIGGY" décor at 964 Old Topanga Canyon Road. *No* sign of Beausoleil's added touch either: the bloody pawprint next to where UCLA grad student Gary Hinman's body was found. *Nothing* about how plenty of knife wounds to Hinman appeared like those inflicted on these illustrious victims: a famous hairstylist, a Hollywood starlet, an aspiring screenwriter, and a corporate coffee heiress who went to Radcliffe and Harvard.

Two LA County Sheriff's Department homicide detectives, Sergeants Whiteley and Gunther—who were investigating the murder of Gary Hinman—did, in fact, speak with the LAPD investigators. They tried drawing their attention to the bloody writing on the wall in Topanga Canyon as matching the wording on the front door in Sharon Tate's blood at Cielo Drive.

They were told straight up, "Nah, they're not connected." LAPD detectives had already latched onto a coincidentally common thread of assumptions reported by the sensationalizing Los Angeles press corps: *If Sharon Tate's husband, Roman Polanski, wasn't himself personally responsible for the murders, he must know who was.* That's the lead they pursued.

Given film director Roman Polanski's affinity for Satanic horror in some of his movies, he was "invited" to take a polygraph test at the police department. The polygraph was conducted and analyzed by Lieutenant Earl Deemer, who asked the widower if he had received any hate mail after his movie *Rosemary's Baby.*

Polanski admitted he had, speculating, "It could be some type of witchcraft, you know. A maniac or something... I wouldn't be surprised if I were the target. Despite all this drug thing, the narcotics. I think the police like to jump too hastily on this type of lead, you know. Because the only connection I know of Voytek with any kind of narcotic was he smoked pot. So did Jay. Plus, cocaine. In the beginning, I thought it was just an occasional kick. When I discussed it with Sharon, she said, 'Are you kidding? He's been doing it for years, regularly.'"

While crazy sex and drug rumors were flying all over the place, and the police were left scratching their heads, Manson opted for the standard narcissist's go-to tactic: the old faithful double-down. Although he thought the evidentiary (copycat) similarities at the crime scenes would appear obvious to the police and the press, Charlie also needed to keep faith with Bobby Beausoleil. By vowing he'd create "reasonable doubt" by going out again without delay.

This time, make the pattern of destruction so *unmistakeably* obvious, there would be no way for LAPD detectives to discount the connection between the murder of Gary Hinman and those at the Tate residence.

August 9th, 1969. Tonight was the night. Manson got word to Bobby and promised he'd lead the random assault himself. Presumably, to demonstrate how to do things more efficiently this time.

Leslie only found out that afternoon, from her close friend Patricia Krenwinkel, about what happened to Sharon Tate and the others. She told "Katie" she didn't want to have to kill anyone herself, but that she believed in Charlie Manson as some kind of a Christ-incarnate fifth Beatle. Therefore, what he said had to be done, had to be done. Everyone understood that.

Manson took Leslie aside that evening and proposed that what happened in Benedict Canyon that morning was just the opening salvo in the predestined Revolution that The Beatles and HE, the fifth angel, had ordained. What he said was, "Are you crazy?" And she said she was.

"Crazy enough to believe in what I say is the way it's coming down now?" Once again, she nodded. "Yes, I'm crazy enough to believe it." Spoken like a true fanatic.

"Are you crazy enough to kill someone for this?" said the Mesmerist.

"Yes," she said that she was. Because that's what he wanted.

As crazy as all of it looked to her years later, Leslie admitted how, in 1969, she was willing to sacrifice herself for what turned out to be nothing more than Charles Manson's delusions of grandeur. Such delusional belief systems had infected more than just a few members of Charlie's cult. How could anyone in their right mind—knowing right from wrong—actually believe in such a crudely posed Apocalyptic cause? They couldn't.

Psychiatrists who testified for the defense insisted that Leslie wasn't capable of knowing right from wrong in the months before and long after August 1969. She had been psychically damaged to such a degree that the belief system the Family shared with each other back then wasn't the same socially constructed reality most of us commonly share.

In 1977, the day before she and I were due to meet face-to-face for the first time, I thought to reacquaint myself with the exact role Leslie played that cataclysmic night. Few people I'd spoken to actually knew or surmised what really happened. What I had to find out for myself, I'm about to share with you now.

9

ECLIPSING
"HELTER SKELTER"

Around sundown on Saturday, August 9th, 1969, at Spahn Ranch in Chatsworth, California, Charles Manson told complicit veterans from the previous night—Watson, Atkins, Krenwinkel, and Kasabian, plus rookies Steve "Clem" Grogan and Leslie Van Houten—to bring a change of dark clothing and meet him back at the bunkhouse.

Then Manson told Leslie to get in the car and do what she was told. Exactly as she and the others were programmed to do like wind-up toy soldiers in denim, leather, and cotton.

Charlie's plan was to divide the group into two separate assault teams. Each, he said, would take a different house and not leave any witnesses. Leslie had little doubt there would be killing and that she herself may have to die for the sake of igniting Helter Skelter. She was anxious to prove her loyalty to Manson, and for her and the others, nothing else mattered. That's why she got into the car that night.

What Leslie didn't know yet, however, was what her exact role would be. Or how far she would have to go to please Charlie.

During his tactical debriefing of the Tate massacre with Tex Watson—who had spent the past day snorting meth with Susan Atkins—Manson complained about the chaos, panic, and noise of the midnight before. Tex insisted the problem was that Charlie hadn't outfitted him properly with weapons to kill so many people. Manson insisted, "That wasn't the problem. Last night was too messy. This time, I'm going to show you how to do it."

Charlie and Tex armed themselves with a gun and a knife-bladed bayonet. None of the others were given weapons.

The teams drove around LA for a couple of hours, with Charlie at the wheel part of the time and other times riding shotgun alongside Linda Kasabian, acting as her navigator. After getting lost a couple of times—and aborting three or more random attempts at committing violence—Manson suddenly became deliberate in his directions.

Somewhere near Griffith Park and the Golden State Freeway, he told Linda Kasabian to stop the same old '59 Ford they'd used the night before. Linda immediately recognized the house, and so did Susan and Pat. They'd been there before for an "electric Kool-Aid" peyote test that ended rather abruptly. Especially from the point of view of this ex-con with a penchant for holding grudges.

The house they'd stopped in sight of was oddly numbered 3267 Waverly Drive, next door to 3301. The place once belonged to Rolling Stones' roadie Phil Kaufman, another ex-con who knew Charlie from when they did time together at Terminal Island prison. The friend who moved in after Kaufman, and who threw all the wild parties, was a guy named Harold True.

Harold was known for the huge psychedelic soirées he'd promote with flyers and maps of the location. The house right next door belonged to the LaBiancas.

Manson was known that summer to take some of his cult on "creepy crawl" tours of Harold's tony neighbors' houses. The homes that kept their backdoors unlocked. Sneaking in and moving items around while the occupants were sleeping. Petty theft, mostly, or reconnaissance training. There was no way of telling for sure all that Manson may have been up to or why.

According to testimony given by Mrs. LaBianca's twenty-year-old daughter by a previous marriage, Susan Struthers, what is known for a fact is that a few weeks earlier, Rosemary LaBianca told close friends, "Someone is coming in our house while we're away. Things have been gone through, and the dogs are outside the house when they should be inside."

One night that summer, during a particularly loud, raucous party with scores of hippies, someone called the police to lodge a complaint about all the loud music and suspicious goings-on next door at 3267 Waverly. The LaBiancas stood outside as the police arrived and ordered all the partygoers to leave. Charles Manson's entourage had been among them.

Now, close to midnight on August 9th, pointing to Harold True's place at number 3267, Linda asked Charlie, "You're not going to do that house, are you?" To which Manson replied, "No, the one next door."

Like the night before, Charlie chose the venue at 3301 Waverly Drive because he already knew the layout. And quite likely because he could settle some opportune rancor at the same time. Armed with a gun, a saber, and an angry grudge, Manson disappeared alone into a stand of trees between the two houses while the others remained in the car. When he came back a few minutes later, he signaled Tex with a quick nod to get out of the car and come join him. The two men quickly vanished back into the darkness.

The backdoor was unlocked. Once they entered the living room, they could see Mr. Leno LaBianca passed out alone on the sofa. Beside him were scattered racing forms and pages of newspapers describing the Tate killings in Beverly Hills strewn on the pillows.

Suddenly startled awake, Leno jumped to his feet. "Who are you? What do you want?" asked the stunned business exec standing barefoot in his pajamas.

Waving his gun in Mr. LaBianca's direction, Manson told Leno to sit back down and be quiet. Nobody was going to be hurt if he did what he was told. Holding the heavyset man at gunpoint, Manson asked if anyone else was in the house while Watson secured Leno tightly with the leather thongs they brought for that purpose. "My wife is upstairs in the bedroom," Leno said, and Charlie sent Tex upstairs to find her.

Watson found Rosemary LaBianca seated in bed in her nightgown. He told her to put something on over her nightgown, then ordered the terrified woman downstairs to the living room with the end of his bayonet. He bound the couple tightly together, back-to-back, by their wrists and ankles. Manson held the couple at gunpoint the whole time and kept reassuring them that if they remained calm and did exactly what they were told, no harm would come to either of them. "This is only a robbery," he kept repeating.

After ten minutes, Charlie and Tex returned to the car on the street below. Charlie was carrying some items he'd taken from the house, including the couple's purses and wallets. He tossed Rosemary's driver's license and the couple's credit cards on the front seat beside Linda and told Katie and Leslie to get out of the car. "Do whatever Tex says." Then, turning to Tex, he said, "Don't let them know you're goin' to kill them. After, make sure the girls leave the scene shocking and witchy as hell. Paint a picture like no one has seen."

Once they finished with their mission, Manson told the gang to hitchhike back to the ranch where he would meet them. Just before driving off, he whispered to Tex, "Make sure everybody does something to get her hands dirty." Then Charlie and his second unit drove off with Susan, Linda, and Clem, leaving the first detail alone to carry out his orders.

Inside the house, Charles Watson untied Mrs. LaBianca, demanding she find more money. Rosemary searched feverishly and found a small box of collectible coins that she handed the girls, saying that was all she had left. Patricia Krenwinkel went to the kitchen as Watson instructed and returned with a serrated eight-inch knife and a tined ten-inch carving fork. Armed with these utensils, she and Leslie were told to take Mrs. LaBianca upstairs to the bedroom and keep her there pinned to the bed. Tex told them to put a pillowcase over her head and use the lamp cords to tie her up.

Once they were gone, Tex pushed his captive flat on his back and pressed against the sofa with his hands bound and defenseless. Mr. LaBianca sensed what horrors were coming. Watson ripped open the man's pajamas and began plunging the bayonet into his body. Leno LaBianca's last choking words were, "I'm dead, I'm dead." Only he wasn't, not yet—even though Watson thought so at first.

Hearing the blood-curdling shrieks of her husband, Rosemary LaBianca had begun to struggle with Leslie and Patricia. Tex heard the loud crash as the woman broke free from Leslie and knocked over a table lamp. The terrified woman demanded to know, "What are you doing to my husband?"

Despite Leslie's attempts to restrain her, Mrs. LaBianca picked up the lamp and started swinging it at her assailants to keep them at bay. Pat had her knife out. During Rosemary's scuffle with Leslie, Pat tried to stab the woman from behind. Only the knife struck a collarbone, and the handle broke off in her hand. She shouted for Tex to come help.

Leslie let go of Rosemary and fled from the room, standing frozen in shock on the threshold, staring into an empty hall.

Still frenzied and soaked with amphetamines, Tex Watson bounded up the stairs like the state's champion hurdler he once was. His attack on Mrs. LaBianca was so ferocious that each of the seven bayonet wounds he inflicted penetrated deep enough to have ended her life on their own.

Leslie had no memory of watching Mrs. LaBianca dying. All that she remembered when she stepped up beside Tex and looked at the body of Rosemary LaBianca lying face down on the floor was seeing that she was dead and no longer moving. The ultimate shock.

Charles Watson later confessed that he'd already killed the woman before he ordered Leslie to "Do something!" Implying he might carve her up too if she didn't. In his 1978 book with Chaplain Ray, *Will You Die For Me?*, Watson wrote that Leslie was not a willing participant in the murders of Leno and Rosemary LaBianca.

"The lady was dead," Tex said. "I pushed Leslie down beside her. She shook her head. I turned her face up toward me. I had blood all the way up my arms, and I had a knife in my hand. She was one scared girl."

With Watson standing over her, Leslie took the knife he handed her and stabbed the woman's lifeless body more than a dozen times in the back and buttocks. Tex said later he didn't believe Leslie showed enough craze and fury. From the autopsy examination of Rosemary LaBianca's body, it was determined that of the total of forty-one gashes inflicted, approximately sixteen were shallow post-mortem wounds to her lower back and hindquarters.

Watson could see that Leslie had been hesitant all along to take part in the carnage. He was still high, deranged, and focused on only one thing: Manson's directive not to leave any witnesses. Pat later said she was afraid that what Tex had done to the others, he might do to them too. Manson wanted a bloody, horrific scene. If she held back, Tex would tell Charlie, and Charlie would kill her just to make his point to the others.

When Patricia Krenwinkel returned to the living room, she discovered that Mr. LaBianca was still alive, if only just barely. Once again, Katie alerted Commandant Watson.

Leno LaBianca would have undoubtedly bled out in a matter of minutes, but just to be certain, Watson stabbed his body some more. After which, Pat carved the word "WAR" into his abdomen. Krenwinkel also testified to sticking the long-tined fork into Mr. LaBianca's stomach and just leaving it there, watching it wobble. LaBianca was also found with a small kitchen knife Pat left lodged in his throat.

Still upstairs and stricken with shock, Leslie wiped everything down. Including the insides of the drawers and things none of them had even come close to touching. Although there was plenty of loot in the way of expensive cameras and pricey guns to be had, the gang took nothing more than the small bag full of coins Rosemary handed over.

Patricia Krenwinkel misspelled the phrase "HEALTER SKELTER" when she wrote it in Leno LaBianca's blood on the refrigerator door. Katie had heard The Beatles sing "Helter Skelter" on a record player over and over but had never seen the words written inside the album cover. They also wrote "Death To Pigs" and "RISE" in blood on the living room wall, alongside the framed family photos.

Leslie had no bloodstains on her clothes, so Tex told her to take off her jeans and hand them over. Leslie found a pair of Rosemary LaBianca's shorts that fit, which she changed into after taking a shower.

Before leaving the house, this trio of wild Manson-cult zombies left watermelon rinds in the sink after feeding the LaBianca's dogs. The intruders hid in the bushes for a while before making their way toward the Golden State Freeway. They tossed their bloody clothes in trash bins far from the house.

From the freeway, they hitched a few rides back to Spahn Ranch and got there ahead of Charlie, who was still somewhere near Venice Beach at the time. The last guy to give them a lift came back to the ranch a few times after that asking for Leslie. She always hid when she saw him coming.

After Manson and his second assault team drove away from the scene at 3301 Waverly Drive, Charlie took the wheel with Linda beside him. Clem and Susan sat in the back. "Sadie," who participated in the torture and smothering of Gary Hinman—as well as the stabbings of Frykowski and Tate—was known as the most unstable member of the Manson cult. An unpredictable force of nature that Leslie remarked was, "Almost infatuated with death. She kept sharpening the knives; getting them real sharp."

It's worth noting that Susan Atkins never once mentioned any *race war* during her testimony to the grand jury on December 5th, 1969. In fact, not once in those entire hearings—in which twenty-two witnesses were called—was there any mention of a race war. You wouldn't know that from reading Bugliosi's book on the subject.

The term "Helter Skelter" was vaguely discussed, but only as it pertained to the title of The Beatles' song, written in blood at one of the crime scenes.

The remaining Manson crew stopped at a service station in a neighborhood Charlie told the others was a good place to leave Rosemary LaBianca's wallet and identification. He said a black person would find it, use the credit cards, and get caught. Leading the police to suspect black people with militant political ties took part in these murders. Bingo! Once Linda hid the wallet inside one of the washrooms, Charlie drove the gang directly to Venice Beach for some reason.

During the trial in 1970, the prosecution argued that Manson's motive was to murder one or two more random persons in order to keep the Helter Skelter myth going. First, to frame black people for the slaughter in Los Feliz; and second, to connect the same gang of black culprits to the night before in Bel Air. And lastly, for police to make the same connection back to the stabbing of Gary Hinman.

Deputy DA Bugliosi's version of what led Manson to Venice that night coincidentally lined up with his star witness, Linda Kasabian's account, which others, including myself, maintained serious doubts about. Kasabian's immunity-protected tale of the events, in essence, went something like this: Linda indicated that when Charlie asked if she knew anyone in Venice, she mentioned that she had a friend there they could go and kill.

Linda told Charlie how she and cult member Sandra Good recently met an actor while hitchhiking who took the girls back to his apartment on Ocean Front Walk. This was the standard *modus operandi* for Charlie's angels when trolling for guys with means enough to own their own automobile. Thumbs out—skirts up—pants down—"Your place or the car?"

Linda told Charlie she had sex with actor Saladin Nader in the bedroom while Sandy took a nap on his couch.

This time, at Nader's apartment building—after Manson and Kasabian went in to check things out—Manson handed Linda a pocketknife and Clem a handgun. Sadie brought her own buck knife (no surprise), so she was all set and itching to go.

Charlie gave the squad their final instructions. Linda would knock. When Nader let her, Sadie, and Clem inside—Clem would shut the door behind them, turn, and shoot. Then the girls would slit Saladin's throat. Manson demonstrated precisely how Linda should do it. Then, after leaving more bloody tidings in ongoing Black Panther motifs, the Venice crew were told to hitchhike back to the ranch as Charlie had directed the others at Waverly Drive in Los Feliz.

Linda claimed later she picked a door at random and knocked. When someone answered, she said she must have the wrong apartment building. Her story didn't make sense really. But then juries can be as unguarded as a dozen donuts sometimes, I suppose. In fact, so much of Deputy DA Bugliosi's case based on Kasabian's testimony never made much sense at all.

Turned out later, both assault teams—the trio from Waverly Drive and the pack at Ocean Front Walk—arrived back at the ranch before Charlie Manson. What did begin to make sense was that Ocean Front Walk was only a four-minute stroll or a minute's drive from 110 Mildred Avenue, at the corner of Pacific Avenue, one block from the beach. *Why?*

In 1969, this apartment building served as the Straight Satans' Venice Chapter clubhouse. The same gang that Charlie had approached to protect the ranch from the Black Panthers. The same ink-slingers that Bobby Beausoleil owed money to.

What if Charles Manson had taken more than just the LaBiancas' wallets and credit cards from the house that night? Maybe more than enough *cash* to pay off the Satans? What if Leno—a notoriously unlucky but avid sports and horserac-ing gambler—kept plenty of cash stashed in the house? Maybe Charlie took that money with him to Venice Beach to pay back the Satans and win back their protection? It's certainly plausible. And it fits Manson's MO perfectly.

The *Los Angeles Times* frontpage headline the next day after the killing of Mr. and Mrs. LaBianca read:

SECOND RITUAL KILLINGS HERE: LOS FELIZ COUPLE FOUND SLAIN; LINK TO 5-WAY MURDER SEEN.

Hearing this news provided Charles Manson with at least some degree of repose. After half a lifetime already dwarfed by prison, now he'd instigated something so savagely gruesome, he had the whole world asking, "Who could have done such a thing and why?"

In 1970, Doctors Keith Ditman (for the defense) and Dr. Joel Fort (for the prosecution), each confirmed that Leslie's use of these drugs—plus Manson's influence over her—played a large role in her behavior that night. They each testified these could have been significant factors causing her to participate in the ho-micide. Stating that any young person like Leslie Van Houten—who had been using LSD under these conditions on a regular basis—was definitely more susceptible to the influence of a sec-ond party.

To which Leslie Van Houten—still crazed at the time—shouted out in open court: "This is all such a big lie. I was influenced by the war in Vietnam and TV." Her crazy denial that either Manson's depraved influence or the drugs had any effect on her was clearly a lie. Though the bit about war and TV partly rang true. Overall, I thought this only reinforced Maxwell Keith's theory of temporary "diminished mental capacity."

I was also beginning to see how any one of us might be influenced by the extraordinary scrutiny of the news media, making us more likely to *pretend* to be whatever others imagine us to be. For Leslie, being on trial meant being publicly made to feel ashamed of herself. Assumed to be that someone who others made her appear to be. Her response at the time, in 1970, had been to play along as a bluff of defiance. Although she was being made out to be someone who wasn't who she was now, she was still held responsible for the shadow she no longer was as a person.

If it could be the other way around, after a while, we'd all be better off leaving some parts of the worst of our pasts behind. Free to be the responsible person we are now instead of that shadow.

In 1977, just knowing that Leslie had come out of her delusions after serving nearly eight years of a life sentence already, I felt differently about her spending any more time in prison than the others. Like Manson and Watson, especially. Perhaps Atkins and Krenwinkel too. I'm sure it had something to do with the way Leslie looked in her photos, but not in the familiar way we tend to view other people as objects.

Reading her letters, I already had a glimpse into the way she looked at the world and herself. Imagining what possible role she had to play in those transfigured times we were amidst. That's what struck a chord with me. Not just a flickering picture on TV or a stagnant snapshot in some magazine. Not only that. Something more.

Her view of what was important was—I suspected—in sync with the way I was beginning to see the possibilities that lay before our entire generation. There was this allusive, mystified sense I had that summer. That once I got to meet Leslie Van Houten close up and in person, I'd know for sure if we were on the same track or not. Once our eyes met. You know, when your brain comes to the surface to have a good look around.

My dear and trusted friend Tricia Woodbridge already knew the basic facts if not many details. She reminded me of some of the things concerning Leslie Van Houten that we'd talked about many times before now. She listened politely as I did my best to fill in the blanks. She had an intuitive sense of what counted for fairness and social justice. One cluster of the many things I admired most about her.

On the ride over to drop me off to meet Leslie's friend Linda Grippi, who would take me to the county jail, Trish told me, "No one likes to be the least preferred choice. Look, Peter. I'm not blind or stupid. I think I see what's going on here. I can see Van Houten's become an important person to you, so you do what you must. Don't worry 'bout me.

"Maybe once you meet her in person, she might not match your infatuations." Trish was brusque but not angry.

Slightly smarting by her last remark, I admitted, "What you say is fair. And honest." Tricia smiled a smidge, gave me a kiss on the cheek, then pulled over in front of the Century Wilshire. Where I was meeting Leslie's friend and sentry, Linda Grippi.

Afterward, Trish would come back and pick me up. In the meantime, she said she had errands of her own to rush off to.

I could see Linda Grippi's BMW parked outside the hotel when we got there. I'd reached for the handle just as Trish pulled the car over. "Catch you later," she said, holding me back an instant longer. I gave her one last, gentle kiss on the lips and got out of the car. Outside the bright summer sun was shining unimpeded, but my interior barometer was in free fall. Suddenly, I felt strangely nervous like a schoolboy. An odd illusion to occur right at that moment, I thought.

Linda drove the same route to Sybil Brand County Jail as before. Heading slowly east in traffic on the Santa Monica Freeway, she mentioned having recently spoken to Leslie over the phone. "She's excited to see you," Linda said.

"What a coincidence. I feel the same way," I kidded. "Sorry, I don't mean to be smug." I was nervous, excited, undone.

Linda handled our getting through all the LA County Jail rigmarole like an old pro. She knew the ropes, and I skipped along right behind her. There were rules posted every which way you looked. Lists of "Visitor's Instructions" printed on black, blue, and red plastic panels were drilled to the walls and wired to the fences. Armed guards sat in glass and steel cages where we had to "Wait Behind the Green Line" for our passes.

Once inside, I could hear distant bells ringing like they do in most factories and high schools. There was this constant, ghostly din of intercom voices echoing down the hallways I imagined to be "labyrinths of solitude." The place smelled like a combination of industrial-strength disinfectant and vomit.

I could see visitors in the queue ahead of me perched to enter a room lined with two rows of less than ten hard, round wooden-top stools. I could taste the steel on my tongue with the sound vibrations of the heavy lockbolts clanging shut. There were cubicles facing both sides of steel-meshed glass windows.

On each side there were similar setups; each stall with its companion headset hung on a cradle. Inmates and guests had to talk over institutionally monitored phone sets, watching through what looked like TV-drama bulletproof glass. The atmosphere wasn't inviting.

Then, I saw Leslie.

I remember the exact moment in time. What figured most from out of the pale, lusterless background was her great, big, miraculous smile. Which I could spot at forty paces. She was lining up like a kid at the head of the class waiting for recess. She had on a tattered-knit navy blue sweater that hung at odds on her mighty-thin shoulders. Underneath that, she wore a dreary gray dress made of sack linen.

Even in such a cheerless outfit, Leslie stood alone, looking sunny and willowy among all the blurred-to-invisible guards and inmates surrounding her. I was blinded. Everything else faded into the background.

Leslie gave a wave and another big smile before she sat down and began talking to Linda. Watching me take irregular glances at what she had on, she pinched the fabric of her dress and mouthed the words, "Don't you like it?" She would tell me later when I could hear her, "It isn't Parisian, but it's the best that we've got."

I'm unaware of when I smiled, but I must have been beaming on account of being so immediately taken over by her intrinsic allure. She really got me. Without a shadow of doubt or a moment's delay. Just as I had imagined.

I distinctly remember noticing how Leslie did not look like any of the pictures of her that I'd seen or imagined. Well, whoever does? She was far prettier and pleasingly brighter to encounter in person. Even if her skin did look a bit pasty—gods only knew what they fed her—her hair was a sleek mocha brown. I liked the way something about her glowed through those warm, unabashed hazelnut eyes of hers. I confirmed she was smart, sexy, and fun right from the start. I knew all that already.

As Leslie and Linda continued to talk, I leaned back against the nearby wall and tried not to stare. Watching other inmates and their guests interacting. It wasn't all sad; upbeat for the most part. Both Leslie and Linda seemed to be having a laugh on me occasionally. After a few minutes more, Leslie unfolded her arms and motioned for me to come closer. I scooted onto the edge of the stool next to Linda and asked them both, "What's so funny?"

That's when Linda passed me the headset and Leslie said, "My mother is going to be so surprised. My sister Betsy too. They were sure the pictures you sent were of somebody else. Bets thought you probably got a friend to pose and sent those instead of yourself."

"How is that possible? There's no hiding from you, is there? I'm not sure I'd know how to do it deliberately." Dumb stuff to say, I supposed. Why was I acting so nervous? At the same time, something else noteworthy kicked in. We found ourselves involuntarily starting to talk at the same time.

This happened more than a few times in the short time we were allotted. It's not something one would normally find so enticing, yet there it was.

Before our time was up, I imagined gathering her up in my arms and carrying her off somewhere to be alone. Twenty minutes was too short a time. It seemed we had so much more we needed to cover. But just that short interval of intersubjective reflection on this first occasion was enough to change the way we wrote our letters from then on. As both of us would write each other later, we knew we'd stumbled into some new phase or dimension. One look was all it took. Fancy that.

"Linda can bring you along to the courthouse right away if you want," Leslie said. "I'd like you to catch a glimpse of that scene. How long will you stay in California?"

"A month if my friends let me sleep on their couch. I have to get back to Toronto for grad school this summer session."

"Tor-ron-*toe*. Like the end of your foot. Is that how you say it?"

"Some people who live there make it sound more like *Ta-ronna*," I smiled.

"Got someone back home in Toronto to water your houseplants?"

"I put them outside and left their fate, like my own, to the gods for the rest of the summer. They know what they're doing. *I'm* still in doubt."

"Know what, Peter? Before I forget, want to say I just got the letter where you copied the poems by Mark Strand. *Really* neat poems. I liked 'The Room' a lot. You knew that I would, which is why you sent it, right?"

"I told you I met him once. At Ohio U. in Athens when I was a freshman. He came to read from his latest books at the time, *Reasons for Moving* and *Darker*. I've kept the copies he signed. On the first page of his 'New Poetry Handbook,' he advised us against overpraising the poems of another, so that we might 'have a beautiful mistress…'"

"Oh, so you're looking for a beautiful mistress, huh? I guess that rules me out."

"That's funny, Leslie," I said, smiling so much I tried to stop, but I couldn't. Catching my own reflection under the glistening surface of her eyes.

"I'll talk to Max about you coming in with him one of these evenings. That way, we can talk in a conference room instead of through this weird, smudgy window."

"Maybe get to hold hands?" I suggested, planting thoughts in both our minds. Leslie drew a big smile, and maybe her face slightly flushed. I know mine did. Just as I'd started to hand the phone back to Linda, Leslie signaled me back on the line.

"Will you come visit again?" she asked, and I said that I would.

And she asked, "How 'bout tomorrow?"

10

FOLIE À FAMILLE, FOLIE À DEAU

From the outside, the LA County Superior Court on West Temple Street looked to me like the establishing shot for a popular TV show at the time, *Quincy, M.E.* Linda Grippi picked me up the next day after meeting Leslie, and we went downtown to see her in court that afternoon.

Inside, the courtroom looked the same as you see in the movies, with high ceilings and wood-paneled walls. Banks of filing cabinets flanked the bailiffs. Judge Hinz's executive perch was just below the Great Seal of the State of California, and the rest of us were resigned to a lower tier of hard, wooden benches. The overriding feeling it gave me was of a most profound wasteland.

In contrast to all the chatter going on inside my head at that moment, suddenly the room went deathly quiet. The court bailiff told us to rise and remain standing until the man in the black robes had sat down. I tried not to stare at Leslie the whole time but couldn't help it. Whenever she turned to look my way,

I couldn't help but give myself away smiling. Other than Leslie, the most interesting person in the room wasn't the judge or the deputy DA. It was her attorney.

Maxwell Stanley Keith interrupted his education to serve in World War II as a bombardier. After graduating from Princeton, he returned home to California to attend Loyola Law School in Los Angeles. Now in his mid-forties, Max had mostly wispy white hair. His eyes were set wide apart, and he had sizeable ears that always seemed primed on alert like a kitten's. That day in court, Max wore a dark navy Brooks Brothers suit with his tie knotted loosely. He looked taller than I was—well over six feet.

Even though he would frequently glance at his notes as he stood at the podium, I thought he did this mostly for effect. He argued in such an extemporaneous fashion, it seemed to me he was composing off of the cuff. I hoped and imagined the jury liked him as much as I did.

Linda Grippi told me how, only a few days before—the day I flew in from Toronto, in fact—Max Keith argued in court that Leslie Van Houten was suffering from a severe and debilitating mental impairment at the time of the LaBianca murders. This was (ironically) called *folie a famille*, or "family madness." Harvard psychiatrist Lester Grinspoon was just one of several experts Keith planned to call to the stand in defense of these claims. Dr. Grinspoon later testified that, in his opinion, Leslie was "incapable of meaningfully premeditating murder" at the time the LaBianca couple was killed.

Back in 1971, when Max substituted for Leslie's lawyer, Ron Hughes, he asked the court to declare a mistrial. This motion was based on the fact of his not having been present to hear each of the previous witnesses testify. Therefore, he could not properly assess their credibility. He argued that he hadn't been granted adequate time to absorb the more than 18,000 pages of court documents he had to review.

The judge at the first trial, Charles H. Older, denied Keith's request. In fact, still under Manson's rune at the time, Leslie said that she was against Max even making the appeal, although it was in her own best interest. That's how completely under a madding spell she was. Regardless, Max carried on to present a defense that eventually parted Leslie's welfare from Mr. Manson's.

His contention was that Leslie and other young women in the cult had been effectively brainwashed by a certified lunatic-con man. Therefore, to varying degrees, they were by design incapable of thinking or acting of their own volition.

In his closing argument in the previous trial, Keith pointed out how even Deputy DA Vincent Bugliosi repeatedly referred to Leslie and other members as "robots." Then, at other times when it suited him, the prosecutor billed them all as "free-willed individuals." A flagrant flaw in his case that he should have been called out on.

Keith argued, "If you believe the prosecution's theory that these female defendants were extensions of Mr. Manson, and you believe that they were mindless robots, then they cannot be guilty of premeditated murder." Afterward, Bugliosi admitted that Maxwell Keith delivered the best of the four defense arguments. But to no avail with the judge and jury.

Lady Justice is blind, all right, I thought when I read the transcript. She often fails to recognize what is perfectly obvious to those with their blinds off.

Leslie, along with all the other defendants, was given the maximum penalty: death in the San Quentin gas chamber. When the state legislature temporarily abolished capital punishment a year later in 1972, their sentences were reduced to life in prison, *with* the possibility of parole after seven years.

The average incarceration in the state for first-degree murder was then ten and a half to eleven years. Certainly more if the victims were strangers and in cases where there was deliberate torture or mutilation of the victims' bodies.

I spent every day that week in court and heard University of Wisconsin Professor of Psychiatry Leigh Roberts use the term "folie à ménage" or "household madness," another term used to describe the temporary state of group madness common to most cults. Where fanatics impart the same delusions to one another, therefore fueling each other's beliefs even further.

Roberts and other psychiatrists also used the term *folie à famille* to describe the state of cult paranoia. Because staunchly held convictions such as, "Charlie is really Jesus Christ," were so doggedly held, the cult's delusions were impossible to reason away.

Apparently, even someone as smart as Leslie Van Houten (and lots of other ordinary people), was at risk of episodic, paranoid states of being. Potent psychedelic drugs helped Manson to mimic and intensify these conditions through various means of familiar mind control.

Keith asked Dr. Roberts whether Leslie, as she was in such a state, would be "able to premeditate or deliberate the murder of another human being?" The witness answered that due to her mental illness at the time of the murders, Leslie did not have that capacity. Roberts went on to say, "She was in a paranoid state... as opposed to being a paranoid person...during the time of the LaBianca slayings."

Former Manson Family recruiter Paul Watkins formerly testified that after living with Manson for a couple of years, he "became Charlie...there was nothing left of *me* anymore. And the people in the Family, there's nothing left of them anymore. They're all Charlie too."

Watkins attested to how Manson intimated that he was the second coming of Christ. His opinion from living on the ranch was that Manson's disciples, himself included, were so "thoroughly brainwashed," they believed they could do no wrong—so long as they followed Charlie's tenets of love and death as if they were according to Scripture.

All four psychiatrists who had taken the stand in Leslie's defense so far in this second trial—Keith Ditman, Lester Grinspoon, Leigh Roberts, and Joel Hochman—told the court the same thing. Leslie Van Houten was incapable of premeditation or of willfully taking the life of another human being with malice. Whatever crime she might have been guilty of, it could not be first-degree murder.

Sensing the defense's momentum, Prosecutor Stephen Kay objected to any more psychiatric testimony. Mr. Kay asked the judge to cut the defense's psychiatric witness testimony short, farcically arguing that it could have the effect of "brainwashing the jury." Mr. Keith naturally opposed the request, begging Judge Hinz not to grant the prosecution's motion. Leslie remained calm, but Linda Grippi and I were beginning to shiver.

Judge Hinz wasted no time in granting the prosecution's motion. To make matters worse, he ruled against the defense presenting Charles Manson's psychiatric records as evidence of his malevolent mind control tactics. The judge ruled that however Charles Manson acquired these methods, and however he used them to abolish the self-control of his followers, it would not be heard in his court. There were a few gasps in the courtroom when he said it. I wasn't the only one there who couldn't believe it.

That evening, Linda drove me out to Sybil Brand. That's when I got to meet Maxwell Keith for the first time at the end of a handshake. Leslie and Max told me they thought they were getting somewhere with more than half of the six men/six women jury. Some cause for optimism. Max still had a long list of experts to call.

After too short a visit with Les, Max took Linda and me out to a steakhouse near Fair Oaks and Hope Street in Pasadena. We didn't stay late. Max said he had work to prepare before court in the morning. Leslie was scheduled to take the stand. The main purpose of this little get-together at the restaurant that evening was to give Max Keith and me the opportunity to size each other up. At least that's what Linda thought when I asked her.

The next morning, Tricia gave me a ride downtown to the Security Pacific Plaza on South Hope Street and dropped me off. As I stepped into his office on the twenty-eighth floor, Max's receptionist informed me he'd already left for Superior Court. There was also a message for me from Leslie: *Can you come this evening with Max? Can't wait to see you!*

Right after court, Max drove us out to Sybil Brand in his black Scirocco. I thought the bombardier handled the car okay for an "old guy." It turned out to be a simple drill for getting me in with him when we got there. Max said, "We'll tell them you're a 'legal runner' for my firm."

"What does that mean?"

"Nothing. It means you have a right to be in there. To carry my briefcase." I had to laugh at that; happy to go along.

That evening, while Max read over transcripts and took notes, Les and I got to hold hands under the table in such a way that the deputies couldn't see us. "Does this feel like falling in love to you?" she whispered so no one could hear us.

"If love is like a beautiful girl that smiles at me the way you do, then the answer is 'Yes, I believe it does.'

"Les, do you know the fifties' film *The Bad and the Beautiful*?" She shook her head. "No? Kirk Douglas's character Jonathan tells Lana Turner's Georgia, 'Love is for the very young.'" Leslie frowned, then smiled again right away again only slightly.

"That can't be all there is to it," she said in a tone of mock protest.

"No. Later on in the film, in fact, a cynical but *fatally* attractive Lila, played by a sultry Elaine Stewart—who reminds me of you by the way...'

"Me? I'm not *sultry*, am I?"

"*Very*," said I. "*I* think so. Anyway, what was I saying? Oh, Lila reminds everyone that, 'Love is for the birds.'" Leslie laughed but said nothing more for the moment. She turned in her chair so no one could hear us.

"You remember the second time you came to see me? You came alone."

"Sure. The day your high school friends also came to show off their newborn baby boy. I remember. I kept him with me while they went through the whole photo and fingerprint rigmarole. I had him cradled half-asleep in my arms. Why?"

"That's them. I didn't tell you, they've been sweethearts ever since they were frosh in high school. I think that's kind of wonderful. That sort of thing can last, don't you think?"

"Look, Les, when you saw me holding that cute, chubby baby, the first thing you did was to put your fists on your hips, tilt your head all the way to your shoulder, and shake your finger at me while mouthing the words, 'You didn't tell me you had a baby!'" Even Max, who overheard us, looked up and laughed.

"So, what's your point, mister?"

"It was very funny, that's all. And it's great these kids are in a romantic mood right now, and I hope it lasts. It's lovely. If it doesn't, it can't be helped.

"Times change, and one of them will be sure to put the other on too high a pedestal sooner or later. Then feel destroyed when they stagger. It's inevitable. And if one of them should ever have their head turned by another admirer, they'll end up despising each other."

She laughed but not genuinely. "For some people, maybe. But I'm not the jealous type. Or maybe I am...," Leslie started but stopped.

Toward the end of our visit, Les and I went back to discussing plans for me to meet some more of her family and friends. Next on the list was for me to call a young reporter named Judith Frutig, western bureau chief for *The Christian Science Monitor*. Van Houten family friend, who worked at the *Los Angeles Times*, Glen Peters, had introduced them to Judy.

"I'll give you the number to call," Max, who wasn't listening, said.

A couple of days later, Tricia took me on a tour of Venice Beach before dropping me off in Westwood to meet Judith Frutig. Judy picked me up at the corner of Le Conte and Westwood Boulevard, near the south entrance leading in and out of the UCLA campus. She was driving a dark-brown Datsun 240Z with expired, out-of-state plates.

She was about the same age as Leslie and me but seemed a bit older somehow. She wore her brown hair cut short in a Scout Finch-type of pageboy.

Once we got to talking during the ride, I recognized how very bright and verbally active she was. She told me she had studied journalism at Wayne State University in Detroit. Overall, Judy appeared a tidy, courteous—yet ambitious—young woman in a sort of Midwestern way. Reminded me of people I'd met during the two years I was in Athens, Ohio.

On our way out to the jail for a visit, she told me about a recent series of stories she'd been running on Leslie and Max in the *Christian Science Monitor* since before the retrial began.

After a quick twenty-minute visit with Leslie, Judy dropped me back in Santa Monica and promised to take me for oyster shooters the next day on a tour of Marina del Rey. She let me drive her car as fast as I felt like the whole time we were together. "How long are you planning to stay in Los Angeles?" she asked.

"I start grad school this summer. In the meantime, I'm living out of a gym bag and sleeping on my friend Trish's couch."

"You could stay with me and my sister if you like. We have a fairly spacious condo in Silver Lake, with a spare bedroom and bath you can have to yourself. And the car. I'm out of town a lot. It's just a few blocks above Sunset Boulevard. There's a really big comfy bed, a big desk, and plenty of bookshelves."

"Any books on them?"

"Lots," she smiled. "It's a fairly large living space. Our balcony faces southwest toward Culver City. I'll show you."

"Sounds great." And it was.

Judy called me at Tricia's the next day and said, "You and I are invited to dinner in Monrovia Friday night to meet Leslie's mother, Jane. Our hosts are Glen and Doris Peters—friends of Jane's who would like to meet you. Okay?"

Tricia acted cool with my moving to 1707 Micheltorena Street when I told her. I hadn't paid much attention or been very good company lately. As self-justification, I supposed she had another beau waiting in the wings. I tried to make believe I was clearing a space for her and him, when really, I was only making room for myself and Leslie.

The next day, Trish came with me to the trial. After court ended, she drove me and my bags over to Judy's that afternoon. That evening, Max Keith picked me up at Judy's, and we three went out to the jail to see Leslie. I was anxious to hear what she thought of the move. "This brings me closer to you, kind of," I told her.

That's when she asked me, "What do you call it when you can't wait to see someone or ever stop dreaming about being together?"

"The prelude. Lasts a week, maybe. I hope that I'm wrong." Leslie's eyes glistened a bit and so did mine, I'm sure.

"Can't it last?" A short pause. "Always, it doesn't?" she asked.

"Don't ask me, hon. I'd rather be in love myself than become an expert on it." A long pause while we each stopped to consider the facts.

"Linda said you told her you've taken a lot of LSD," Leslie said by way of changing the subject.

"So have you. Like the poet Leonard Cohen sang, 'It did some good, did some harm.' I think I wrote that poem out for you weeks ago."

"So, you know what was up with life at the ranch... I wasn't sure. You've been polite not to ask too many uneasy questions."

"Look, Les. We've discussed this before. I've had more than my fair share of most things." Which was a lie, of course. "I'll always be honest with you and open to anything you have to tell me. I'm in no position to judge." Which I wasn't.

"Boy this is embarrassing," she said. "You've read all that. Charlie'd dole out the acid and start preachin' and dancin' and singing his songs. He was a trip if he got dancing. I can't believe it now, how I ever...

"How did I ever believe it! I still don't know. It's like a lot of it didn't really happen. I just thought it did. Dumb?

"Peter, I know what I did then was horribly wrong. But I believed it wasn't wrong when it was happening. I honestly didn't. But how could that be? I was convinced it was the right thing to do because that's what Charlie said was coming to pass. Does that make any sense? Not much, huh?"

"Yes, in a way, it sounds just like a nightmare. Which everyone knows is a real event for those finding themselves in the midst of one. The more important point is when and how you snapped out of it."

"I was still in isolation," she said. "Some people from the ranch came to visit. They were still spewing all of that Manson pseudo-philosophy, and I thought they were nuts. I realized I'm nothing like you, and you aren't making any sense.

"I'll be glad we can talk on Sunday. Peter, it sure is fine having you help me weigh these things out. I need you and you know that now. I can see how we really have gotten into talking about things. Sharing opinions. I miss you so much when we're apart, and it's even worse the more time we're together."

"Les, how do you think life will be different once you get out?"

"A lot like it is for you now. Only with me popped into the picture."

Whenever Judy was home, she and I'd talk non-stop for hours, drinking mugs of black tea out on the balcony. There was always a great sunset horizon, and after dark, we used to stay up late to watch the city lights in place of the planets and stars. Respectful, at first, of her staunch religious bearing, I was astonished to find myself politely discussing Edward R. Murrow and Mary Baker Eddy.

One day that week after court, Judy said that she and I were invited to another dinner at the home of old friends of hers, Gil and Terri. They lived a mile or so south of Mount Lee, within view of the famous HOLLYWOOD sign. Gil was an architect and Terri a lawyer. They had a quaint little bungalow with a single garage and a fair-sized concrete patio that was covered with wisteria and dotted with cactus and potted flowers.

After dinner, Terri and Judy squeezed into the jump seat of Gil's green Alfa Romeo Spider Veloce—a space equivalent in size and comfort to a couple of side-by-side toilet seats without any room on the floor for your feet.

To my surprise, Gil buckled himself in on the passenger side—handing me the keys and inviting me to take the controls. I wasted no time turning her on to let her warm up. While Gil and I pulled the top down and I adjusted our seats forward to make room for the girls.

We tore off for a quick spin down the Hollywood Freeway, weaving in and out of slower traffic the whole way downtown. Got off somewhere near the strip and found a place to park in a lot on Franklin Avenue. From there, we walked along Hollywood Boulevard toward Grauman's Chinese Theater.

The lineup for *Star Wars* looked as though it stretched for half a mile in every direction. I had little idea what the hubbub over Luke Skywalker and Darth Vader was about. I had been expecting Stanley Kubrick's *2001: A Space Odyssey*.

The four of us threw an impromptu picnic of smoothies and banana bread on the sidewalk where we sat on the Hollywood stars of Dick Powell and Darryl Zanuck. During one phase of our interminable wait, Gil gave a young street entertainer two quarters to sing us a cover of the Everly Brothers' "When Will I Be Loved?" This fine-looking young man with a winsome smile started to dance and sway to the rhythm of that sad song, which began, "I've been made blue, I've been lied to..." I recall his mood sounded comfortably stoic rather than cruel or pathetic.

The next day, I was poolside at Judy's, reading a signed copy of Lester Grinspoon's *Marihuana Reconsidered*—that he'd presented to Leslie with the inscription, *To Leslie, with best wishes and the hope that win or lose you will continue to grow. Lester.* I'd just finished chapter six when I heard that unmistakable echo-sounding exhaust note of a lonely herd of one hundred Pomigliano d'Arco horses.

When I looked over the fence to see for sure what it was, there was Gil parking his Alfa Romeo on Effie Street beside the pool. I walked out to the street, and right as I did, Judy pulled up in her Datsun with Terri. To my amazement, Gil said he was lending me the use of the Spider for the next couple of days if I wanted while he and Terri went away to San Francisco on a "business vacation."

Having the use of Gil's Alfa Spider for a few days was a dream. I must have gone through two tanks of gas a day. My arms and face were sunburned. Nice as sunny-summer Southern California days can be, there's not a lot of shelter from the glaring sunlight, especially if you never put the top up. When moving at speed in a lightweight two-door convertible, the burnt-orange soot of LA smog can sandblast the paint off the hood of your car.

I was happy to get away from the city on Friday night with Judy. It was a special night for me, especially since it was the first time I met Jane Van Houten, Leslie's mother.

Monrovia is seven miles east of Pasadena. Glen and Doris Peters' house was on South Fairgreen Avenue. Right away as Glen and I shook hands, I could sense their trepidation. First appearances aren't everything, but in those days, it was as if we were all wearing uniforms.

Glen looked to me like another Fred Foot, only this time with a brush cut. Whereas I wore a jean jacket and my long hair was always tussled, Mr. Peters' shirt, tie, and demeanor signaled something opposed, not only different. It wasn't only a matter of comfort or fashion that stood between us. There was a great divide between generations, culture, and politics—and probably a whole lot more I wasn't aware of.

The Peters said how they were old friends of Jane's and her ex, Leslie's dad, Paul. Glen told me that he worked in senior management for the *Los Angeles Times*, which led me to assume that journalism was his connection to Judy. Predictably, they asked a lot about my family background and what church we went to. I could *not* contain my surprise.

"My grandmother and aunt Rose still practice Roman Catholicism," I said.

After a pause without applause, someone whispered, "That's nice."

Jane Van Houten arrived about twenty minutes after Judy and I got there. My first impressions never changed from the moment she stepped through the door. I immediately recognized the resemblance to Leslie. Jane was what I would have described as an exceptionally handsome middle-aged woman. She had wavy white hair and an engaging smile in her eyes, though her lips were downturned a tiny bit at the edges. She appeared completely comfortable in herself.

It soon became obvious that they may have all shared a profound and longstanding community faith in Christian Science. Although I couldn't sense anything certain about Jane. The

Peters had known Leslie ever since she and her siblings were kids growing up in Monrovia.

As the evening wore on, my assumptions about Glen holding a religious-right military dogma about him led me to imagine how he must have responded to Leslie's running off to join up with the Manson Family. Something in the way Mr. Peters looked at me convinced me he was accustomed to hiding unfavorable scrutiny with a smile.

If Jane felt the same caution with me as the Peters had, I didn't notice. I was perfectly taken in by her poise, warmth, and charm. Given the way she smiled at me throughout the evening, I was certain that she liked me as much as I found her striking and fun to listen to.

In the days that followed, I got to meet more of Leslie's friends and spent some days in court with her tall, handsome brother David and pretty, hip, younger sister, Betsy. I also visited and talked on the phone with Leslie as often as possible.

Our time was limited, so we still counted a lot on exchanging letters. I wasn't too surprised to find out I wasn't the first "pen pal" she'd had. A couple of days after meeting her mom and Glen Peters, a letter from Leslie arrived that read in part:

Tomorrow, "Pete" [Glen Peters] will probably come with Mom for a visit. Mama says, by the way, to be sure to tell you "hello" and said to send you her love. She wants you to call her. Pete said on the phone he hadn't got my letter yet—the one I told you about—but wanted to see me in person. I know one thing we need to discuss is what to do about Frank Andrews and the letters/publishing scene. Max is mad about it too. Tomorrow, I will discuss it with Pete, but then I have a huge hunch that attorneys will be getting into the matter. Talk about exploitation…. I find it ironic how "perfect" this is all supposed to be, when I don't know a damn thing about it. And how "wrong" anything else I say is. It will straighten out. I need to make a list so I can clue you in on all the happenings.

* * *

Frank Andrews walked out of prison after thirteen years served of an original fifty-five-to-sixty-seven-year sentence. He served hard time for a series of armed robberies and an escape attempt in which he wounded a sheriff's deputy. Andrews was thirty-seven years old—ten years older than Leslie—when he started to write her in prison. He'd already spent half his lifetime in one kind of jail or another. As had Charlie Manson.

He sold his first short story to a journal in 1967 and co-edited an anthology of prison writing, *Voices from the Big House,* in 1971. Andrews became a leading light of a cynical "type" from within the gray walls of the New Jersey State Penitentiary.

"The parole board asked me if I might be tempted to go back to crime," Frank Andrews said at the time *Voices* was published. "I told them I never made more than a hundred bucks in any job I ever pulled. Now, I can double that by just sitting down at a typewriter for a few hours."

Andrews contributed to at least two more prison anthologies. In one, *Prose and Cons,* there was a particularly charming story, "Ima Fibbin" written by Leslie Van Houten.

* * *

I picked Jane Van Houten up at her home on Sefton Avenue at 8:00 a.m. We drove out to Sybil Brand to visit Leslie in Gil's Alfa Romeo. I left the top up to keep the wind out of Jane's hair. Right from the start, she took to calling me "Honey," which I adored. We only had half an hour to visit. It seemed to make Leslie happy to see us together.

When I dropped Jane back at home in Monterey Park, this time, she said for me to pull into the alley. She made me brunch while I washed and waxed Gil's car in her garage. I stayed all day talking to Jane about Leslie, her childhood, and how some dreams come true while others inevitably fall apart.

After Mexican food with Les's adopted sister Betsy and next-door neighbor Georgie Calhoun who had both dropped over for dinner, I spent the night in Jane's guest room. The wallpaper was made with bamboo.

The next morning, Terri dropped Gil off at Jane's to pick up his car. He let me drive him and the Spider one last time back to Silver Lake, where I traded his Alfa for Judy's 240-Z while she was away on assignment. It was the first time Gil and I ever discussed anything other than cars or movies. Most of the time, he and Terri were around Judy, and when I was talking about Leslie, I noticed Gil had stayed out of it.

"Peter, I want you to know, Terri and I think it's wonderful that you've taken such an interest in Leslie's case and have lent your support to Judy as well. We haven't met her ourselves, but from what Judy tells us, Leslie seems to have found herself again somehow. In prison, of all places!" He looked surprised.

I nodded politely and shook his hand before handing back the keys to his Alfa Romeo Spider. Suddenly, I felt sure I would have one of my own someday. I'm crazy that way.

After driving back to Judy's, I inexplicably felt like going for a slow run to explore some of the up-and-down terrain in the Silver Lake neighborhood.

Started out jogging west on Effie Street, then swung right on Griffith Park all the way past the Rowena Reservoir. Then, quite at random, I turned left onto Waverly Drive without reading the signpost. And there I was.

Glancing up a steep, familiar-looking driveway at number 3301. The whitish stucco house with bright-red Spanish roof tile and two lampposts at the foot of the drive with the street number on the left column. I looked to my right at the exact spot at which the car with Tex, Patricia, and Leslie had been parked that horrible midnight, waiting for Charlie.

Things were very quiet and still, and I must have stood there for a very long time. I never told anyone about it. Not even Leslie. No reason to, really. What could I say that she didn't know? What was once a peaceful space that a family called home was now the vacated site of a catastrophe. It felt to me as though I was standing at the end of the road where a bomb had gone off that left nothing but numbing dissonance and emotional ruins.

It was a slow walk back to Micheltorena. I'd spent the whole time thinking about Rosemary LaBianca and her children. Noting that she was born around the same year as my own mother.

After a prolonged and icy-cold shower, I drove out to LAX to pick up Judy. On the way home from the airport, we stopped somewhere near the beach for wine, cheese, and oysters to put on the bread and crackers. She asked me why I was looking so glum. I had no idea for an immediate response.

When we got home and stepped into the condo, Judy's sister Jennifer told me there had been a phone call for me while I was away. "Someone named Martin wants you to call him. His number is beside the phone. He said it was urgent."

When I called, Martin picked up right away and told me he had tragic news from back home.

11

"WILL YOU DIE FOR ME?"

Jim Buchanan had been instantly killed in a car crash. He and another friend of mine were on their way north from Kingston to Ottawa when they were struck head-on by an eighteen-wheel tractor-trailer. The truck driver survived the collision, but Tiit Romet, who was asleep in the back seat of the car Buck was driving, woke up in the hospital a day later. He had a concussion and a broken arm. Tricia and I both had a good cry when I told her.

As an accomplished world-class athlete, Buck's passing caused me to reflect on the simple yet twisted fate of being in the wrong place at the wrong time. Death seems an outrage you can't be prepared for. The consequences of having the physical forces of nature conspire against you in such a brutal and sudden way.

I also thought of how easily it could have been me who got into the car that night with Buck and Tiit after the track meet at Queen's. Just as it could have been me who got into ranch hand

Johnny Swartz's yellow Ford alongside Leslie Van Houten under similarly injudicious circumstances.

* * *

The summer of '69 that Leslie spent on Spahn Ranch with the Manson Family, I had dramatically lost interest in hockey after getting my face stitched and nose straightened again. I had already started taking a greater interest in reading more twentieth-century European philosophy, taking road trips in my Lotus Elan, and riding my BSA Thunderbolt motorcycle.

Spent a weekend's unwholesome adventure at the Satan's Choice motorcycle club's farmhouse and headquarters in Agincourt, Ontario that summer. Where a friend and I rode in with a couple of girls whom we met who had invitations to the Satan's Choice Field Day Event. They had Motorcycle drag races and jousting competitions where the riders drove at each other, and the passengers tried knocking off the competition with broken hockey sticks taped with foam padding.

Later that Saturday night, I remember sitting on some rocks around a burning fire pit while tripping at a mighty clip. I'd shared a large button of peyote with one of the girls to have with spoonfuls of strawberry ice cream. That's when this "leader of the pack"—who appeared to me at times as a live caricature of Che Guevara crossed with a raw-boned Alice Cooper—started rapping to me about joining his band of demons.

I recall the next day, thinking how effortlessly I could have stayed a few weekends out of some hedonistic, psychedelic-amplified curiosity. It wouldn't have taken much more wild abandon on my part to stick around to see how that set and setting collided. *If...*I didn't have a commitment to Ohio U. to look forward to that fall, I may have fallen into a slot pocket the wheel of dark Destiny had dropped me in.

Disillusioned by my early, soured family life and braved for any new raw adventure, I might have easily stumbled into such a powerful disease of exposure as Charlie Manson. After meeting Leslie, I wondered, what if he had imbued me with the same deceits as the others? I also tried to imagine if I'd been in Tex Watson's shoes and met Manson and Leslie when he did. We had both played football and been track stars in high school, though we held nothing else—other than Leslie Van Houten—in common.

Outside of his leading role in the murders, all I knew of him so far was from what I had read. Charles Watson grew up near Copeville, Texas. A tiny place called Farmersville. He dropped out of high school and ran off to Los Angeles. One day, he stopped his truck to pick up a hitchhiker.

The guy with his thumb out was none other than Beach Boys' drummer Dennis Wilson, whose Ferrari was in the shop. Wilson invited Watson back to his house on Sunset Boulevard. When they got there, it was Dennis Wilson who introduced Tex to Charles Manson and the slew of half-naked girls skipping and tripping around the gardens and pool.

Tex quickly took to the girls, the drugs, Wilson, and Manson himself. Charlie soon had a devoted protégé he could control and pass on his years of experience in petty criminal trades, including enforcement through violence. Among other things, Watson had advanced tutorials in pimping, guns, drugs, knives, different ways to rob banks, and how to survive in the desert.

Other reference guides Manson studied in prison besides mistaken Beatles' lyrics and Biblical quotations were: L. Ron

Hubbard's *Scientology*, Robert Heinlein's novel *Stranger in a Strange Land,* and Dale Carnegie's *How to Win Friends and Influence People.* These books gave him plenty to work with. For example, one of Dale Carnegie's basic tenets was to "Let the other fellow feel that the idea is his."

That way, for instance, Charlie was able to convince Tex to help get their co-conspirator Bobby Beausoleil off for having killed Gary Hinman. Manson told him something like, "Maybe copycat murders will get the pigs to believe the real killers are still out there roaming free?"

Charlie asked Tex whom he thought they might get to lead novice female combatants on such a mission. "Which target seems right to you, Tex? Is there some secluded place with some rich pigs we can cut up to look like Gary's place?" Then Tex may have reasonably answered, "How about somewhere like Terry Melcher's place?" After all, Tex knew the way there and the lay-out. He'd been there before when he and Charlie went looking for Terry.

From Tex's point of view, it was his own idea to pick someplace private from where he could get away undetected. Someplace where there were sure to be rich and famous people that would make a big splash in the news. Like Charlie said, *They'll be laying on their lawns dead.*

* * *

August 8th, 1969, at Spahn Movie Ranch began like so many others, as far as the girls were concerned anyway. Their job was to look after the men—cooking and cleaning up their mess—then take care of the kids, livestock, and gardens. All except Susan Atkins. She reportedly spent the day snorting grams of powdered methamphetamine with Tex Watson, who had already been trip-ping for days on regular hits of acid.

In the evening, less than twenty miles away, Sharon Tate and her houseguests Jay Sebring, Abigail Folger, and Voytek Frykowski met for dinner at the El Coyote restaurant on Beverly Boulevard. Coincidently, Voytek had been on a forty-eight-hour drug binge himself. Same sorts of stuff. Everybody in LA was on one kind of junk or another. However much you took of whatever.

You can never get enough of what you really don't need.

"What a great idea, Tex. Atta boy, way to go," Manson might have told him.

Then, point-blank, Charlie asked, "Will you die for me?" An easily misperceived tribute to someone like Tex, who so desper-ately sought Manson's approval. Tex said that he would.

"Take three girls with you," Manson told him. Susan Atkins was a good bet since she'd been with Beausoleil and Brunner when they killed Hinman. He should also take Patricia Krenwinkel and Linda Kasabian. After he'd killed everyone at the house, Charlie told Tex to be sure and leave the same sort of bloody writing. He told him what equipment to take with him: an extra change of dark clothes, wire cutters, a length of rope, a military bayonet, and Charlie's .22-caliber revolver.

Then, Manson took each of the girls aside to give them specific instructions. He told them to bring along a change of clothes and their buck knives. Patricia Krenwinkel said at this point she didn't know for certain what was going to occur. But Susan Atkins did, which explains why Manson told Susan to "Do something witchy," same as the last time at Hinman's.

To each of the girls, he simply commanded, "Go with Tex and do exactly what he tells you to."

The Polanskis' elegant ranch-style house at the end of Cielo Drive sat on its own shelf of land in the Santa Monica Mountains. To get there from Chatsworth, Charles Watson would have driven past UCLA along West Sunset Boulevard and wound his way up Benedict Canyon. Despite having been there before, Tex got lost a few times before he could find the right cul-de-sac to turn in on.

He was likely still tripping on acid and clobbered on speed. Riding along in the backseat on the way into LA, Pat said she had the feeling she was being "entwined in the entrails of some monstrous beast."

In those days, Cielo Drive was little more than a narrow dirt road that dead-ended at the gates to what was, until a few months earlier, the home of actress Candice Bergen and music producer Terry Melcher. She the daughter of a famous ventriloquist and he the son of Hollywood film star, Doris Day. With the gates locked at midnight, you wouldn't be able to see far enough up the driveway to where the house was because it sat far back in the hillside.

When Watson saw the closed, wrought-iron gates blocking the entrance, he thought they might be electrified. No matter. He knew what to do. First, he shimmied up the pole by the gates and used the bolt cutters he brought to sever the phone lines. Then he and the girls—Sadie, Pat, and Linda—all dressed in black and armed with buck knives—climbed the embankment that by-passed the fences and gates.

Suddenly, they saw car lights approaching from the direction of the house and crouched down to hide in the brush alongside the driveway. An unlucky eighteen-year-old Steven Parent, who had been visiting his friend Bill Garretson in the guesthouse, was driving the car.

Just as Parent slowed to the gate, Watson jumped out from the bushes and yelled, "Halt!" Then he thrust the twelve-inch-long .22-calibre revolver inside the open window.

Seeing the gun pointed at his face, Parent pleaded, "Please don't hurt me. I won't say anything."

With the teen's arm up to guard himself, Tex slashed Steven with his knife on the forearm. Before pulling the trigger four times. The bullets tore through Steve Parent's arm and chest, and one slug exploded point-blank into his face. The impact of the bullet sending his head violently back toward the passenger side.

After turning the engine and lights off, Tex pushed the car to the side of the drive and told the girls to follow him up to the house. As each of the girls passed by the open door of Parent's car, they could see the young man bleeding to death from the head. He was already unconscious. Now, they were getting an inkling of what was about to happen. No one was backing away.

At night, the Christmas lights that former tenant Candice Bergen had strung along the split-rail fence in front of the house glowed under a heavy darkness. When the attackers reached the house, Tex sent the girls around back to look for an unlocked door or window. Nothing so far.

Then he told Linda to check down the drive and watch out for anything unexpected. Tex used his bayonet to cut the screen on the window to the room intended to be the Polanskis' nursery. It was being readied for the arrival of Sharon and Roman's son, Paul Richard. The baby was due in less than a month.

Once inside the house, Tex opened the front door to let Susan and Pat onto the premises. The invaders quietly entered the living room and looked up to see a spacious loft beneath the high-beam ceilings. Everywhere inside the wood cabin interior, there were piles of books and film scripts strewn about. In front of the stone fireplace, passed out on the sofa, was Roman's Polish friend Voytek Frykowski.

Suddenly startled awake, Voytek yawned and asked, "What time is it?"

Tex responded with a kick in the head. Putting the open barrel of the gun to the man's face, he told him, "Don't move or you're dead."

Startled and groggy, Voytek asked him, "Well...who are you, and what are you doing here?"

"I'm the Devil," growled Watson. "I'm here to do the Devil's business."

When each of the girls told him to give them all his money, he pointed without hesitation. "My money is in the wallet on the desk."

Susan Atkins said she couldn't find it. That made Tex angry. Watson started to beat Frykowski with the wooden grip of the revolver until the man gave way to his blows. Then he ordered Susan to tie him up before dispatching her and Pat to scout the rest of the house for any others.

Abigail Folger was sitting up in her bedroom reading. There were hashish and ten capsules of MDA in a bag on the night-stand. Sharon Tate and Jay Sebring were in the master bedroom sitting up on the bed talking.

Armed with their own buck knives, Susan and Pat herded everyone into the living room, where they were tied up together. Tex ordered the girls to blindfold their captives with whatever they could find in terms of pillowcases and towels.

Then, when Watson ordered everyone to lie face down on the floor—including a very expectant Sharon Tate—Jay Sebring protested, "Let her sit down. Can't you see she's pregnant?"

Jay and Tex started exchanging punches and wrestled each other toward the door. Finally, Tex pulled the trigger and shot Sebring in the armpit.

With a noose tied around his neck, Jay Sebring lay unconscious and bleeding to death. Watson proceeded to stab him several times more—viciously slicing his aorta. Blood sprayed all over the floor, and it didn't take long for Jay Sebring to die in full view of the others.

Sharon and Abigail were absolutely hysterical, crying and pleading for their lives. Watson strung them up with nooses around their necks with the rope tossed over the roofbeams and told the terrified women to "shut the fuck up." They had to stand straight and be quiet or else strangle to death.

"What are you going to do with us?" Abigail cried.

Tex said, "You're all going to die." Then he ordered Susan to kill Voytek to make his point.

"Oh, God...no... Don't...," the man pleaded. Then, with a sudden rush, Voytek jumped up off the couch in an attempt to escape. Susan tried to tackle him, and the two continued to wrestle as he made for the hallway leading to the front door.

Voytek started swinging Susan around by her hair to make her let go. Before she lost her knife in the fracas, Atkins managed to stab Voytek several times in the legs and once in the back of the lung. He staggered, smearing blood on the walls as he went through the doorway.

In all the chaos, Pat was now struggling with the two tied-up women. Tex had become distracted with stabbing Jay Sebring, and it took several seconds before he heard Susan Atkins' screams for help with killing Frykowski.

When Tex caught up with the wounded man, he immediately began clobbering Voytek over the head with the butt end of his gun. Using the full force of his grip and swing-arc of the extra long barrel for leverage.

Beaten and bloodied, Frykowski fell into the bushes outside on the front threshold of the house. Linda Kasabian saw him stand again for a moment before Tex tackled him onto the front lawn. Hitting and stabbing him senseless.

Standing over the fallen man like Ali stood over Liston, Watson shot him once in the back before the gun misfired the second time. Then, Tex proceeded to club Voytek with the butt of Manson's Buntline revolver so ferociously that the grip handle broke off. Tex shot him once more for good measure.

All the while this carnage was happening inside and outside the house, Linda Kasabian claimed she just stood in shock and watched as Watson repeatedly stabbed Mr. Frykowski's fractured body until all his tremors stopped.

Frantic with terror, Abigail Folger had managed to twist free of her restraints and rushed through the hallway and into the master bedroom, with Patricia Krenwinkel in close pursuit. Abigail burst through the back doorway that opened out onto the pool patio. Patricia gave chase with her knife held high overhead and finally set upon Ms. Folger out by the lawns and gardens.

Abigail raised her hands in defense, and the sharp knife blade tore gashes in her hands and the left side of her face. The victim continued to struggle until Watson, who had just finished his annihilation of Frykowski, ran over and slashed Abigail's throat with his bayonet.

The girls later testified that the instant before Tex cut her off at the neck, the woman looked up at him and whispered, "I give up. I'm dead. Take me."

When Tex shuffled back inside, he saw that Sharon Tate had slipped free and ordered Susan and Pat to finish her off. With each of Sharon's houseguests already dead—all the while she was left alone to beg and plead for the life of her unborn child—Manson's operatives continued stabbing and deriding the helpless woman.

Susan Atkins looked her straight in the eye and said, "Look, bitch, I don't care about you. I don't care if you're going to have a baby. You had better be ready. You're going to die, and I don't feel anything about it."

Meanwhile, Watson—according to specific orders—made certain everyone else was either dead or dying before he finally strode over to where Susan was holding Sharon's arms behind her back. She was sobbing uncontrollably when the blood-soaked, meth-crazed fanatic from Farmersville, Texas, thrust his bayonet through the woman's lung and heart, ending her vale of tears forever.

Charles Watson had effectively destroyed five human souls in a matter of minutes.

In the aftermath, he told the girls to take turns mutilating their victims' lifeless bodies. Sadie admitted later they considered cutting out the unborn baby but decided instead to smear Sharon's blood all over her swollen belly. Then took a towel with her blood and used it to write "PIG" on the front door.

The whole assault lasted approximately half an hour. Then, everything returned to the same quiet as before. Linda Kasabian would later testify that when the assassins returned to their car, Watson still had a terrible look in his eyes. "They all looked like zombies covered with blood."

The entire crew stopped a few miles away from this site and used someone's garden hose to wash off all the gore. They changed into clean clothes and tossed their bloody clothing down a washed-out ravine. After which, they drove back to

Spahn Ranch around two in the morning. Charles Manson was standing in the same spot he had been when they drove off only hours before.

Watson told him how most of it went according to plan. For instance, he reported that there were butchered bodies lying all around the property inside and out. Inside, the walls inside were splashed with gore. There were large pools of dark blood beginning to jell beneath each of the ripped and ravished corpses. Someone draped an American flag upside down over the sofa next to where Sharon Tate's body lay in the last of her blood.

Tex, still rushing on meth, had the audacity to complain to Charlie about the inadequacy of the weapons he gave him to do the job, which he blamed for all the screaming panic, fighting, and overall chaos.

Manson asked all four of his assassins: "Do you have any remorse?"

All shook their heads and said, "No." Then, Manson told each of them to go straight to bed and be sure not to say anything to the others. Not yet anyway.

Leslie at Linda Grippi's apartment

At Leslie's mom's house

Surprised by the ring I gave her

Leslie at McDonald's

Getting ready for bed

Me before my interview at UCSB with professors Brown, Shapiro and Phillips

Agincourt, just outside Toronto

Writing to Leslie from my mom's house

Me on the left, sprinter Jim 'Buck' Buchanan in the middle, and triple jumper David Watt on the right

Ohio U, August 1969

12

JUST ASK ROMAN POLANSKI

Which fallen angels haunted my sleep, I didn't know. These spirits seemed to find me trudging knee-deep in a desert of snowdrifts, shivering with cold. In this dreamscape of unmemorable colors, I wondered how nice it would be if it were warmer. In a flash, I recognized that it *could* be summer if I wanted it so.

The trespass of ice suddenly vanished, and in its place, I willed a landscape of melded summer greens, yellows, pinks, and blues into view. Things came alive but only for a moment. An instant later, a blizzard had started when, out of nowhere, a motorcycle cop came alongside, shouting, "Do you know Jim Buchanan? He's dead." I woke with the telephone ringing in my head.

Martin Bijaux said he had a next-day flight out of LAX in the morning and asked if I could meet him for breakfast, then drop him off at the airport. He picked Canter's Bakery and Delicatessen on North Fairfax between Melrose and Beverly.

Canter's Bakery was a lot like a typical Montreal-style deli or Yitz's on Eglinton West in Toronto. There was a familiar Neil Young song playing as I walked in at ten past eight in the morning. Martin was already there in a booth having coffee. We both ordered rugelach to have with our second cups.

"For some reason, 'Hurricane' always reminds me of Leslie," I said.

"It reminds me of a bar in Ottawa," Martin responded.

"Speaking of Ottawa, I want to thank you again for getting the message about Jim to me when you did."

"Did you know Buchanan well?" he asked.

"I knew him for a couple of years on account of track and field at Toronto. He was probably the most popular guy on the team. He was an outstanding overall athlete; it would have been scary if he'd spent more time learning other sports. He was too late coming into hockey, for instance."

"Have you spoken with anyone close to the family?" he asked.

"I spoke with Andy Higgins and Bruce Kidd on the phone, and to Carl Georgevski. That's it so far.

"Everything disappears with one's death, doesn't it? It's nothing deep or profound, just how it appears to me personally. A year ago, training here in LA, Buck had a personal best in the long jump. Somewhere in the 7.82-meter range. And now, the spirit that propelled that achievement is gone. It's just gone."

Not so inclined to think about spirit and death bosh as I was, Martin asked, "How good a jump is that?"

"In the world? Look at it this way: All the men who jumped over 7.80 in Montreal advanced to the final. There are maybe twenty in the world who can accomplish this feat."

We talked about other things too. Like about where Martin was flying to later that morning (Detroit), and what kind of story he hoped to write (on the history of Motown Records). Listening to this only as background, I was still thinking about Jim's life and death at that time. Conscious of nothing at all really—only his absence—as well as the ever-present threat of my own.

"What's going on with the Van Houten case?" he asked, seemingly quite out of the blue.

"I'm learning new things all the time. Mostly just from hanging out with Max Keith and Judy. Bits of history that fill in more of what's missing in other accounts."

"For instance?"

"Well, for example, I didn't know that the average length of time served in California for first-degree murder was ten and a half to eleven years when this happened. Bugliosi himself had guessed the girls would serve fifteen to twenty years, the men, with the exception of Manson, a like number...at least twenty-five years."

"Sounds about right," he said, glancing down to look at his watch.

"Do you think so?"

"What does her lawyer say?"

"Max said that by law, one could argue that Leslie may be guilty of manslaughter—which doesn't carry with it a life sentence. But she is not guilty of first-degree murder."

"On what is he basing this defense?"

"Well, first of all, by reason of 'diminished capacity' due to mental illness, prolonged drug use, and cult conditioning," I answered. By his look, I could see that Martin remained unconvinced.

"Don't make faces..."

"I'm not," he said. "Go ahead with what you were saying."

"In this new trial, the prosecution remains hellbent on tying Leslie to the 'conspiracy' to murder Sharon Tate—even though Leslie wasn't aware of either the killings or the planning for what happened at 10050 Cielo Drive. She didn't learn of it until the day after it happened.

"Max Keith admitted that Leslie participated in killing the LaBiancas. Which forced the prosecution to concede that she *hadn't* participated in the Tate murders. Kay may need some other sleight of hand to con the press and the jury," I said, leaning back to stretch away the sudden tightness I felt in my shoulders and back. "Maybe not," I added with a frown.

Martin didn't say anything more right away, and neither did I for a spell.

"Time to go?" I asked. Martin looked at his watch and said, "No."

After a long pause—and before we got to talking about anything else *besides* Leslie or Manson—the last thing Martin asked me about was the killing of "Shorty" Shea.

"Donald Shea," I answered, "was the ninth and final victim in the Manson murder spree that began one month before, beginning with Gary Hinman. Just two weeks after the murder of the LaBiancas. How much do you know?"

"Just that Shea was a foreman at Spahn Ranch. And that he and Charlie never got along."

"That's what I've read," I said. "Shorty was continually trying to convince George Spahn to run the Manson Family off. Charlie found out it was Shorty who was informing on him to both George and the LA County Sheriff. Stuff about all the drug dealing, car theft, and rumors of all sorts of über-strange and sinister goings-on.

"Manson enticed Shea to take a ride with Tex and Clem (Steve Grogan) up the Santa Susana Pass into the mountains to pick up a stash of stolen car parts. Then convinced him to drive the parts to LA, where Tex had arranged to exchange them for money. Charlie promised there'd be something in it for Shorty.

"Shea was behind the wheel. Clem was seated behind him. Watson sat in the front beside Shea and told him to pull over on a deserted pass west of Topanga Boulevard. Then, right as Charles Manson and Bruce Davis were pulling up in another car behind them, Watson got out and pretended to look for the stash of car parts in the bushes.

"Clem froze at first when he got the signal from Tex. He swung the pipe Charlie had given him and hit Shea with a glancing blow. Shorty jumped out of the open door on the passenger side and made a break for it with Watson drawing his bayonet and giving chase.

"When Tex caught up with him, he wasted no time thrusting his knife into Shorty's back. The other three men gathered to watch. Charlie Manson, ever needing to make everyone complicit—saw to it that each of the killers took turns beating, taunting, and slashing Shorty Shea. Until he stopped breathing.

"Clem helped drag the corpse to a shallow grave where they buried his remains and covered the site with bushes."

"What about rumors of decapitation?" Martin asked. "I heard that somewhere."

"From what I've read, Shea's body was not dismembered. Part of his left hand was missing from the shallow grave where it was discovered in 1977. The coroner concluded he'd died from several skull fracture blows to the head, along with multiple chop and stab wounds to the rest of his body.

"Bruce Davis also remains in prison, of course, but Steve Grogan became the first and, so far, only Manson Family member convicted of murder to be released from prison.

"Grogan served fifteen years for his role in the killing. The judge decided he was 'too stupid and too hopped on drugs to decide anything on his own,' and that it was really 'Manson who decided who lived or died.'

"Grogan later drew the authorities a map to where Shea's body was buried, and that's the reason he was let go in 1985. Why do you ask?"

"Just curious. To complete the picture in my head, I guess."

Martin signaled it was time to get moving.

We tossed his gear into the back of Judy's car and went barreling down Highway 405 mostly in third and hard on the throttle. When we hit traffic, I shifted up a gear to relax the engine, as well as Martin. That's when he started talking again.

"Where did you get hold of this swift car?" he asked with excitement. After which, I explained about Judy Frutig and her connection to Leslie by way of family friends intent on promoting Christian Science and journalism. Among other things.

"Speaking of which, have you been keeping up with the news about Roman Polanski?" Martin shouted over the whining engine. "He's been back to court, you know. The judge, Rittenband, thinks Polanski's a pervert, so he denied a petition to have the rape charges dropped.

"Doping and raping a drunk, precocious thirteen-year-old girl, if convicted, can get him fifty years in the big house."

"I don't think he deserves that," I said. "Polanski may be a slightly warped swinger, but he's probably nowhere near midfield of the lot of them."

"Nor the last of them, I imagine," Martin added. "He's an artist, he claims. That doesn't give him license to be twisted around a minor. His films may be on edge, but he shouldn't be. Although, she *was* there with her mother's permission. Having her picture taken for *Vogue*."

"Maybe Roman needed a way to put the right pout on her face that he wanted?" I asked him, rather facetiously.

"Do you know how old Sharon Tate was when Polanski seduced her?" Martin asked and then answered his own question. "Twenty-two. I heard they were both tripping on acid."

"Everyone wants something wicked some time. No one's immune to human nature," I guessed.

We were just pulling into the airport. Inside the LAX World Way terminal loop, I dropped Martin and his two pieces of luggage off by the curb outside the United Airways departures desk. From there, he was headed to Detroit via Chicago. I wished him a safe journey home.

He surprised me when he said, "Wish Leslie good luck for me, will you?" I nodded and said that I would. "And say 'hi' to Jean when you see him back in Toronto. I'm sorry about your friend Jim."

Back in court the next morning, I heard Deputy District Attorney Stephen Kay keep harping on testimony Leslie had given in court six years before. Kay insisted on reminding this jury what Leslie said in 1971, when she was asked if she felt any remorse for the part she played in the killing. Leslie famously answered, "Sorry is only a five-letter word."

This day in 1977, she admitted, "I feel very ashamed.... I don't feel the same way today."

Stephen Kay, naturally, implied she was lying.

When I asked her about it later that evening, Leslie told me, "When I said what I said about 'sorry' being only a word, that wasn't meant to sound unremorseful, you know? At the time, I really felt these murders had to be done. That's what Charlie said. That's how messed up I was."

* * *

Facing the death penalty in 1971, Maxwell Keith vehemently argued that Leslie Van Houten deserved to live. In his closing, he said, "Mr. Bugliosi tells you that 'if the death penalty is not appropriate in this case, it would never be appropriate.' Well, I wonder if it ever is appropriate.

"I am not asking you to forgive her, although to forgive is divine. I am asking you to give her the chance to redeem herself. She deserves to live. What she did was not done by the real Leslie. Let the Leslie of today die... She will, slowly and maybe painfully. And let the Leslie as she once was live again."

In his conclusion, Judge Older said, "After all of the hyperbole has been indulged in, all that remains are the bare, stark facts of seven senseless murders...seven people whose lives were snuffed out by total strangers. I have carefully looked, in considering this action, for mitigating circumstances and have been unable to find any.

"It is my considered judgment that not only is the death penalty appropriate, but it is almost compelled by the circumstances. I must agree with the prosecutor that if this is not a proper case for the death penalty, what would be?"

Then, speaking directly to the defendants, the judge added, "The Department of Corrections is ordered to deliver you to the custody of the warden of the state prison of the State of California at San Quentin to be by him put to death in the manner prescribed by law of the State of California."

A tooth for a tooth after all.

Here's something I hope never to see the inside of—I'm told the San Quentin gas chamber contains a couple of side-by-side perforated seats like you would expect to find on some old farmer's tractor. Two guards strap each of the prisoners into the chairs and attach belts across their legs, arms, and chest. Beneath the chairs are bowls filled with sulphuric acid, and there's a pound of sodium cyanide pellets suspended in a gauze bag just above that.

After the door to the death chamber is sealed, the warden gives a signal for the executioner to pull the lever that drops the cyanide into the acid pool under the seat. The chemical reaction immediately causes hydrogen cyanide gas to be released into the chamber.

In medical terms, victims die from "hypoxia," which means the supply of oxygen to all vital organs, including the brain, has been cut off. At first, this results in muscle spasms and seizures due to increasing suffocation, but because of the straps, involuntary body movements are minimized. The prisoner doesn't lose consciousness right away either. It can take one to three minutes to completely pass out, during which time the pain is akin to a respiratory/cardiac arrest.

The horror, they say, continues to intensify until the eyes bug right out of their sockets. Skin turns a bruised purple and blue as a stew of blood and froth flows from the nose and mouth. It can take between nine and twelve minutes before the heart muscle finally grinds to a halt. Exhaust fans suck the gas out of the compartment, and the bodies are robotically sprayed with ammonia.

After half an hour, staff enters the chamber wearing gas masks and rubber gloves. Their training manual advises them to be sure to ruffle the victims' hair before taking their corpses away on a tray in a body bag. Poison that strong tends to linger.

In 1972, the California State Supreme Court rescinded the death penalty, noting that execution by means of containment in a cyanide gas chamber met the criteria defined as "cruel and unusual punishment."

Although the state reinstated the death penalty four years later, it did not affect Leslie or any of her co-defendants because the new statutes were not retroactive. And since legislation handing out life imprisonment without the possibility of parole wasn't in place yet, this meant that, according to state law, the "Manson murderers" were entitled to the possibility of ensuing freedom.

Then as now, according to the law—when each individual no longer poses a threat to society—each parole would be decided on a case-by-case basis. That sounded fair to both Leslie and her attorney. Then as now.

13

JOURNEY OUT; JOURNEY HOME

On Thursday, June 9th, 1977, I was in court when Leslie testified about how things changed so dramatically at Spahn Ranch throughout 1969.

When asked by Max Keith about what life was like when she first joined the Family a year before that, Leslie said, "At that time, it was a mellow situation. It was an easy, slow life. No one had any ambitions or goals in life, other than to get rid of our thoughts and live only for the moment. That's what Spahn was all about then. Manson's songs and lyrics were about loving your fellow man. It was what I had been looking for."

She also testified that by the spring of 1969, there was an increased mood of fear and anger surrounding Manson that replaced all the peace and love that had gone on before.

Leslie said she only stayed with Manson in the first place because she was seeking a spiritual advisor to lead her on the path to enlightenment. Then, by '69, he not only kept them completely isolated from their families and friends but would also malign or abuse any girl who dared to behave independently.

Manson didn't want girls who were totally wrecked—only fractured.

Another cardinal rule Manson learned from the more experienced crooks and pimps in prison was to never allow the girls to carry their own money. That way, they couldn't pay for a phone call to friends or relatives or buy themselves a bus ticket home.

Then came more testimony about Charlie's obsession with The Beatles' *White Album*. Former cult members spoke about the "delusional belief system" Manson created for them to accept his word on every subject as gospel. Several admitted they believed Charles Manson was the actual figure of Christ and that The Beatles were in on this secret. Disguising this message in their lyrics.

During her time on the stand in 1977, Leslie described herself as a huge Beatles fanatic long before she ever met Manson. She said the cult was astounded to learn their leader was *so special* that The Beatles encoded messages meant only for him and the Family. That's how special they were made to believe they were. And, by repeating over and over how The Beatles were charging him to trigger an inevitable race war called "Helter Skelter," Manson convinced her and the others they were destined to raise from the smoldering heap of ashes left after the war.

Leslie admitted under oath, "I felt he [Charlie] was more special than anyone I had ever met and felt that everything he said was the truth..."

She, at the time, said she believed the Manson Family was destined to rule over the world and restore it to peace—just like it said in the published lyrics to the *White Album*, or so she and the others believed with all their hearts. Why is that so hard for some folks to imagine?

Sometime later in June 1977, the jurors were also told about how, at the time of the investigations into the Tate–LaBianca murders in December 1969, LAPD Detective Mike McGann offered Leslie immunity protection. The police also promised her a reward in exchange for all she could tell them about the slayings. Even though this would have saved her from prosecution (and therefore the death chamber), Leslie declined their offer. If that isn't crazy, what is? I wondered.

When Max Keith asked her "Why?" on the stand, she answered, "I felt kind of like I was sitting in the seat of Judas. I knew if I needed twenty-four-hour protection, I would be doing something that wouldn't please Charlie. I just played games with him [Detective McGann]."

* * *

Friday morning, June 10th, 1977, Glen Peters, who told Leslie he had something urgent to discuss with her, had me bumped from the visitor's lineup. I suspected it had to do with the publishing deal he had brokered between Frank Andrews and Leslie going sour. But this had nothing whatsoever to do with me, unless she asked for my opinion.

After a four-set workout with a curling bar Judy's neighbor lent me, I went for a run and cooled down in the pool. Jane Van Houten called and invited me over for lunch, where I met Leslie's brother David's wife, Shannon. Les's sister, Betsy, whom I was already friends with, was also there. My social space was expanding. That evening, I went out with Judy and Max for dinner in Pasadena.

It was just after midnight when Jude and I got back to Micheltorena. Her sister, Jenn, left me a message, asking me to call Glen Peters when I got in. But being so late, I didn't return his call.

The telephone ringing woke me at 7:10 a.m., when Jennifer brought the handset into my room. It was Glen. He said he wanted to see me that morning and asked if I could meet him at his office in the *Los Angeles Times* building at First and Spring streets.

Glen took me for soup and sandwiches in the remarkable Pablo Picasso Room, where we sat at a table alongside portraits of whom I was told represented Marie-Thérèse Walter, Dora Maar, and Jacqueline Rogue.

After an overture of polite chitchat about modern art, Glen finally finished stirring his soup and said, "I won't waste your time or mine, Peter. I'll just say this. Okay? I'm concerned for Leslie and for you. I don't want either of you to be hurt or fooled by the fantasy picture frame in which you see yourselves."

"Picture frame?" I challenged, thinking it best to put on a good forecheck before he got started. "Do you mind me asking how so?" I asked in response to his tone.

"Cut it out, Peter. You know what I mean. That glass window you and Leslie see each other through at Sybil Brand every day. That picture can be very seductive. I hope you aren't fooling yourself."

Seeing the sneer and hearing the pitch in his snub, I put down my soup spoon and imagined myself picking up his butter knife to jam his toast with.

Glen sensed the look coming from me and said, "I've invited you here to lunch as a courtesy. I'm trying to help you here, not start any trouble. I know Jane and Max seem to think well of you." The way he said it made my blood boil. I'd met his type and seen this type of lame groove before.

"Has Leslie told you anything about this book business with Frank Andrews?" he asked.

Ah, now, here comes the real reason for the free lunch, I thought to myself. Glen pursed his lips. I looked away and noticed that the expression Picasso gave Dora Maar looked very similar.

"Frank Andrews? Not really. I've heard his name mentioned, that's all. Something to do with the book, *Prose and Cons.*"

"I'm just telling you to be careful. You could find your feelings hurt. Leslie can be very charming, but she can be a tough cookie too."

I kept quiet.

"Has Leslie said anything to you about writing her book with Judy? What do you know about that?"

"Look, Glen. This is all very interesting. But none of my business. As far as Judy writing Leslie's book…I don't see how that's possible. It seems to me the only person who can write Leslie's book is Leslie."

Then, pushing my chair away from the table, I got up to leave. Glen said nothing, but I could see he was steaming. I turned to face him.

"I know you mean well and all that," I said faintly. "Thanks for the caution or…whatever. I may be young, but I'm not stupid. Here's the thing, though. Whatever you think…*I'm* not the one writing a book or publishing a newspaper story. That's not my thing. It's yours. And Judy's.

"Whatever you believe or imagine, I'm here as Leslie's friend. At her request. I leave in two weeks. Keep me posted."

"Rude bastard. Who do you think…?" Glen started.

Only I skipped out of earshot without taking a whole breath until I stepped onto Spring Street. All I could think of was how much my arrogance fueled my anger. It wasn't Glen I was mad at. It was that awful, weak, angry part of myself always threatening to let go of the beast's bridle.

Leslie called me that night from the county jailhouse. I told her what happened with Glen. She said she was weary from all the intrigue, plus all the peripheral junk about coauthors, letters, lawyers, and publishers. I gave her my side of the events, which was largely hers to begin with.

"What're you doing now?" she asked, sounding in need of cheering up.

"Daydreaming about you and me…naked," I teased.

"Liar. No, you're not."

"Writing you a letter…and reading. Just started Truman Capote's *Breakfast at Tiffany's*. I'd been meaning to read it for years. And I've finished rereading *In Cold Blood*. Time to take notes. I found it on Judy's bookshelves. She has a very respectable library, by the way. Can't wait for you to see it…naked."

"Peter! I started to write you a letter. When I got this one from you today, I thought I'd take a chance and just call. It's about Erich Fromm's theory of… What's the book called? *The Dogma of Christ*? I'm still unsure what it's about. Tell me."

"You said something in court about how 'all of us girls *worshipped* Charlie.' It sounded so real, it was shocking. It goes to show how unaware you were at the time that what you were doing was wrong. Or the consequences.

"What Fromm is doing in his chapter on the dogma of Christ is to put Christianity and—especially, Catholic dogmatism and authoritarianism—in its social, historical context," I said.

"Manson liked to say how he was all about love. About how love is for everyone. But he sure put you down if you showed too much ego or doubt about him. So, he used fear the way he used love…. Oh, darn it…

"Honey, I got to go," she said, sounding rushed. "Tell me more in your next letter. My time is up. But will I see you tomorrow?"

The next day, I did go to see Leslie with her mom Jane in the morning. I saw her again from a distance on Monday when she testified in open court. I couldn't see her that evening, though, because I had to pick Judy up from the airport again.

For the rest of the month of June, at least, Les and I were able to keep up our regular routine of daily courtroom glances, phone calls, near-daily five- and six-page letters, and evening visits with Max every chance we could get.

The last time I saw Leslie on that leg of the journey was on Tuesday, June 21st. I'd spent the afternoon at the Huntington Library, Art Museum, and Botanical Gardens with her mom. It's a magnificent campus around ten miles from downtown LA with individual libraries, halls, gardens, and education centers.

There were some wonderful sculptures outside in the court-yard that practically came alive. Not as many paintings as I had imagined there would be. Mostly British and European art from the fifteenth to late-nineteenth centuries. I remember Thomas Gainsborough's famous portrait of *The Blue Boy* in the picture gallery, but personally, I could not see what all the fuss was about. It looked like the still portrait of a spoiled brat in the eighteenth century. What was I missing?

Jane and I held hands as we walked through the gardens up and around the water fountain in the North Vista and chatted. Being with Jane always helped calm me down. No matter what state of mind I was in, troubled or not—she was soft and gentle with me, always.

"I'm going with Max to see Les tonight at Sybil Brand," I told her.

"I know. She said you were worried about the way the trial is unfolding. What's the matter, honey? What's worrying you?"

"Not entirely sure where this anxiety is coming from. I don't want to spread it to her. But I'm surprised Max hasn't made it any clearer to the jury. The potency of Manson's 'program' and the effect that it had on her state of mind."

"Don't let it worry you, hon. I'm sure Max knows what he's doing."

"I'm sure he does. I'm more concerned with not knowing what Stephen Kay is up to. I'm worried he's hiding something. Or keeping something hidden from the jury. It's frustrating having him cast aspersions on Leslie's upbringing and lack of respect for you and the rest of her family."

"I think the jury can see through that, don't you?" she asked.

"No, I don't." Then, just to expel some spontaneous effect, I took three quick strides, gathered my arms, and jumped vertically to touch the hanging branches of a tall chestnut tree. Jane smiled brightly when I turned around and waited for her to catch up with me.

"Was Leslie much into sports as a kid?"

"She was. She was good in school too."

"What was her favorite sport?"

"She loved to dance. Would you count that?" she asked, and I laughed.

"Of course! What else was she good at?"

"Besides school and the church choir, she was a very good archer."

"Jane, I hope you won't hate me for saying anything disrespectful about one's faith in religion…. I was in the choir too. Until my voice changed and I stopped believing anything the sisters and fathers told me was true."

"I'm not insulted, honey." We stopped walking and sat side-by-side on the rim of the fountain in the shade of the trees.

"Our church in Monrovia was an important focal point for the community we lived in. Leslie took it very seriously and was active in lots of church groups. Then, after Paul and I divorced, Leslie lost faith in a lot of things. Including her parents.

"Drugs were a new thing. She started avoiding friends she grew up with and got involved with people we didn't know. You know, she became pregnant and believed strongly that having a baby was the 'right' thing to do. She was only seventeen and I opposed her."

I could see the genuine sadness this memory brought back and regretted mentioning religion. I reached out to hold her hand in mine again.

"Every one of us is a maze of contradictions," I said. "We make plans, then do the exact opposite. We treat some episodes as if they were permanent conditions. It's absurd the way a loving parent and child can suddenly turn away from one another."

"My heart still aches," Jane sighed. "We wanted to make her as comfortable as possible. The procedure was performed in our home. In my day, our parents would have married us off as soon as possible."

"Which might have been worse," I said, smiling.

"Let's head back," she said, standing and letting go of my hand for a moment.

Then, seemingly out of the blue, Jane added, "She had already started experimenting with psychedelic drugs. I couldn't understand. I thought we needed to get her help from outside the church. Nothing we tried seemed to work. We argued more often; we weren't relating. Then, she just disappeared."

"How did you hear about her involvement with the killings?" I asked.

"Glen told us once the *Times* had her name and a picture."

"Glen thinks Les and I are living in some kind of 'fantasy picture frame' and fooling ourselves into believing we might have a future together," I said.

"He and Doris are old friends of ours. After the divorce, Glen stepped in to help protect Leslie after Paul had gone. Don't worry, honey. He'll come around when he sees how happy and independent she's become."

"He's very protective of her; I respect that," I said, biting my tongue. As much as I trusted Jane, I skeptically thought of something to add but thought better of it.

That evening in the conference room at Sybil Brand, Max, Leslie, and I got to talking some more about whether the jury seemed to be getting the picture as to the potency of Manson's combined approach to brainwashing through music, religion, and psychotropic drugs. I asked if the reason might be on account of too many equivocal plotlines in their heads about "insanity pleas" gleaned from TV and the movies.

"You know," Leslie said, "I did get to say for the record how one time, while on LSD, I'd actually experienced my own crucifixion. I'm not sure they believed me or understood the experience I was talking about. But that was a turning point for me in terms of my stupid devotion to Manson."

"It's hard to believe how real an experience an acid trip can be unless you've been there yourself. I thought you did a good job of describing the experience."

"Yeah, well, it was a hard chargin' trip. I saw myself bleeding from my hands, my feet, and from right here just under my heart," she said, pointing to the exact spot.

"Like all the blood was draining out of me, and I just kept seeing Charlie's face in front of me the whole time. My whole world became Charlie, and the ecstasy I felt led me to him. I thought he was the holy spirit of Christ for real."

Leslie waited for my reaction, and I frowned.

"Hey, what's wrong?" she asked, sounding concerned about my expression. Max got up to stretch his arms and legs for a minute.

"What? No, nothing. I was just thinking how much I hate leaving you in the middle of all this right now. The timing is wrong. I don't want to go back to Toronto. Not now. Not unless you come with me," I added, checking Max's reaction.

"It's okay, honey," Leslie quietly said. "You know you need to go back and finish what you had planned to do before I came along. It's important to you and me too. Of course, I hope things will work out like we hope. Maybe it will and maybe it won't. Time will tell. But we need to be prepared if it doesn't."

The next day, I packed up my things from Judy's. Sweat suits mostly. Along with some borrowed books, stacks of letters, notebooks, and shoes. I was sure to give Tricia Woodbridge a last call to say "Hello, goodbye" again. Judy was out of town. So, I made sure her car was polished and topped off with fuel, oil, and water. I left a bouquet of flowers and a thank you card on the driver's seat.

Judy's sister Jennifer gave me a ride over to Jane Van Houten's place in Monterey Park. That's where I spent my last night of this stint in LA, watching an old movie on TV with Audrey Hepburn and Albert Finney: *Two for the Road*.

Jane and her best friend, Georgie, drove me out to the airport first thing in the morning. I had three empty seats all to myself on the way to Vancouver. By the time we landed in Toronto, just after nine o'clock, I had begun marking up the margins in three-quarters of Truman Capote's *In Cold Blood* with my pencils.

I had also begun a letter to Leslie regarding Capote's account of Perry Smith and Richard Hickock, two savage young men who, in 1959, broke into a stranger's home in Holcomb, Kansas, and senselessly shot-gunned all four members of the Herb Clutter family without any obvious motive. There was nothing to rob.

A false tip by a prison inmate led Smith and Hickock to think there would be a safe filled with money. There wasn't. They could have just left without harming anyone.

The murders, wrote Truman Capote, were "a psychological accident, virtually an impersonal act. The victims might as well have been killed by lightning, except for one thing. They [each of the victims] had experienced prolonged terror, they had suffered." That meant retribution.

Toward the end of the book, the author reported on expert testimony that suggested this crime would never have happened except for a certain "frictional interplay between the perpetrators." In other words, *folie a deux*. Referencing expert psychiatry on the subject, Capote claimed that neither Perry Smith nor Dick Hickock would have, or could have, committed such barbarism all on his own. Not without the complex interplay of each other's personal madness.

Before going to bed that first night back in Toronto, I went for a long walk in the dark and mailed my letter to Leslie. It included my response to the page she sent me of her repeatedly writing her name as *Leslie Chiaramonte,* (presumably) to see how it looked on paper.

I told her I wished I could honestly say it was good to be home, only it wasn't. Not entirely. It wasn't just as though something was missing exactly. It felt more as though I no longer belonged where I was. Maybe it was time to go about getting my roots down in firm *terra nova* once and for all.

NO VERDICT IN DOUBLE MURDER

The end of June was a good time to be in Toronto. The ground was green, and the cool morning air was perfect for running. I spent my first week back home hanging around the track and Andy's office in Hart House. Like everyone else who knew Buck, I couldn't help thinking about how much I missed him. Carl Georgevski said he kept expecting him to show up for practice.

"I keep calling, but he doesn't answer."

On Monday, July 4th, I registered for two three-week summer courses at the OISE: "Program Planning" on Tuesday and Thursday mornings and "Facilitating Adult Learning" in the afternoons. When I got back from the campus bookstore, there was a letter from UC Berkeley waiting for me, along with the one I'd been expecting from Leslie.

As I requested, the Regents in Residence Matters, University Hall, Berkeley, forwarded catalogs and application forms for two graduate schools of education: Berkeley and Santa Barbara. After reading my mail and looking over the various program offerings at the University of California—I made a phone call to my landlady, giving her a month's notice.

Later that week, Bruce Kidd invited me to join him for a run around Queen's Park for a few laps before we headed off to have lunch with Andy Higgins and Carl Georgevski in the Great Hall at Hart House.

After our cool-down around the park, we went inside to eat before heading downstairs to the showers. Andy and Carl were already there. I recall waving "Hello" to my old prof. Thomas Langdon, who was having lunch in the upstairs faculty lounge with Marshall McLuhan. Professor McLuhan let me audit his course once when I was still living with Jackson Tovell, but I doubted he'd remember me.

When we sat down, Carl asked me, "What are you taking at OISE this summer?"

"Two of the most boring courses imaginable," I said. "We're reading Malcolm Knowles's theory of andragogy, and it's putting my feet to sleep. Same with Saul Alinsky. *Rules for Radicals* read better seven years ago than it does today."

"It's called growing up," Higgins said. Kidd smiled in a way that suggested he agreed with Andy.

Bruce qualified this by saying, "If you weren't a socialist when you were twenty, you'd have no heart. If you aren't a capitalist by thirty, you..."

"You haven't any brains... Yeah, I've heard that one before," Andy said and everyone but me laughed.

"I'm not sure I'll go on with OISE this fall," I announced out of nowhere. "I've applied to Cal Berkeley and UC Santa Barbara instead." No comments right away—just strange looks of surprise. First at me and then at each other.

"And what will you do in the meantime?" Andy asked.

"First of all, I'm heading back to LA in a couple of weeks. I should get back in time for the end of the Van Houten trial."

Carl asked, "You don't honestly think she'll get off, do you?"

I wish I had a nickel...

"She'll plea to a lesser charge when one is offered," I guessed. "Probably manslaughter or second-degree. She could be out in a year, maybe less." I paused to chew my grilled cheese sandwich.

"Probably *not*," said Andy. "You must be dreaming. At this point in your life, you want to chance your existent future on intrigue and illusions?"

"She's already served nearly eight years in prison. Ain't that enough?" I tried pointing out.

Bruce said, "Some people think none of the Manson Family will *ever* be let out of prison."

"Some people think differently," I responded.

"Hear him out," Andy said.

Bruce continued. "You've told me before that Van Houten took part in a fight with this woman, Rosemary LaBianca. Who ended up brutally murdered. Whatever her defense, you know the justice system's penchant for punishment. The system's designed to exact retribution." On that point, he had my full agreement.

"But when is enough, enough?" I found myself often repeating. "Before that night eight years ago, Leslie had never been known to be a danger to society. Same goes for her time in prison. Prosecutors, politicians, juries, and judges inflict punishment..."

"Out of respect for the law," Bruce interjected.

"More often out of vengeance and rage," Andy suggested. "The motive for punishment is deterrence, right?"

"And justice," Bruce added.

"That's still missing the real point in all this," Carl finally got a word in.

"Which is?"

"The real point," Carl continued, "is the misplaced emphasis on punishment and not on rehabilitation. Which should be the real goal of justice in the first place."

I agreed with him. It reminded me of something Leslie's friend Karlene Faith said about "reciprocal vengeance" in the justice system. She said that "Manson and the state reflect one another," and I agreed.

A truly civilized society would reject such vengeful policies like they do in some European countries. Where the justice system is pointed more toward accomplishing rehabilitation. Returning prisoners to society better off than when they left— not simply more damaged, hardened, and resentful. Like Mr. Manson.

That summer Saturday evening, Gabrielle called. She and Jean invited themselves over to my mom's place. They brought high-potency "Columbian gold" cannabis flower like we hadn't seen much of before. Fifty an ounce was very expensive in those days.

As I recall, we got pretty hammered on Henkell Trocken sparkling wine also, after which Gabe decided she'd cut my hair. Twice. Once she messed up the first time, she tried again and messed it up worse. I accused her of doing this on purpose, but she denied it.

Jean put on side one of David Bowie's album *Diamond Dogs*.

Exhaling blue-gray smoke from the small bong he brought with him, Jean got around to asking, "This lawyer of Leslie's... How will he get around the question of premeditation? You know, her decision to join his cult in the first place."

"With the girls at least—in the beginning, Manson wasn't preaching violence and aggression. Mind control delusions take time to cultivate. Things emerge out of necessity. He used what he needed when he needed to keep them in line. It takes time, repetition, and isolation to get rid of free will and break down the ego."

"Oh...come on, Peter," Gabe broke in. "How about her plain willingness to get in the car in the first place? When she knew it would mean taking part in murder? She knew what happened to Sharon Tate and the others."

"Are we going to relitigate all of that now? We should be about how much *more* time she must serve. Not what she was thinking when she was a teenager. Free will? What is that really? She's served her time in a prison when she should have been in a mental clinic instead. Like a university!"

Gabe shook her head. But Jean cracked a smile.

"We like to think free will is a cornerstone of society," he said. "We like to think we act by conscious choice at all times, but that's all an illusion."

"That's right," I agreed. Turning to Gabrielle, I added, "And that's what Manson sought to destroy. Conscious choice. Leslie did not make the choice to murder those people. She was taken along to carry out orders and take the fall for the boys if they were caught.

"As for what happened at the home of Sharon Tate—it seems to me, Charlie Manson hoped that by killing whoever was in the house where Terry Melcher lived, he'd be sending him and friends like Dennis Wilson a message.

"Manson held a monster grudge against both Melcher and Wilson. For Terry not signing him to a big record deal; and Dennis, for changing the lyrics to one of his songs and not acknowledging his contribution on the record or its royalties.

Soon after that, Gabe turned to Jean and pronounced that they had to get going. Just as my guests were leaving, Jean passed me an eighth of an ounce of his Columbian stash as a gift. I rolled some of it into a joint right away and started another dispatch to Leslie. In the background, the Diamond Dogs were howling, "making bulletproof faces, Charlie Manson, Cassius Clay..."

The next night at 11:30 p.m., the telephone rang, and it was Leslie. She started by saying she was calling to tell me how much she missed me. I told her I felt the same way about her. I also told her about Jean and Gabrielle's visit.

"What did you talk about?" Leslie asked.

"Among other stuff, we talked about shoring up one's ego instead of getting rid of it, living for the moment, and all that jazz.... But how was your day? What happened in court?"

"The usual. Typical Stevie Kay day. He's still tryin' to rile up the jury to hate me. Showing 'before' and 'after' pictures. Sharon Tate happy. Sharon Tate dead."

"You weren't even *there*."

"He did the same with pictures of the LaBiancas. Max objected, of course. But Kay kept bringing up all the stupid things I said at the first trial. Just crazy. Now he's acting like it all happened yesterday or something.

"Hey, how long will it take you to get here in your car? I liked the pictures of you and your darlin' British sportscar. What does MGB stand for?"

"Morris Garages. Longbridge, UK. The 'B' part comes after the MGA preceded. The company's founder worked for car magnate William Morris."

"The convertible top looks like a lot of fun. Are you going to miss all of your friends? Will they hate me?"

"I'm missing you a lot more than anyone here will miss me. I have plenty of friends, but there's only one Lou-Lou!"

"You lie. I bet you have lots of girls," she teased.

"I've hung my skates up," I stated with extant certainty.

"I got a call from Judith on Sunday. One of the things we discussed was your living arrangements when you return. She said you could go on staying with her and Jennifer for as long as you need. She said for you to give her a call." I called Judy right after Les and I had to hang up.

I told Judy, "Until things are settled with Leslie, it might take a few months before I find out if I've been accepted into graduate school at UCSB. I hope that it's all right with you if I stay with you and Jen until then?"

"Yes, of course. Though, just so you know, Glen says he's disappointed you haven't applied to a school here in Los Angeles. Maybe Cal State LA? He knows people in the Cal State system. Why not let him help you out? He has a friend with good connections at Dominguez Hills. You have a better chance of getting in there than you do the University of California.

Besides," Judy added, "don't you want Leslie to remain close to her family?"

"I'll send Glen my CV. Thanks, Jude. That's a good idea."

"Glen said to include descriptions of the courses you've taken. He'll carry things forward from here. You can trust him."

Hmm.

Eventually, sometime after that, we got back to the subject of Leslie. For one thing, Judy caught me up on what was happening in court.

"Same old courtroom rhetoric from Stephen Kay, of course. He's such a flake. On Thursday, he said something like, 'Even

Houdini or Clarence Darrow couldn't get Leslie off the hook for first-degree murder.'"

"Sounds like he's mixing his metaphors. Has Max gotten to his closing argument, or aren't we there yet?" I asked.

"Just beginning that now," Judy said. "You know Max. He's being his usual sensible, fatherly self. He told the jurors he doesn't expect them to acquit her of any wrongdoing. He's simply asked the jury not to punish her for any more serious crime than she's guilty of."

"What does he expect them to come back with?"

"Max conceded a lesser verdict of manslaughter would be in line with the doctrine of diminished capacity."

"How well was that received, do you think?"

"Nnnn...not sure if the jury can get the distinctions between murder and manslaughter or premeditation *without* malice."

"Whoa. You're beginning to sound like a lawyer," I said.

"But *it is* their job to get it. We'll get Max to explain it to them," she said. "Things are wrapping up now. Max seems to think the jury will decide sometime this week or next. When are you coming back?"

On the 19th of July, a week before I set out for Los Angeles, a large envelope arrived from Judy. The return address was printed on Glen Peters' *Los Angeles Times* letterhead. The envelope included a copy (dateline July 12, 1977) of an article by *Times'* staff writer, Kathleen Hendrix. The headline read: "Van Houten Jurors Reach No Verdict in Double Murder."

The piece opened with an overview of the sixties counter-culture in terms such as these: Flower children. Hippies. Pot. LSD. Tuning in. Turning on. Dropping out. The Beatles. The Beach Boys. Guitars. Vans. Communes. Gurus. Mysticism. The breakup of the family. The sexual revolution. The turn against organized religion. Against the establishment. Race riots. The war in Vietnam. Alienation. Runaways. And beyond that, the Manson family looking for people to kill...

"It was all here in the courtroom of the '70s," Hendrix wrote. "A 'concatenation of events,' one defense witness, Dr. Lester Grinspoon, called it a linked chain of 'people, places and drugs which conspired to take this vulnerable girl and left her enmeshed in a system of delusional beliefs.'"

General details of Leslie Van Houten's life were cataloged: Daddy's girl, twice homecoming princess in high school, an IQ in the top 5 percent of the nation, achievements in school government, and so on. After her parents divorced, Leslie experimented with drugs, sex, and counterculture. Who didn't?

She and her boyfriend tripped out. Leslie lost interest in school. She got pregnant, and her mother arranged for an abortion. She briefly turned to Eastern religion for solace. She temporarily quit sex and drugs. She studied meditation. She even tried to become a Buddhist nun. But after the breakup with her boyfriend, Leslie met Bobby "Cupid" Beausoleil, who introduced her to Manson.

Hendrix described Deputy District Attorney Stephen Kay as "bandbox neat" with a "wearing nasal voice" and an expression that seldom changes. "He wears away at a witness with phrases like "by the way...isn't it true?" again and again. Kay is often sarcastic, and it does not seem natural to him. He describes Leslie Van Houten as coming to the courtroom "all dolled up" and tells the jury that if they believe her testimony, "I'll sell you the Brooklyn Bridge after the trial."

What a card.

According to the *Times*, Kay's most dramatic moment was when he passed the jury "before" and "after" photographs of all seven Tate–LaBianca victims—first presenting a picture of each person alive and then each one of them dead.

"If psychiatrists made decisions in criminal cases," Kay added, "I'd be out of a job." He was probably right about that.

When Maxwell Keith asked the jury to recognize the legal implications of Leslie's delusional mental state at the time of the murders "as a good soldier carrying out orders," Kay shouted out, "Was Sirhan Sirhan doing his duty as a good Arab killing Bobby Kennedy? …To call them the LaBianca manslaughters would be a travesty of justice."

Stephen Kay said in his closing: "When you go into that jury room, you're not going to be alone. Society will be watching that jury room. So, society will be watching you."

I'm not a lawyer, thank the gods, but even I know you can't say crap like that to the jury.

Judge Hinz had to contradict Kay's inflammatory statements and reminded the jurors of their obligation to judge Leslie Van Houten solely on the evidence presented in court—"…regardless of what society as a whole thinks of this case." The judge ordered them to judge Leslie Van Houten as an individual and to base their decision on the evidence alone.

Stephen Kay must've fretted he was losing the case because he was. Even he could see how both the public and members of the jury had come to see Leslie as she really was, not as he liked to portray her. His fibs were as phony as he was.

My last day of classes at OISE was on Tuesday, July 26th. I'd already loaded my teal blue '73 MGB the night before. There was only room enough in the boot and the jump seat for a few clothes. Lots of books and my trusty Smith Corona Super 12 electric typewriter filled the passenger side of the cockpit.

Tuesday afternoon, I topped off the fluids, kicked the tires, and said my goodbyes once more to family. Headed west on Highway 401 for 250 miles to the border at Windsor and Detroit.

As always, I was hassled by young, short-haired, military-type US Customs agents at the Ambassador Bridge. They grudgingly granted me a six-month visa to check out graduate schools in California. I don't remember if I told them about my girlfriend or not. I spent that first night in a motel just off Interstate 94, somewhere outside of Chicago.

The next morning, there were thin, high-level clouds on the eastern horizon that turned magnificent shades of orange, yellow, and blue when the light came up in my mirrors. I kept my rig pointed west, pitching and plunging across summer hills and dry, open plains with the top down. With The Rolling Stones blaring, I was joyfully clear out of my head and hungry for substance and adventure.

The day I left Toronto was the same day Judge Hinz ordered the jury to begin deliberations all over again. They were to start on Monday, after an alternative juror replaced the one who became ill. The composition of the jury was now seven women and five men. I didn't learn about this until later since I was in transit.

Varying my speed between seventy and ninety mph—depending on traffic conditions and the threat of police patrols—I pretty much stuck to the fastest routes on interstate highways. I took I-80 west all the way through Illinois, then straight across Iowa into Nebraska.

Each time I stopped for gas, it took longer to wash and wipe beetle juice off the windshields than to fill the tanks and pans with gasoline, water, and oil. The chrome bumpers and headlamps were all caked with bits and pieces of fresh and dried bugs. I just hoped not to hit anything larger.

At the Colorado state border, I took I-76 and set my bearing more to the southwest than before. Better for tanning for one thing. Up until now, my right side was relatively pale by comparison with the left side of my face. Turning a darker pink than tan.

After such a slow start in the morning and some carburetor problems lugging up the mountainside to Denver, I still made it through to I-70 past Vail and as far as Grand Junction, Colorado. The hotel I checked into was downtown near North Third Street and Main, two or three blocks from the Museum of the West. After checking in, I jogged around the block just to loosen up before passing out on the bed.

Woke up the next morning without a sunstroke hangover, which was a blessing. I drew open the curtains right before sun-up. I was glad later for having the foresight to eat a good, early breakfast of steak and eggs with brown toast and honey.

That final day on the road was the longest, hottest, and harshest of the entire journey. Eight hundred miles in eleven hours. It started out well enough, though. Thanks to the last four joints I had stashed in my sock, which lasted me as far as the plateaus and basins of Utah.

The rest of the way, I stayed on I-15 south through Nevada and the wide-open vistas beyond. I throttled through Las Vegas, not even stopping for water, sensing the end of my journey was within reach if I kept pushing hard.

Although the landscape surrounding Las Vegas had its charms, I was unhappy to see a Nevada State Police Highway patrolman creeping up in my mirrors. I kept it down to seventy-five mph as far as the McCullough Pass. Then, just a mile from the state line with California, I opened her back up.

Nearly burned out in the Mojave Desert. At one hundred miles an hour, the air feels like the blast in one of the furnaces they use in brickyards. I completely scorched my arms and the entire left side of my head, never thinking to wear a hat or put the top up.

It was well after nightfall when I finally arrived within sight of my destination—city lights, mazes of highway traffic, short and tall buildings, ballparks, and shopping mall clusters of oases and nightlights inside the Los Angeles city limits.

In spite of how thirsty, starving, hysterical, sun-sick, and half-naked I was at the time, it was always a thrill to be back in the City of Angels. Running low on gasoline and carbohydrates, I got off the highway somewhere very near Cal State LA and gave Judy Frutig a call from a phone booth—munching on Cracker Jacks.

She didn't pick up, so I left a message, then called over to Jane Van Houten's. Jane invited me to crash at her place, which I accepted gratefully. I was especially happy to see her after such a long haul in an open car with no one but my lonesome self to talk to.

As deadbeat and crippled as I was right before bed, I got up at dawn out of habit. Never one to sleep in very much, I would be sure to collapse sometime after I'd been to see Leslie, my love. Took a long hot and cold shower, shampooed, and shaved. Flipped through the *Times*, made toast, and brewed enough coffee for six thirsty people.

Jane and I drove in my car to Sybil Brand for a visit that morning with Les. Twenty minutes were all we were given. Leslie asked if there was something wrong since I was so two-faced, wind-bitten, and worn. I didn't say much the whole time we were there, which was unlike me.

When Jane passed me the phone, all I could do at first was to whisper, "It goes to show without saying, you see just how much of a fool I am for you, girl."

There I was feeling clichéd and shameless. But glad to be close again. Despite the limits.

One week later, on August 5th, after twenty-five days of deliberations, the jury in the Leslie Van Houten first-degree murder case reported to Judge Hinz that they were "hopelessly deadlocked." Five votes for manslaughter and seven for first-degree murder was the final tally. I was there when the judge declared a mistrial and set a September 12th hearing date to determine if and when Leslie would be put on trial yet again.

One of the jurors, Alphonzo Miller, told reporters that although he agreed that Leslie was "believable" at first, he was in favor of convicting her of first-degree murder. But because of the court's instructions on "reasonable doubt," he said, he changed his vote to second-degree. Alphonzo then changed his verdict again, this time to "manslaughter" on the final ballot. Alas, the story of a man gradually coming to his senses.

That's what deliberation should be about. Rather than true, deliberate consensus, what we usually get is "groupthink" for the most part.

"It was impossible for us to unanimously decide on whether she [Leslie] actually was responsible for her actions," Miller said. "And I doubt if you will ever find a jury that could."

In fact, I believe that never before in California history had a hung jury in a first-degree murder case led to a further trial. Things were beginning to look up for Leslie Van Houten. Was it reasonable to expect a reduced sentence on a lesser charge? Fair, just, and simple. That's what we hoped. That's what I thought.

I was at Jane's, hanging out with Betsy, David, and Dave's wife, Shannon Van Houten, when a very excited Leslie called the house in response to the news. People lined up to say, "Congratulations."

Everyone seemed to believe Leslie was one giant step closer to impending freedom after eight years in prison. When it was my turn on the phone, she said that she was "pleased but also exhausted."

That weekend, Jane's place on Sefton Avenue was frantic with telephone calls. Well-wishing visitors came by the house by the score. It was nice—sounds cliché—only it really was nice. I don't recall what time it was on Saturday night when Max finally showed up with two more bottles of Mumm's. The first toast was "To a most deserving and humble gentleman, Maxwell S. Keith."

Max said he needed time to prepare for his meeting the next week with District Attorney John Van de Kamp, so he left early.

"There might be a realistic chance," he said, "for some sort of reduced sentencing deal."

The next morning, even the guards at Sybil Brand—who'd heard about the hung jury—were more noticeably friendly toward Leslie than before. Instead of the usual twenty-minute visit, that next day (on Sunday) was the first time the deputies left us alone from eight until nine without interruption.

A tired-looking Leslie said, "No use trying to guess what will happen next. Not at this point. We'll know more once Max sits down with the DA."

"Don't worry, Les. They won't gamble the cost and bad press of another trial. That would be senseless and stupid." Then again...

"Okay, let's talk about something else, honey, please," she said. "What are you up to? Did you get my card? What's in the news besides me? What are you doin'?"

"Me? Nothing of any remarkable interest. My lifestyle's blushing bourgeois at the moment. My days consist of long, leisurely runs around Griffith Park and reading Charles Bukowski by the pool. Soon you can join me. I'm sure we can find better things to do than just hang around in the hot tub like I do."

"Oh, yeah? Such as what? Speak for yourself, mister. I could sure do with a hot tub right about now." She took a long pause to soak in the notion. "Judy is coming to visit tomorrow. She called Mom. She's been away... Judy has, you know... I keep forgetting you live there!"

Neither of us said anything more after that right away. Leslie had a look of weariness in her eyes while we talked about possibly having to go through yet another trial if Max and Van de Kamp couldn't agree to a lesser plea than first-degree murder. For once in a very long time, I sat quietly. Just watched and listened.

"I dreamed all last night of you and me," Leslie said. "And you were teasing me about being so skinny. You were thumpin' your chest and acting so strong. We had a lot of fun pinching each other. You can imagine. It felt so good to be kissed and touched gently by you. When I woke up, I wanted to go on dreaming, but the noise in this place is too much to sleep through.

"Peter, I think since you and me have come together, I look more alive. I believe it's true. I was tripping on the changes I feel. One thing I noticed is that I am a lot calmer. Not with regard to the case... That's intense. But I'm more settled in my inner-life thoughts. I feel pretty and wanted because of the way you make me feel."

"Are you kidding? You're absolutely incredible. Not to mention fall-down, knee-buckling gorgeous. It's not just the way that you look at the world around you that pleases me. That's what 'good-looking' really means." Glancing around at the bars, guards, visitors, and inmates, I added, "What an incredible place in which to go about falling in love."

"Tell me something special and soft before you go, so when I close my eyes later on, I can put these jailhouse vibes out of my mind. How 'bout a Beatles song?"

"John, George, or Paul?"

"John."

"Why?"

"*Because.*"

.

15

AU PAYS DE COCAINE

The night before his first post-mistrial meeting with Los Angeles District Attorney John Van de Kamp, Max Keith invited Judy Frutig and me to dinner with four other guests at the Valley Hunt Club near Pasadena. The Hunt Club was a century-old social club rooted in blue blood, gold stock, and old-fashioned manners.

Judy went with Max, and I drove my own car. When we got there, the maître d wouldn't admit me into the dining room—not without a jacket and tie. Max had a suitcase of "emergency courtroom supplies" in the trunk of his car. I slipped on a necktie and put on a new white shirt with sleeves that were too long. The blazer, I got from the coatroom. No one other than the daughter of one of Max's friends, an attractive young woman named Lisa, noticed I had no socks on inside my loafers.

We were seated outside on the patio. Max seemed in high spirits right from the start. It was great to see him in such a good mood for a change. I paid little attention to the others at our table except Lisa.

Besides appearing to have aligned herself with the *avant-garde*, there was plenty of intrigue in the space around her. She was, in that moment, a pretty but sad-looking woman I guessed to be somewhere mid-way through her "trying twenties." There was also something hidden that I sensed may be audacious and daring about her.

All throughout dinner, others were asking Max some version of: "What're you expecting to get out of that tight-ass Van de Kamp?"

"Plea to a lesser charge."

"Leslie's time served is already longer than the average in this state for second-degree murder," Judy added. "This last trial cost the state more than a quarter of a million dollars, and what did it prove? Half the jurors agreed she was guilty of manslaughter, not murder."

No one present seemed to hold any doubt. Nor had anyone much to add to subjects other than Leslie Van Houten that evening. Though some, including me, often tried. I'd had maybe four glasses of dark-violet wine. I had a pretty good time up to that point, despite the stiff shirt and mosquitos biting me on the ankles.

Around nine-thirty or ten, Lisa asked me if I would give her a ride home. I asked her father if it was all right with him. We'd all been drinking, but I assured them I wasn't suffering from "diminished capacity." Everyone laughed except Judy, who shot me a keen look of doubt.

Max assured Lisa's dad it would be all right to trust me. Judy said she'd see me later.

"Good night and good luck." We waved goodbye, I left the jacket, and we made for the exit.

Outside by the sculpted hedges surrounding the parking lot, Lisa and I sat and chatted while my modest 1.8-liter roadster warmed up.

"Do you want to get high?" she asked me, very nonchalant. In those days, it wasn't an uncommon presumption to make about someone our age, even at places like the Valley Hunt Club.

"Of course. But I don't have anything with me."

"I have a friend who can get us whatever we want. Do you know how to find your way to Echo Park?" I wasn't sure, but I didn't admit it.

"Do you mind if we stop at my place first?" I asked. "I'd like to get some cash to if your friend has any good marijuana to spare. I'd also like to change out of this shirt."

"Do it now." You had to love the way that she said it. But I'd learned the hard way before. Girls say a lot of things, don't they?

After a quick stop at the condo for a further change of wardrobe (two UCLA sweatshirts and blue jeans), we wound our way back along Echo Park Avenue to the top of Park Drive. That's where Lisa told me to stop the car.

There was a rock and sand garden with a path leading to the side entrance of a beige stucco house where her friend lived. I could hear rock music inside and sirens far off in the distance. The lone occupant took his time answering the door. When he did, he sure looked happy to see Lisa.

He and I exchanged looks of suspicion, which I thought a prudent response.

Lisa's friend Lyn was a tall, skinny guy with a black ponytail tied tight with a postman's elastic. He reminded me of a cross between Geddy Lee (the lead singer in Rush) and the comic book character Ol' Injun Joe in *Tom Sawyer*.

Inside the house, the main living space was cluttered with predictable drug paraphernalia. There were plenty of pipes, candles, and grinders lying about on the tables. Other than that, it was a plain, empty space with one stupendous exception.

In what would normally be called a "living room" hung a mattress on a plywood slab that was bolted with chains to beams in the ceiling. The whole contraption swung like a hammock four feet off the floor. There were also stereo speakers hung from each of the room's corners. That was something I hadn't seen before.

Lisa told Lyn that I needed to pick up an ounce of pot and that we were in a hurry. I thought that was brusque. He took out his scales from a cupboard inside the kitchen and left for another room down the hall. A minute later, he was back carrying a mustard jar full of golden-brown bud in one hand and a box of plastic bags in the other. He weighed out an ounce of marijuana and asked me for fifty bucks.

Lisa got up off the sofa and put a Tom Petty disc on the table. Then I watched her follow Lyn down the hall, where I heard them go into one of the washrooms. That left me alone, getting high with the quadraphonic sound of the Heartbreakers playing. I had faint premonitions of excitement and trouble to go with the traces of petroleum ether that suddenly breezed in the air.

They came back into the living room several minutes later, before the end of side one. This time, Lyn was carrying a plate of something that looked like a polished slab of petrified forest. He laid the plate flat on the table in front of where Lisa and I had been seated. From his hip pocket, he took out an amber vial and knocked some rock and powder into a metal grinder.

After a dozen turns of the crank, Lyn unscrewed the bottom and tapped out the fluffy, pinkish-white powder onto the plate. Then, with a carpenter's blade, he drew out six long, thick, parallel lines of cocaine hydrochloride.

In the meantime, Lisa rolled a twenty-dollar bill she'd taken out from her cross-body wallet. She drew each of two lines up into her nostrils, one right after the other. Ladies first. Then Lyn signaled to me it was my turn. Lisa passed me her straw.

"Peruvian flake," he announced, gesturing toward the glittering ridges of crystals. First, I turned to watch Lisa sink back into the cushions. She was smiling and her eyes glistened brightly.

Once I drew the lines up into my bloodstream, it took a moment for the drug to breach the brain barrier. The sense I had then was of blowing myself into thousands of pieces. It was a far more full-on, whole-body rush than I could have expected. Never before had I experienced anything so primal or sudden—nothing so pared to the bone.

Just as I began to regain some semblance of conscious control of my senses, my conscience besieged me with ruinous thoughts. Floodgates of excitement gave way to provisional fight-or-flight paranoia. What will Leslie or Max's friends think when they hear of this night's misadventures? Depends on what happens next, I supposed.

For the second time in ten or fifteen minutes, Lisa stood up and followed Lyn down the hall. I heard the far-away ringing of water pipes and the echoes of seemingly discarnate voices. When those two came back a few minutes later, I could see that some form of seduction protocol had begun. Lyn held her close for a kiss, and I couldn't blame him for trying.

I pretended to pay no attention at first, but in a way, I was grateful for the chance to get away clean and leave Lisa to her friend's care. Such as it was. But what happened next came as no real surprise. I watched Lyn piece her off with a gram she quickly tucked away in her wallet.

Lisa turned toward me and announced, "It's time for us to be leaving. Ready?"

Yes, I was, especially now since I knew she was holding. Seems we both had what we came for.

Reaching out for the crook at her elbow, Lyn pulled Lisa back for another kiss. When he finally released her, I heard her say, "Your kisses taste bitter with coca."

Hearing this as encouragement, he tried once again to embrace her. This time, all she said was "Please, Lyn, let me go." And he did right away. Saved me from having to hurt more than his feelings.

"*Buenos noches*, Injun Joe," I said as we left in a hurry.

Following Lisa's directions, I took the Hollywood Freeway north to Ventura Highway headed west. My trip odometer already had fifty miles on it by the time Lisa told me to turn south onto Topanga Canyon Boulevard. I knew from the maps in the pages of *Helter Skelter* that we were only a few miles in either direction from the old Spahn Ranch site and Gary Hinman's house.

"You're going too fast... You're going to miss it!" Lisa shouted into the wind that tangled her wispy blonde hair.

She was right, of course. I should have slowed to a stop and turned about instead of trying to hold tight in the corner. The back end broke loose, and my rear wheel spun onto a side bank of gravel. We didn't hit anything, but we came pretty close to a tall mountain pine near the end of her driveway.

I turned off the engine, and we walked arm-in-arm up the steps of the grassy embankment leading to Lisa's house. Once inside the front hall, she turned on the light. I could see from our

AU PAYS DE COCAINE

mirrored reflections just how much we'd each taken on a pasty-like pallor. Lisa drew out a few fat lines for herself and two for me on a mirror. I didn't like the look of myself up the nose.

Right after the cocaine rush plateaued a bit in my blood-stream—like the noble gentleman I was—I said my goodnights to the lady.

Lisa thanked me for the ride with a cutesy peck on the lips, and I stumbled down the black path to my car. I drove two and a half miles back up Topanga Canyon Road and parked, more or less by chance, at the foot of the hill below number 964. Gary Hinman's old address and the place where he died.

I did this all on the spur of the moment without premeditation. It was dark all around, and the only ghosts on the prowl were my own demons. When the coke started wearing off, I thought about heading back to Lisa's to pick up my sweatshirt. Soberly, I thought better of it.

After a prolonged, scalding shower first thing in the morning, I had coffee with Judy on the balcony at Micheltorena. We went together to visit Leslie from eight until nine. As far as we knew, there was nothing happening on the plea-bargain front. Max was still meeting with District Attorney Van de Kamp. We didn't discuss much of anything else. Judy and I learned to trust one another early on, but it couldn't last.

Despite our differences in background and attitude toward the world and our existence, we both tried getting along for Leslie's sake. I kept quiet about my time spent with Lisa. On the way back to her place, Judy asked whether I'd made contact yet with Glen Peters' friend at Cal State Dominguez Hills. I told her I hadn't.

She also asked about my night out with Lisa. I left out the parts about Echo Park and my visit to Hinman's. Whereas, in the beginning of our relationship, I thought it amusing how Judy tried to appear hip when she wasn't—especially regarding music and psychedelic drugs—it was beginning to look like we were coming at all things from hopelessly different directions.

Why is it that people with the least direct experience about something claim to know the whole truth about it?

When she called later, I didn't tell Leslie that part about Hinman either, but I did mention everything else. I was compelled to be brutally honest and begged for forgiveness.

"No, nothing happened," I said over the phone. "Just some negligent, semi-anesthetized driving unbecoming someone who should've known better. No sweat. I got the girl home safely before midnight, Cinderella."

I'd promised Les I'd play it safer from now on. Subject to the whims of the gods or rules of good conscience.

"I could tell something was up with Jude," Leslie said just before Max and Judy came through the front door and I had to hang up.

"Hey, Max," I said, "what's up? How did things go with Van de Kamp?"

I was curious to hear of this meeting.

"Nothing to shout about," he said, looking tired and somewhat disappointed. "I was just saying to Judy how I hoped he'd have more to say than he did."

"Can I get you a drink?" Judy asked him while already starting to fix his bourbon and water.

"Do you think Van de Kamp's made his decision yet?" I asked.

"Impossible to say," Max sighed, taking a seat at the dining room table.

"I heard what Stephen Kay had to say to the press," Judy said. "He's claiming the last jury followed their emotions instead of the law."

"What a lame excuse," I had to laugh. "What is he trying to say? That it wasn't his fault?"

"Emotions, hah," Max snorted. "This coming from the guy who fixated the jury on the most gruesome pictures of the crime scenes imaginable. Including those he knows Leslie was never there to lay eyes on."

"Do you mind if I go with Max tonight to see Leslie?" Judy asked me.

"That's fine with me. I just got off the phone with her when you stepped in. She'll be anxious to hear about Van de Kamp."

I excused myself and went for the walk I had planned along Sunset. When I got back, Judy and Max were gone. So, I rolled a couple of joints of the grass I got from Lyn. Put on Marc Bolan's *Tanx* pretty loud, and sat on the balcony writing notes for a letter to Leslie.

Once Judge Hinz declared a mistrial in August 1977, more people than ever were interested in visiting Leslie Van Houten. There's no denying I felt the pangs of a general wariness stirring. At first, I felt obliged to stay away to make time for the old guard who knew Leslie longer than I did. There were some of her old friends whom I became close with, though at times I begrudged them the time lost with "my girl."

Among those I got along best with was one of Les's college teachers from when she was in state prison at Frontera, Professor Michael Malone.

Michael had been an adjunct professor at a few English departments in City College and prison programs when he met Leslie at the California Institution for Women in the mid-seventies. She told me that Professor Malone was her favorite teacher. So, if for no other reason, I accepted the Malones' invitation to spend a week at their home on a hill near the coast of Laguna Nigel, fifty miles south of Los Angeles.

Their place was less than a mile from the coast off the Crown Valley Parkway, where the hillside was splendid. I turned around and parked in front of the house, with my front tires turned into the curbside on the steep downslope of Grand Canyon Drive. The large, open house was well forested in front and back with eucalyptus, stone pine, a single live oak, and lemon trees on one side of the driveway.

There was a classic Mercedes camper van parked on the other side, and as I walked past the open garage, I could see their classic white Mercedes 190 SL, with red leather seats and its canvas top folded down.

The Malones heard me pull up and had come outside to greet me. Mr. Malone looked to me like a smiling, gray-haired, fifty-something Richard Burton. Gray sideburns too, very handsome. So was his wife, Jane. She had a kind of Liz Taylor thing going as well. Pitch-black hair and faint burgundy mascara. We shook hands and hugged like we knew each other well.

"I'm so pleased to meet you at last," I told them. Leslie had told me quite a bit about them already. They said they'd heard a lot about me from her as well. I could sense right away how our mutual trust in Leslie's judgment sped up our trust and openness with one another.

We did the usual "getting to know you" kinds of contextual bearing. I remember wanting to ask Michael about how he got to be close to Leslie. What she was like as his student. That sort of thing. Both he and Jane seemed interested in hearing about how the negotiations between Max and Van de Kamp were going.

I asked why they left Europe for California. I was always surprised when someone mentions getting away from any potential war zones. That's how naïve I was.

When I told them about the apparent stalemate involving the "persecution"—my new term for the prosecution—they didn't seem too alarmed. I might have guessed from looking over their bookshelves for clues.

Michael watched closely as I thumbed through a few of the titles while he mixed us ice-cold cocktails and Jane laid out a variety of tostadas, guacamoles, chips, and salsa.

"The history of the concentration camps is not as simple as victims and persecutors," Michael said, handing me a tall margarita. I admitted I didn't at first understand what he meant. I stood when we clinked glasses, and he sat down on a chair across from me.

"During the Second World War, even within the SS, not everyone who took part in the Holocaust took part equally. The punishment by the perpetrators on their victims wasn't doled out symmetrically. The range of choice each faced was totally different."

Jane pointed out, "Hannah Arendt documented how any measure of evil is not banal. Still, it must surely be obvious—that Leslie was clearly less culpable than each of the others."

"If Les had been tried in Canada, or anywhere else besides the third world or the United States, she'd most likely be free already," I said and watched while Michael poured me another margarita from the cold, sweating pitcher.

"Anyone could become a killer under such circumstances," Michael said, sitting down beside his wife. "Peer pressure sets moral norms." And so, we went on talking and drinking like that long into the night.

The next morning, I could hear the phone ringing when I came in from my jog up and down the canyon. Loosening up and taking in the ocean air. I could tell Jane was on a call with Leslie when I stepped into the kitchen to pour myself a cold iced tea.

When it was my turn to get on the call, Leslie asked how I was "loving it so far?" I told her the truth. Wishing I had longer than a week to stay getting to know the Malones. She reminded me of a meeting I promised to be back for.

Later, I explained I had an appointment to meet with Mr. Glen Peters back in LA. Otherwise, I'd join them for a quick trip down the Mexican Baja, which they had planned for. They went alone but promised to take me along the next time I was sure to visit.

The Lawry's Center was on the historic site of the old spice packing plant northeast of Los Angeles Dodger Stadium. The center had several lush flower gardens, water fountains, and a hacienda-style restaurant only minutes away from downtown LA. It so happens that District Attorney John Van de Kamp's grandfather, Walter, was one of the original Van de Kamp's Bakeries and Lawry's Restaurants' founders.

Glen arrived before me and pretended to be friendly for the first ten minutes after I arrived. But I could see his shoulders starting to tighten when I ignored him to chat with Canadian tourists at the next table, who said they were on vacation from their government jobs in Montreal.

"Judy tells me you and she were at dinner with Maxwell Keith at the Hunt Club. She said you were drinking and driving…"

"Is that what she said?" I asked calmly.

"She said you were drunk when you left the restaurant with a guest's daughter."

"What's all the fuss about, Glen? I know you'll think it rude of me to say this, but who appointed you guardian of everyone's business? I wasn't the only one who had wine with dinner."

"She said you'd all had a lot to drink. That's not the point."

"Then why bring it up?"

No reply for a second. "I'm concerned with what I see as your self-destructive nature, Peter. I'm worried for Leslie's sake. You two are like moths drawn to a fire. You're gonna get burned, let me tell you." I frowned as he said it but stopped short of growling.

"Aren't you concerned where all this could be leading?"

"What would you know about it?" I challenged.

Glen suddenly blinked in rapid succession. "I know you take too many chances. You've admitted as much to Judy."

"Have I? You do or don't approve. Which is it?"

"What if Leslie were to get out of prison a year from now? Will you still be around then looking for trouble?"

"Look, Glen. What happens *then* will be up to Leslie."

I started speed-eating my tortilla casserole as a way of keeping my tongue tied. I decided that moment, I'd had enough of Glen Peters. The feeling was mutual. No need to shout about it.

"Look at me, will you?" he persisted. "Would you try and take her away from her friends and her family? Is that the plan?" he persisted.

I wanted to sock him right in the guacamole.

"My plans are my own to decide. The same goes for Leslie."

"What happened at Dominguez Hills? Did you see Brad like I told you?"

"Forget that," I said. "Please tell your pal Brad, thanks all the same. I've decided to apply elsewhere for grad school."

Folding my table napkin, I said, "I've got to get going, Glen. Thanks awfully for lunch. I hope you'll excuse me." I stood up, tossed the napkin on my chair, turned, and marched away.

"Which 'elsewhere' might you be going to, might I ask? Back to Toronto?" he called after me.

He only *wished*.

Glancing back nonchalantly over my shoulder, I said, "UC Santa Barbara."

"Good luck getting in *there*," Glen said with a simper.

I couldn't hear what more he said after that since I was halfway out the door when he said it. Adrenaline clouded my judgment. To myself, I put it this way: We have to stop meeting and parting this way. When I finally found my car, I drove off right away without warming her up. I didn't get high until later. That's when I sobered up.

Leslie's siblings David and Betsy Van Houten had first dibs on the next morning's visit to see their sister at Sybil Brand. I met up with them later for lunch at their mother Jane's house.

After that, I gave Betsy a lift back to her apartment in Hermosa Beach. It was a fair-size, three-bedroom, second-floor flat close to the ocean, near the corner of 34th Street and Palm. I stayed a couple of hours that afternoon while Betsy unpacked some of her moving boxes.

Noticing me taking my time looking at pictures of them all growing up, Bets told me, "Leslie always has something in her hands. Something to knit, sew, or turn the pages of in some book or magazine.

"She was always busy making something. Leslie liked to do things for others. She wasn't selfish."

"Did you ever fight?" I asked.

"That I'll tell you about some other time. First, I need your help moving these boxes."

That evening, Betsy and I went with her roommate, Sara, and her boyfriend to a Hollywood cinema to see Martin Scorsese's *Taxi Driver*, starring Robert de Niro. What impressed me more than the bloody ending everyone was raving about was how poignantly the end of the film strange-looped back to the beginning.

Afterward, I recalled reading screenwriter Paul Schrader's remark that the last frame of the film could be spliced to the first and the movie started all over. I wrote to Leslie suggesting she might find it worth exploring the ways different writers used this structure as a narrative form. For instance, the way surrealist Julio Cortázar did with his novel *Hopscotch*.

Betsy Van Houten called the next day and asked if I still wanted to move out of Judy's. I'd spoken with her about this more than a few times before. She said I could stay with her and her roommate Sara at 122 34th Street in Hermosa Beach and share the apartment—at least until things sorted themselves out with her sister.

Later that evening, I drove over to Sybil Brand with Max Keith to tell Leslie the news of my moving in with Betsy. We only had forty-five minutes to talk, so I promised to relay the rest of my thoughts when I had time to write it all down in a letter.

August 23rd, 1977 was Leslie Van Houten's twenty-eighth birthday. A beautiful young woman coming into the prime of her life. Human rights activist Karlene Faith (who worked with Leslie's, Patricia's, and Susan's deprogramming from Manson's psychic stranglehold while in prison), was in town and took my usual 8:00 a.m. slot at the jailhouse.

Betsy Van Houten and I spent the morning walking the beach, talking and taking pictures to send to her sister. Once the pictures I'd taken with Betsy and David were developed, I put the best of the lot in with what I would soon regard as a most embarrassing letter I'd sent to Leslie—some of which read in part:

No offense against Jude as a writer. I'm in no position to judge her reports. I've read her pieces about you in the Monitor, and I believe that you are the more daring writer. Why don't you try writing your story yourself? Or, if you feel you need her for just talking to, that also makes sense.

Just remember: Judy spent the sixties in Bible Camp! She's curious about the counterculture but never took part. From what she tells me, she went to some sort of Christian Science prep school while you and I were in search of alternative, sentient adventures. If she and Glen want to publish a series of "have faith in God" stories about you for their congregation, that's one thing. But a biography of Leslie Van Houten can only be written by you. No one but you. That's whose voice people need to hear, not some story "as told to a reporter."

Hey, you know what Mark Twain had to say about Christian Science? He said that Mary Baker Eddy was head of a "greed-infested tribe of superstitious buffoons." He said not a single material thing in the world is conceded by them to be real, except the all-mighty dollar. "Long live the Prince and the Pauper."

* * *

David Van Houten and I took his boss Milo's van to Micheltorena Street first thing in the morning to fetch the last of my things from Judy's apartment. Judy and her sister Jenn were both away, so there was nobody there to say goodbye to.

When I called later that evening, Judy said she was surprised to find some of my personal papers left behind on the balcony.

She said she had something important to discuss and asked if I would come over.

An hour later when I got there, it was obvious that Judy was pink-faced and upset about something. After the cold but customary salutations and prattle, I asked her, "What's wrong?"

"Why don't you sit down, and I'll show you?"

I sat on one of the stools beside the kitchen counter. Jude handed me a legal pad with what were obviously my own notes. I took a quick look at the top page of notes and put them down on the counter.

Judy asked, "Would you care to explain this?"

Pushing the pad a few inches away on the countertop, I said, "What's there to explain?"

"Try explaining why you are telling Leslie not to write her book with me. What business is it of yours to interfere with my job?"

"You're right," I admitted, "it's none of my business. What Leslie decides to do about her book is up to her and you, or whomever. It has nothing to do with me."

Judy said nothing, but I could see she was steaming. All I wanted was to escape from the scene.

"Yes," I said as if I were talking to myself. "It was fainthearted of me to leave this lying around. I'm sorry you found it. I should have said what I thought of your project and would have if you had asked me."

But the truth was, I felt better now that she knew. Time heals all wounds, or at least toughens the scars used to cover them over. I told her to please tear up the pages, and let's try to start over. She said she felt betrayed.

Who could blame her? Judy marched down the hall and shut the door to her bedroom behind her. I thought to toss all but one page into the trash bin, the one I kept for my scrapbook, but decided to take them all away with me.

Stepping outside to where my MGB was parked, I had the unexpected feeling that some invisible tax had been lifted. I was in a much better mood when I got back to Hermosa Beach and stayed that way for days while exploring this modish seaside district. *Idyllic.*

The next time I heard from Judy Frutig was on Wednesday afternoon, August 31st. She called Betsy's apartment with breaking news concerning the DA John Van de Kamp's resolve in the case.

"I've just spoken with Max," Judy told Betsy and me over the phone. "Van de Kamp's office just announced their decision to prosecute Leslie a third time for first-degree murder."

16

TURNING POINTS AND TUMBLING HORIZONS

Leslie returned to court on September 12th, when the judge set the new trial date for January 16th, 1978. She was in court again on Monday the 19th of September for a bail hearing. The jailhouse door wasn't fully ajar just yet. Bail was set at $200,000. Family and friends (including my own) began working behind the scenes, canvassing those we thought could help us raise the fee for securing her freedom.

Another month after that, Richard C. Paddock wrote in the *Los Angeles Times* about District Attorney John Van de Kamp's decision to retry the case. The headline read "Third Leslie Van Houten Trial Scheduled for Jan. 16: Smiling Cheerfully, Former Manson Cultist Waives Her Right to Go to Court Within Next 10 Days."

I found it noteworthy of Paddock to point out that "If Miss Van Houten had been allowed to plead guilty to a charge of second-degree murder, she would have been eligible for parole almost immediately...the LaBiancas were apparently selected as targets at random by Manson."

Perhaps I was reading too much into these facts, but it led me to feel more confident in Max Keith's defense strategy. I wasn't so sure of the law. If the LaBiancas had been selected at random by Manson, and if an experienced con was in *total control* of his cult, then how could a brainwashed, teenaged Leslie Van Houten be entirely held responsible for the part that she played? She couldn't, could she?

Whatever crime she committed, it couldn't be *first-degree* murder. Given the facts, that charge couldn't hold, could it?

At this point, Leslie did not stand convicted of any crime whatsoever. Even her prosecutors were of the opinion that, of all the former Manson Family defendants in this case, she was seen as the one most eligible for release on parole.

I knew it was important for Leslie to see her supporters in person, so I made time for visitors to take my place in line. My personal deprivation was offset by the fact that Les would call me during the evenings and catch me up.

We discussed her prospects with the new trial in three or four months. It seemed to us that, ever since Leslie's admissibility for bail, a more liberal sentiment had begun to appear in the press. This indicated to us that she might be headed in the right direction with momentum.

Looking back, those were remarkable times for our "baby boom" generation. There had been some underground sense of social and cultural change that we were a part of. Actually, getting her free on bail seemed like the next inevitable step toward gaining her lasting independence.

To turn the key in that lock, all we needed right away was 20 percent and a valiant bondsman willing to help bail her out.

* * *

Most autumn mornings, if I wasn't visiting Leslie, I'd spend my time either reading on Betsy's couch, writing notes in my diaries, or composing letters to post home and abroad. Once or twice a week, I'd help David out with his job at Milo's. I ran on the beach and lifted weights by the pier. I even went sprinting, hopping and bounding on the grass in Cypress Park. Most evenings, Betsy and I would either eat out at some place on the beach or at home. Or else ride over to her mum's place in Monterey Park and chow down with the rest of the family.

One night, after Glen and Doris Peters had already left, Jane introduced me to Leslie's father, Paul, and her brother, Paul Jr. and his wife, Marge. Judy was also there but left to have dinner with Max somewhere else after cocktails. I'm certain I didn't make much of an impression on Les's dad and older brother. I'd felt that same chill from my own dad and uncles.

The next morning, I was back in line with the rest of the lonely hearts waiting to visit inmates at Sybil Brand County Jail. Leslie, at first, seemed to have something urgent to tell me. But it seemed to take her a while to sort herself out.

"Are Mom and Dad coming later on? I want to talk to them before I mail the letter I've written to Pete. I guess I need to get it together." ("Pete" was Leslie's nickname for Glen Peters.)

"What is it? What's wrong? What did you have to tell him?"

"Just to lay off. Let me claim my own personal space for a change. Stop intruding into my affairs...that's for one thing. I'll write you about it later. Some of it was about you and me, of course. I don't want to waste any more time worrying about it.

"Honey, let's change the subject. Anything going on out there in that great big world of ours?"

"Just gossip. I think I told you that my friends back home, Jean and Gabe, are breaking up."

"Oh. Yeah, you predicted something like that in your letter. Well, the last letter I *got* anyway."

"It's no surprise...their breaking up, I mean. Just part of a general epidemic."

"Peter, I feel we've made a promise to one another. Haven't we? And now, with that comes responsibilities. Please say you agree."

"I guess. Please say what they are." I nodded.

"All we decide to do from now on we should decide to do together. I've been giving this a lot of thought. If you don't get accepted into Santa Barbara, you'll get in somewhere else, and we'll make it work regardless. I love you, and I am committed to you and you only. Once this damn trial is over and I'm out, I want to support you, and I want you to support me. Now, I have said it. Do you want it in writing? I'm committed to us, aren't you?"

"It matters to me that you want this too," I told her sincerely.

"Now, I feel I can be completely open with you. I want to share my feelings. I couldn't always. In a sense...I haven't any secrets. Well, I do. What I mean is, a lot of what's been said or written about me just wasn't true. I want you to know everything."

"Is this about your old boyfriends? Maybe I don't want to know. It will drive me crazy with jealousy."

"It's because you are driven and want to protect me, but you can't. Because you want to defend me from my past, but you can't. So, honey, please let me set your mind at ease.

"You asked me about Tex. I didn't have that many...what you would call 'boyfriends.' Not compared to you and all the girlfriends you've told me about."

I cringed a bit, thinking that over. What a strange way to try to impress a girl. I was a moron.

"Tex was a square kind of a guy. Nothing like you. I guess from things he told me about where he was from, I figured out that our high school pasts must have been similar. We got close that summer at Spahn. I had been hung up with the whole biker scene. I was getting a bit freaked out by it too. Charlie picked up on it and suggested I not hang around that scene anymore. And, about that same time, Tex asked me to help him do things around the ranch. So that's when we first got together."

"What sorts of things did he need help with?"

"Nothing too special. Just ordinary things such as helping him fix up the dune buggies and other stuff Charlie wanted done. Tex was always an up kind of guy. Sometimes, I felt very close to him. Not always, though. I honestly thought then that I loved everyone, but I know now that wasn't true. It's like...I can't remember the guy, but the one that wrote about the whole acid scene..."

"Ken Kesey? You mean Tom Wolfe, *The Electric Kool-Aid Acid Test*."

"Yeah, that's it. It was all detached like that. Love wasn't real. Although sometimes I thought it was. For a while, Tex was catatonic, and I was really concerned for him. I'll tell you more in my letter, I swear. Or, better yet, sometime soon when we won't be interrupted and censored. Let's not discuss it now, or all of our time will be used up."

After a pause, feeling some tinge of jealousy stirring, I reflected, "Listen, Les, I don't want us messing this up. I can't help wanting you all to myself. Is that wrong?"

"We aren't going to mess this up, Peter. I feel the same way you do. Just, please try not to get so rattled by what others say to rile you. Or get angered about stories you've read concerning my sordid past. You need to trust me and hear me out."

"What happened a decade ago isn't what gets to me. It's the more recent junk about you and Frank Andrews getting married...," I growled.

"Well, I told you how Pete got involved, and how confused everything got after that..."

"I'm not talking about book deals or whatever. Just the part where he went on national television to say that you and he were going to be married. Were you just leading him on? Doesn't bode well for me then, does it?"

After I made this last crackling remark, everything in the subterranean dynamo stopped. The deputies started to rustle us up. Bad timing. Our visit for that day was over. This wasn't the best place for us to stop. All Leslie had time to say at the end was to repeat, "I'll write you about it, I promise. I'll go do it right away now." All there was left for me to do was to hang up the handset and covetously wait for her letter.

Hi My Darling, My Honey, My Love!

Wow! I thought I'd already rapped Frank to you, but now I will tell you the whole situation. When we started to write, he was the first person other than Jean Carver on Death Row that I would write or speak to. Pete saw it as a way to draw me out. I saw it as, "Why not? Nothing to lose." He was fun to write with. I was full of opinions about people. My understanding had been cut off philosophically—so Frank's past being similar to Charlie's years inside prison all made it seem OK to write him. I was still messed up from before.

His letters were fun. Funny and clever. I didn't know much about people. We wrote letters all the time. He was bitter over his years in jail. He was from a different time. He missed the whole sixties scene. These differences at the time weren't important because we were both locked up and had that in common. I can't remember if we ever really discussed anything very deep.

As time went on, he asked if I'd marry him. I said I felt it was a bit premature. He got weird. I wanted the fun letters again. So I said "yes." He got out. I asked him not to say anything because it wasn't for the public. I encouraged him to find another love interest. I didn't want to hurt him and thought it would just die out over time. Marriage didn't mean anything to me. A piece of paper. Maybe because of Mom and Dad. I don't know. Also commune life. It seemed square. Dumb. Unnecessary. Only now, with you, and all you're teaching me about alternatives, have I come to realize the beauty in accepting this alternative for us.

The thing is, those letters were good for its time. It could have been a good book. Anyway, in the article, Frank also went into all the money he'd make—then it got to the money I'd make. Ugly scene. I told him I was tired of him trying to speak for me. Only I didn't present myself forcefully enough. Then, when he returned to New York, our letters had already dwindled down to not much. All he did was complain. No money for this or that. He lived above his means. We were not together in any respect.

Then Frank went off about Pete. There was this big falling out. That ended it for "us." I saw that I had become nothing more to him than an opportunity to make some money. Same old story. Just another con. He said it was so I could get F. Lee Bailey to defend me.

The last time I spoke with him on the phone, I politely asked about the woman he'd been living with since he got out. He played like there was a bad connection. That's it. That's the whole story complete. I know I was wrong now to have been so careless as to say "yes," because with you, I see how really special marriage can be. You are my only man.

You ask me how do I know it ends with you? Every living bit of me knows it to be so. You are all my dreams come true at once and for always. A man who loves me for me. A man who wants to protect me and to teach me how to learn things for myself. To hold me close enough to be safe but also let me adventure on my own. I want to discover my own way of being free the way you are. I want us to challenge each other the way Olympians spur each other on. Isn't that what you're always telling me about? What humans can be? That's what I want us to be. I love the thought of you and me together.

* * *

Martin Bijaux called and left a message at Betsy's. I called him back to say, yes, I did get a call from our friend, Jean Cousineau. Jean said he was coming to Los Angeles to visit Martin and me. Out of the blue, it appeared the two of them had put together a plan for a two-week road trip down the coast to Acapulco. What was the occasion for that, I wondered? I had opted out for obvious reasons. Plus, I had plans to get together with Trish.

Trish and I had planned to spend the afternoon together walking around the oceanfront and playing touch football with some guys and gals we met in the park. Instead of the park right away, we sat down inside a café near the corner of Melrose and Crescent Heights.

"It's nice to see you take refuge in a few simple pleasures for a change," she said, watching me hum as I used a spoon and passed her my fork to share a slice of "pecan delight."

"It beats my taking refuge in other distractions, you mean?"

"No, I'm just glad to see you in such good spirits. You look good. You must be happy."

"And you look absolutely glowing. Who is he this time?" I asked as if I were joking.

"Oh? And what about you? Van Houten still burning a hole in every room? I see in the news she's trying to make bail. How is she feeling?"

I took my eye off the last of my pecan pie to check her expression. Trish wasn't looking particularly intent on an answer. She sat up straight, looked for something in her bag, then smiled at some guys in a booth behind me. I turned to see them passing glances. I smiled at Trish, and she shrugged nonchalantly. Happens all the time.

"The last time Leslie and I spoke she was in a positive frame of mind."

"Have you and she made any plans as to what you might do if she gets out on bail?"

"As a matter of fact, we have" was all I said. Sensing she wasn't terribly interested. "What is it, Trish?" She looked up directly into my eyes when I asked that.

"We'll always be friends, Peter. You know that. I'm just curious about what's next on your itinerary."

"I've decided to go back home to Toronto for six months. Or at least until this trial is over. Find work to help pay Leslie's bail bond if I can, until June. I'll need to do something legal for money until I start grad school again in the fall."

"Where are you planning on going?"

"Our first choice would be to live in Santa Barbara. I'm going up there to check things out before I leave California. A lot will depend on what happens when Leslie gets out, of course. But, for now, we've decided against hiding out like fugitives in LA. If I can't get into UCSB, I may try other UC campuses. *Not* UCLA. Right now, we've got our hearts set on living in Isla Vista."

What's so amazing about Trish, I thought to myself, was and remains present in what I find so amazing in all the other women I'd ever been "serious" about. Besides holding real affection for one another, she was the proud possessor of an open mind and well-above-average intelligence.

"Tricia, you know that you and your world can do without me. But with Leslie, for the time being, at least, she cannot do without me. Or so it seems.

"I don't mean absolutely. I mean in terms of what I can offer that she doesn't have in the world she currently occupies. Or the one she's bound to re-enter, either with or without me. But for now..."

"What's so special about her? Or are you just using one woman to get over another?"

"What's special about Leslie will become clearer once she's given a fair chance at showing the world something about herself—and ourselves—in terms of the underlying, peaceful counterculture she adheres to. Maybe that's what frightens the power elites so much about her.

"Instead of rejoicing in her resurrection, the punitive spirit of the law seeks retribution. Evidence of her redemption be damned. What do they want? She has been behind bars for 70 percent of her life already. How much thirst for vengeance do the sententious elites have left?"

Trish put her purse in her bag, stood up as if to signal her impatience, asked me to kindly pass along her "best wishes" to Leslie, and left.

Watching her turn and walk away, I whispered, "It was great seeing you again too," under my breath.

* * *

Friday, November 11th, and my MGB was back in the shop for a tune-up. My plan was to leave the car at Leslie's mom's. I took a bus to Silver Lake and hitched a ride from there to Sybil Brand with Judy Frutig. She dropped me off and then left right away to make an appointment with another potential bondsman.

I'll give her this, Judy was a diligent emissary in that respect. She was better at talking to bankers than anyone.

"Let's hope Santa Barbara comes through soon," Leslie said during our visit. "We can maybe start planning for when I get out. I know I can start work right away in Max's office. Or, if you find a good job in Toronto, do you think they would let me into the country?"

"They will if we're married. If not, we stay here. What's so bad about *Santa Barbara*?" I teased. "I know that's what we both want. I got another letter from UCSB yesterday. The office of student services is asking for proof of my teaching credentials, previous US student visas, and marital status.

"Apparently, being married to a California girl has certain in-state advantages I wasn't aware of."

"In-state? That's funny. It means something different to me," Leslie said. "Honey, just try to continue your studies and keep training hard for the future. You'll feel better with more important stuff to do than hang around here listening to all this legal mumbo jumbo.

"Believe me, I know what a bore the courtroom scene can get to be. It's all about preparation. Isn't that what you're always telling me? Try and concentrate on... What did you call it? 'The Science of Living.'"

"That's right. Alfred Adler," I said.

Leslie bowed gently. "Concentrate on three things, philosophy, teaching, and me. But not in that order. I can make money when I'm out. I may be a bit rusty, but we'll manage somehow. Don't worry so much.

"Know what?" Leslie continued, "I've been thinking. I've been thinking about what our first place should be like. Want to hear? It should be small and modest. Little compartments with one large room for gathering..."

"A library!" I enthused, getting with the mood of her vision.

"Right. And a small earth space beside the kitchen, where I can grow herbs and flowers. It will be cool."

"I want my own bedroom," I said.

"Not a chance."

"Then how about my own closet?"

"Stop. Listen, if it turns out that bail is beyond our reach—which half the time, it seems it is and half the time not—all this still counts as far as state time anyway. I hate thinking about it this way, but we have to be realistic. It might still take a year or more," Leslie said, looking distracted. Whereas she seemed all lit up only moments before, now she suddenly turned somber and sad.

"Before you, I was alone," she said. "I was looking...not even knowing how mixed up I was about so many things. You've given me a reason to be all I can for you and for us."

"I appreciate your saying so, Leslie.

"Thank you for explaining that business with Frank Earl Andrews, the venerable author. And Tex. It's weakness on my part to ask, is that all? I told you my buddy Martin heard the rumor about your getting married and told me about it. Tell me, what should I have said to him in response?"

"Please don't be so angry. I'm sorry now that those letters with Frank are coming out," she bristled. "I guess I knew they would eventually. All I can ask is that you forgive me my past and foolish ways.

"For a while, I thought the whole thing was canned. But I guess that now, because I'm on trial and back in the news, Frank would be wheeling and dealing to have the book of letters on again. Whatever. It's his scheme and Pete's now. It's for them and their lawyers to figure out. I couldn't care less at this point.

"Believe it or not, I have other things on my mind. And so should you, mister."

"Like your book deal with Dutton and Judy?" I asked. "Is that another Glen Peters' church of salvation enterprise too?"

"That I don't know about either," she said. "See what I mean? This all infuriates me. If I could stop it, I would. The letters, I mean. But I can't. Maybe it will all just fade away. Now is not the time to worry about that, is it? Please, won't you calm down?"

"I'm sorry, Leslie, I don't know for sure where that comes from." Or at least I wasn't certain.

"When will you be going back to Canada? If you're still going?"

"In a week. I mentioned that already. Should be in time enough to see about that job at U of T Andy and Bruce wrote me about. I'll meet with them when I get there. Though, to be honest, I'd rather teach English lit than coach any more track at this point. Right now, we need the money. I'll do whatever it takes to get my end together.

"Look, Les. There is something else about Santa Barbara I wasn't going to mention until I heard back again. On Wednesday, I spoke with someone in the faculty of education. Provided I have the MGB fixed in time. I've made an appointment to drive up and meet Professor Copeland next Thursday. Probably just filling in forms. He's not the one I originally wanted to see, but he's the only one there who can see me before Christmas."

"That's fantastic, Peter. See? This is what I mean. Things are moving our way. Can't you feel it? Try to go with the flow."

"Les, I'm sorry for what I went off about before. It's good to see you excited this way. I don't want to nix or to jinx things…"

"Hey, what's the matter? What's wrong?" I asked, watching her expression change, sensing her mood had taken a step back into the shadows.

"The thought of your leaving for Canada has me uptight. I'm going to miss you…." She paused and sat up straight on her stool. "We need to stop acting like a couple of crumbs and be brave. We have to do what is right for each other, remember? You will come back to me, won't you?"

I raised her chin with my hand, looked into her eyes, and said nothing, just smiled.

LESLIE VAN HOUTEN FREED FROM JAIL ON $200,000 BOND

Spent my last night before leaving LA with David Van Houten and Max Keith. I forget where we started but remember ending up at Max's apartment on South Oakland Avenue in Pasadena. I liked the fact that in place of a lot of law books or trophies, Max's city residence (he lived on a ranch near Paso Robles) had piles of *Time Magazine* and *National Geographic* all scattered about.

David and I were slightly high on Rojo Mezcal, with lemon slices and Mexican sea salt. Max stuck to his tried-and-true Early Times Kentucky Straight Bourbon. We'd been talking that night about Leslie, of course. I discussed feeling torn about leaving her during the midst of her trial. My heart wanted to stay, but my gut said I needed to go. We had plenty of time to sober up before Davy drove himself home. I spent the night under a thin blanket on Max's couch.

Max dropped me off at noon the next day in front of the Air Canada reservations desk at Los Angeles International Airport. We waved goodbye and he sped away in his gloomy Scirocco. I spent most of flight no. 792 staring out the window at the slow-moving landscape below. The rest of the time, I either read or wrote letters. After the mountains and deserts came winter plains, then, at last, more familiar lakes, frozen rivers, and deciduous forests. There was plenty of time to catch up with my diary.

The plane touched down on time at Pearson International Airport in Toronto at 9:00 p.m. The tarmac was wet from rain, sleet, and melted snow. It took the best part of an hour to clear customs. My brother Mike picked me up. When we got home to our mum's, she welcomed me with a smile and a huge hug, of course. Right away, she told me that Mr. Tovell had called. So, I called him right back as soon as I had my boots off.

Jackson Tovell, my high school principal and surrogate dad, put me onto a job opening in Scarborough. Teaching high school English literature, Western culture, and mass media studies. The school was the West Hill Collegiate on Morningside Avenue, fifteen miles east of Toronto.

Jack told me they had already begun to review candidates, but he was sure they hadn't decided on anyone yet. He arranged to get me an interview with the head of the English department right away.

There was a blizzard on the fifth of December, and no mail was delivered. Les called me from Sybil Brand. The news wasn't what I had been hoping to hear. A couple more bail bond proposals had either been dissolved or delayed yet again.

The next day, I had an appointment to meet with Andy Higgins and Bruce Kidd at Bruce's office at University College next to Hart House. They said they had a proposition to discuss. I only got as far as the bus stop at the end of the road. I had what can only be described as a "panic attack." Right as the bus came, I turned around and dragged my sorry ass home into a thickening snowstorm. We rebooked our meeting for Friday.

I took the bus and subway downtown to meet Higgins and Kidd at 10:00 a.m. Andy and Bruce were courageous enough to offer me the job of club administrator (and sprints/relays coach) with the University of Toronto Track Club.

They knew I'd already applied to the University of California. Even if I had asked for some time to think it over, they'd know that was bullshit. High-caliber track and field coaching demands more of a long-term commitment than I was inclined to make in that moment. There was no use starting something I had no real intent on finishing.

We talked about their plans for the track team, and they politely asked about my plans regarding UCSB. In the end, with regret, I declined the honor. Although I expected to feel relief at coming to my decision, for no reason I can explain, I felt uncomfortably anxious instead. Now I was nowhere. In some other way, I felt free to find another way forward toward an even greater, uncertain destiny.

* * *

Leslie and Max were back in front of Superior Court Judge Gordon Ringer on Friday, December 16th—requesting that he reduce the amount of her bail to $50,000. Max told the judge he would stake his professional reputation on Leslie's keeping her promise. He assured Judge Ringer that she was the last person he'd have to fear ever leaving the jurisdiction.

Naturally, Prosecutor Stephen Kay opposed the request. His rote resistance was, quite literally, a no-brainer default. Mostly, I think he was most afraid of Leslie proving him wrong.

"She is not going to run," Max told the judge. "She is not going to engage in misconduct. Her present mental status is normal. Not one psychiatrist feels or believes Leslie, at this time, is a danger to society or that she presents a threat to herself or to others."

The judge replied, "I think the temptation to flee might well be irresistible in a case of this seriousness. Motion denied." Judge Ringer, however, did grant Max's request for a delay in the start of the trial, and a new trial date was set for the second of February. I'd hear the rest when she called.

* * *

The interview Jack Tovell set up for me at West Hill Collegiate took place on December 22nd at 10:30 a.m. I met first with Mrs. Marg Minter, the head of the English department. Then with her colleague, Bob Gentile. The interviews ended just before noon, and Mrs. Minter said she would call back the week after Christmas. She wrapped things up by explaining that Mr. Ron Budd, the principal, was unfortunately 'too busy" to meet me that day. I took this to mean it was he who was calling the shots.

I walked back to where I parked my mom's Camaro RS in the visitors' lot. The engine was cold, so I let it idle with the autochoke on. While she warmed up in the meantime, I pulled out a small bag of weed I had stashed in the glove box and started to roll a joint on my lap. Just as I was about to light it up, there was a rap on the snowy driver's side window.

I rolled down the window, and Mrs. Minter asked me if I would like to come back inside to meet Mr. Budd after all. They must have been desperate.

Maybe I should have waited until after I'd had the chance to smoke that joint before I signed anything morally binding. But by 1:15 p.m., I had a contract. I'd agreed to teach from January to the end of June—for a total of fewer than eight thousand dollars. I acted pleased. However, my quick decision was clouded with doubts.

Whenever I've stooped to do something solely for money, it never works out. Mr. Budd told me I'd be replacing some fellow named Lilly but neglected to say what happened to him or why he was gone. No matter now. I knew I'd struck a deal with the devil, but a gentleman's word is his bond.

When I told Leslie about this new twist of fate the next night over the phone, she agreed it wasn't an ideal situation. All other moral and bad-faith deliberations aside, the cold hard fact of the matter was that we needed the dosh.

* * *

As 1977 was coming to an end, and the New Year was upon us—I read more about the confluent education program at UC Santa Barbara and began thinking about how I might go about changing the world for the better. I went searching the stacks for copies of George I. Brown's *Human Teaching for Human Learning* and *The Live Classroom*.

I had them sent via inter-library loans, photocopied select chapters to include with my notes, and mailed copies of some of them to Leslie. Along with a copy of Professor Brown's introductory pages, I asked what she thought of the ideas contained within.

George Isaac Brown was a professor of education at the University of California at Santa Barbara. He earned his PhD from Harvard, where he taught before moving to California. He and his wife, Judith, studied with the re-founder of Gestalt therapy, F.S. "Fritz" Perls, at the world-famous Esalen Institute in Big Sur.

As for his Gestalt theory of confluent education, what struck me first was how, on the one hand, *constructively* Brown and his colleagues wrote about the current confusion, suspicion, and despair in education. As well as the sometimes-innocent expectations of academic cultures in general. I liked their critique of the state of the art of the entire discipline.

What interested me most and would eventually become the concentration I pursued for the doctorate was the authentic attempt to do something humanistic, holistic, and psychologically healthy about institutional leadership and the governance of universities.

In my next letter to Leslie, I wrote to tell her about confluent education. Or at least as much as I understood it so far. Here's a series of what she had to say in response after she read my notes:

HELLO MY LOVE:
NO LETTER ALL WEEK AND I DON'T MIND SAYING THAT I AM HURTIN'. I CAN HARDLY WAIT TO CALL YOU. I miss you. Had another dream last night. We made love and it was really fine. I dreamt we got married and had twin girls with lots of curly hair just like yours. We were married by a guy who looked like Geppetto (from Pinocchio), who worked in an old clock shop.

Then all of a sudden, the kids were grown up and you were playin' football. I wandered on to the field in a daze to watch the game close up. But I got confused and ended up in the middle of the game myself. Kinda spacey. It was rough and I got really scared and kind of froze. Then you saw me and dropped the ball and came to help me safely get off the field. It was an action dream. Freud said every dream is a wish. I think we should teach our children that dreams don't just happen out of the blue but are stories we act out in our sleep, because they have something important to tell us. It's like a hidden part that needs to be heard, isn't that what you believe?

I dreamed all last night of you and you were teasing me. We had a lot of fun. We were alive and we made love again. Then you said something in the dream that you said in your last letter. That you're "tired of waiting." So am I. All we can really do is keep our fingers crossed and hope really hard that our dream will come true. So, tell me a story about the snow in the forests and what I need to do to stay warm in the winter. I have a few ideas of my own (wink, wink).

I got your jeans—they came with the backlog of letters. The officer is going to try to see if I can try them on...they fit! Perfect! How fine they feel. How did you know? You pay attention to details, don't you? You judge my body better looking at me in a gray ol' jail dress than other women are able to do. What I dig is how fine they feel. Super soft—so just by putting them on I can leave these hard times, steel bars, and bad vibes behind for a little while. I try to ignore them, but there comes a time when you can't turn away and still have a conscience. I'll just be extra glad when this whole prison scene is finally over. I'm writing a personal letter asking Judge Ringer for a reduction in bail, and telling him why I believe I deserve one.

Hi Honey,

Linda is supposed to be here. Her BMW keeps breaking down. She's going to start teaching self-defense to her students because they found the 11th victim of the Hillside Strangler. Some maniac running loose in LA. It's scary all right—and I don't know any of that kind of stuff—will you teach me how to defend myself? I never really learned how.

It doesn't appear Linda has made it, so I will make my desk on the bed and begin to answer some more of your letters. I got the one that was all cut up like William Burroughs' work. I'm sorry Linda didn't come tonight. She always sends you her love. I found out she did an interesting thing. Jude told me Linda called her and laid out her various feelings. They communicate better now. I'm glad she did that. She's extremely loyal. I find myself appreciating Linda more and more. For her sincerity, loyalty, directness, and other things. She really digs you and me too. So that's extra special—she gets it! Unfortunately, not everyone does...you know who...

Well, I'll go to bed now. Please let me dream—always and only of you.

Leslie-Lou

254

Hi Sweets—

I've been so depressed. Really down under in a very dark, heavy hollow. I feel like a tired, kicked and beat up old dog. I've been in this dinky cell for almost a year now. But those are my full blues. I want so much for you to rock me in your arms. I have nothing to do. I am bored out of my mind and extremely impatient.

Also, I've been thinking about what you said about keeping our relationship in a "private compartment." Not isolated. Just private, except for those we know we can trust. And our children will be strong because of it too. Family loyalty will be our first priority.

Honey, I want to get old with you so you can hold my weathered hand in yours, and we can watch the sunrise and set together. Is this too much to ask for? Hold me close and kiss me tender. And tell me what our lives will be like when we are in our sixties, watching coals glow in the fire.

LATER—You wanted to know what I thought about Two for the Road with Audrey Hepburn. Well, it's about two people—it's their journey together. He is busy at first being a loner. He doesn't want any distractions like falling in love. She is a free spirit, but troubled. She senses the potential—both for glory and ruin. She realizes before he does that with individual success comes the distance. She doesn't dig that whole scene. Can't wear the success mask or take it too seriously. Realizes what they lost when they gained recognition. He was not being true to him-self and that not only alarmed her but also it hurt her. But she toughed it out. I really dug it. The old MG and all the changes they each had to go through. Hopes and fears. They lace in and out. It was simple yet was able to say an awful lot. And I like what you said about the narrative structure—how the story is one continuous road trip from Calais to the Rivera. It starts with them in the present—then flashes back and forth from scenes from the past to scenes of the present. That was so cool. I love Audrey Hepburn and when I was young used to wish I were either she or Natalie Wood. And no, you do not miss me more than I miss you! Although I do concede it's harder for you to get over (get it?).

##

Mom and everyone here send their love. I am going to try and mail this and hope it gets on its way soon. Oh good! A Carol King song just came on and I'm singing along. "All I want is a quiet place to live—"

I will sing songs to you just as soon and as often as possible. Must warn you, though, once in a while I sing way off key. Sometimes, without knowing the words, you wouldn't recognize the song that I'm singing. I'm supersleepy to-night. Night Night honey—only two more days left until I can call you again. I'll put the request in first thing tomorrow. I love you.

Yer Baby, Leslie-Lou

p.s. Please don't forget me, Peter. You know it would truly break my heart.

* * *

Leslie called me on Christmas Day. She was still concerned about the deputies inspecting our mail and recording our calls.

"I just don't get it," she said. "I've written to you so many times. So, I don't understand your not receiving them." She was as frustrated by the delays as I was.

I asked her, "Do you think maybe all that talk about spending winter in Canada made its way back to the judge?"

"No, let's not start acting paranoid. Who knows? It could be anything. Maybe it was because I went in wearing your blue jeans? They really fit nice by the way. I thought about you the whole time I was wearing them."

"Did Mr. Kay add his usual gentlemanly charm to the proceedings?"

"Kay was his usual ignorant-arrogant self. He said I'd told a psych once that when I got out, I'd move to another state and change my name. This was before I met you. At that point, the judge interrupted him. He said he felt certain I wasn't speaking of jumping bail.

"Then Judge Ringer asked Kay if he'd had the notoriety I had, wouldn't he want to try to lead as normal a life as possible? Kay couldn't answer because he'd have to be *honest*. He came back with some fast lines, way off-topic, so he wouldn't look like a jackass."

"He'll never pull that off," I mumbled.

"Okay. And then the judge denied me anyway. He said he just wouldn't take the chance. I feel shattered. It felt like we were so close this time, it was bound to happen. I guess I was wrong, again."

"Come on, Leslie. That was expected. They can't keep you shut in forever. You're close to the end, you'll see."

"What do they think I'm going to do when I get out? Plot a revolution?" Leslie laughed. "Judy and Max are coming this evening. Jude may have found some new hopefuls to put up my bail. The search continues. We're not giving up."

There were voices echoing in the background.

Then Leslie said, "Hey, sorry, honey. We gotta go. Time to say goodbye. Please say you still love me."

"You still love me."

"No, silly. You know what I mean. I'm going to have Jude call you—"

Suddenly she was cut off in mid-sentence. That was the first time I could remember that happening.

* * *

On Tuesday, December 27th, 1977, I spent the first part of the day wandering around downtown Toronto. I was thinking of giving Gabrielle a call to see if she wanted to go somewhere for coffee. Quite by chance, I ran into Andy Higgins and his partner Linda Hall in Yorkville. We walked over to Allan Gardens to spend some time inside the warm greenhouse.

Andy and Linda invited me to dinner, but I begged off and headed east on the subway to Kennedy Road, then took a bus the rest of the way to Mom's house in Agincourt.

As soon as I stepped inside the front door, my mom—who was absolutely beaming—handed me the phone.

"It's Mrs. Van Houten."

After I said hello, Jane said she had someone there who wanted-ed to speak with me.

"Did you know," was the first thing Leslie said, "tomorrow is the anniversary of the first letter you ever wrote to me? Wishing me luck and hoping we would meet someday when I got out? Well, can you believe it? I'm out!"

I did believe it but couldn't speak right away on account of the shock. *What must that feel like?* was my first thought.

"How soon can you come down? You still want to, don't you?"

"What do you think? Congratulations! Leslie, I'm so happy for you and the whole family. Especially your mum."

I was still reeling, breathless and stunned.

"I still don't believe it. I have to keep pinching myself," she sighed.

"I'll book my tickets as soon as I can and call you right back," I said. "I have to teach all of next week, but I'll check how much time I can get off and call you tomorrow. Will you be at your mom's?"

"No, I'll be staying at Linda's, far from the press and the weirdoes."

"I'll be there just as soon as I can," I said with conviction.

Leslie purred, "Yes? Now that's a promise."

"Les, remember what we talked about. Please don't leave me now and run off with the first other fine scoundrel you meet."

"Stop it. That will never happen. Come here soon, and you'll see you're my only man now and forever. You should know that by now."

The plans we made the next day were for me to fly to Los Angeles on the fifth and return on the eighth to Toronto. Three days and nights weren't a lot. Though my selfishness demanded I have her all to myself, conscience dictated Leslie would need lots of free time on her own to adjust to the light of day without my casting shadows.

* * *

Air Canada flight no. 793 left Toronto at 7:00 p.m. on Thursday night. At the airport, I picked up a copy of last week's *Los Angeles*

Times (dated December 28th, 1977) at a newsstand. The head-line read: "Leslie Van Houten Freed From Jail on $200,000 Bail." I self-consciously gazed around to see if there was anyone looking over my shoulder. After small children, their guardians, and people needing assistance, I was the first eager passenger to board the aircraft.

The L-1011 flew non-stop and landed in LA just after 9:00 p.m. (Pacific Time). Like everyone else, I was in a rush to get off and be embraced by a loved one. Only, unlike some of the others, there was no one to greet poor me, so I wandered around like a dog lost on moving day.

About fifteen agonizing minutes had passed before I spotted Leslie's big smile and long arms waving from across the arrivals' lounge. By then, I'd almost stopped breathing. I rushed through the crowd like a fullback in sight of the end zone and picked Leslie up two feet off the ground in my arms.

The first kiss was just a peck on the lips, but the second kiss lasted much longer. When I opened my eyes, I'd already forgotten where on earth I actually was for a moment.

Linda Grippi, who I hadn't noticed yet, asked, "Is this yours, Peter?" while picking my bag up. "I'm sorry we're late. It was my fault. First, there was traffic. Then, we couldn't find a space to park."

"Well, at least say you're happy to see me," Leslie added.

"Yes, of course, I'm more than happy to see you," I said, picking my heart up from where it had fallen a moment ago.

We found our way out of the terminal to where Linda had parked her BMW. I climbed in back, and Leslie got in beside me. All I remember were glimpses of traffic and mountains between kisses and bangs of hair flying past my eyes. Linda was smiling the whole time she was driving.

Pulling up to their apartment on Victory Boulevard, I spotted my teal-blue MGB in the parking lot.

"Who do you miss most," Leslie asked, "me or the MGB?" When I asked her how the "B" found its way there from Jane's garage in Monterey Park, she said, "I drove it myself. But I still need you to give me lessons."

"Les did great," Linda said. "I drove behind her the whole way and watched that she didn't break down."

We three had a late-night snack of nachos and salsa before Leslie and I drove off alone for a little while. We parked somewhere close, where we got out to walk and stopped to make out whenever we wanted. Back in the car, I put the top up. There wasn't a square inch of open space left with us both ironed into the passenger seat. Each taking turns one on top of the other. Kind of reminded us both of high school.

"This is our first date, remember?" Leslie asked when I started to reach under her blouse.

Now feeling embarrassed, I must have put on a sulk. No doubt Leslie had seen this before. We both expressed feeling uncertain and awkward without too much explanation. I thought I'd better slow the pace down. *Discipline, 007, discipline.*

Once we returned to Linda's apartment, where Leslie's bedroom was a comfortable couch in the living room, I stayed long enough for a nightcap and one or two long-lasting kisses. Then, I drove myself back to Monterey Park to spend the night in Jane Van Houten's guest room.

The next morning, the rest of Leslie's family showed up for brunch at Jane's. David, Shannon, and Betsy all came together in one car. Georgie came in from next door. (Actually, she and Jane had a door cut in the wall between their garages.) And, soon after that, Leslie and Linda arrived with treats they baked for the rest of us.

Leslie looked spectacular in a way that I'd never seen her before. I couldn't wait to get her alone.

We paid our respects to the others, then Les and I went for a ride out to Malibu Beach with the top down. Along the way down Old Topanga Canyon Road, we pulled over to the side and idled at a spot that once was a location site for the television show *M*A*S*H*. Later on, we stopped again on the campus at Pepperdine and walked around for an hour before we got hungry and found a McDonald's. Exciting stuff like that. Only, it was.

When we got back to Linda's flat, Leslie and I were delighted to find ourselves alone at long last. We chanced a long and luxurious candlelit shower together. Her suggestion—or was it mine? Either way, it was a pleasure to discover just how soft Leslie's blushed skin felt against mine.

When she asked me to hold her close, I thought back to an old Groucho Marx line Alan Alda used in an episode of *M*A*S*H*, where he says, "If we could get any closer, I'd be standing behind you." Something like that.

After we stepped out of the shower and toweled off, Leslie put on the nightshirt my mom had sent her for Christmas. She'd sewn the crest of a pumpkin on the front, and Leslie joked, "Peter, Peter…who had a wife and couldn't keep her."

I was still too hot and wet from the shower to put on anything more than sweat bottoms and ankle socks. The scene was confused, of course, since it resembled my state of mind, body, and soul. We were both nervous. To provide warmth from the shivers, I brought the candles in from the bathroom and turned out the lamplight.

"It seems strange just to be with another person," Leslie said, blowing out all the candles but one. Then, just as things were beginning to heat up again, we heard voices and a key turning the lock.

I called out, "Hey, Linda?"

Yes, it was. Thank the gods. I asked her to please give us a minute. Leslie rushed to put panties on under her nightshirt, and I crawled on all fours looking to find where I'd thrown my blue cotton top. I opened the door, and in stepped Linda with a young boyfriend in tow. Both of them were teasing and smiling. They could see what was going on.

Linda's young man was politely introduced. I've forgotten his name but recall him as younger and taller than I was. I remember thinking that he was very good-looking. I handed him twenty dollars to take Linda out for pizza and beer. I made them promise not to come back for an hour.

After what seemed like eons had passed, I, for one, paused to catch my breath and get my heart rate back under 160. Laying her heart against mine, Leslie breathed something ever-so-sweetly: "So, what should we do now?"

I cleared my throat and said, "Whatever you want."

I checked the lock on the door, and then, just to be extra safe, I braced a wooden chair under the doorknob like we used to see done in the old TV Westerns.

When we finally untangled our limbs, we studied each other's faces closely. Once we began talking in complete sentences again, Leslie asked me how I got so many scars on my face, especially around both of my eyes.

"I like the way it makes you look," she said. "Kinda like Marlon Brando, you know. In that movie where he plays an ex-boxer."

"Terry Malloy? Don't I wish *my* scars looked that good!"

Running the end of her finger over the two bars of scar tissue cut across my right cheek, she said, "Do you remember? Once you told me that a person without scars hasn't dared to live. You wrote that in one of your letters."

Brushing her bangs back to reveal the faint "X" she'd once engraved on her forehead, I said, "Yes. Same goes for you." We stopped talking and just rocked gently in each other's arms.

Later, we took some time to discuss our individual schedules for the next couple of months. Leslie had more free time coming to her than I did, which seemed only just. Though, I complained about our having so little time to spend together.

"When are you coming back for your interview in Santa Barbara?" she asked.

"March 17th. Meeting with professors Brown, Shapiro, and Phillips. That's a Friday. Court won't be in session. We can travel up there and spend the night if you want to. I'll have ten whole days and nights off."

"Yahoo! Santa Barbara! Don't you just love it? We can pretend it's our honeymoon."

"Which reminds me," I said. "I have something to show you." Reaching into the right-side pocket of my jeans, I handed Leslie a small, unwrapped gift box made of tin with a tile of polished pink and blue ivory on top. Leslie looked taken aback at first. Then, she opened the box to see what was rattling inside on a cube of cotton.

She started smiling again when she opened it. And then, just as quickly, turned pensive.

"I know it's not much for now," I said. "Try it on. It may need some sizing. Just a sliver of a stone. Still, I hope that you like it."

"I think it's flawless. I love it," she said, slipping the ring on her finger, then turning the thin gold band and bringing the lonely diamond up to the light.

"Just do me a favor and kiss me so I won't have time to start crying."

First, I kissed her gently on the back of the hand, then on each of her cheeks, then over her eyes and, finally, pressed my lips against hers, which were trembling.

"Please don't cry unless you're happy," I said.

"I am...*very happy*," she said. Then, I cried instead.

18

AN ACADEMIC PREPARES

American Airlines flight no. 50 left Los Angeles International at 12:45 p.m. and arrived in Toronto just past 8:05 in the evening. I was so sick on the plane that it spoiled the in-flight movie for me—*The Deep*, starring Jacqueline Bisset, Robert Shaw, and the rebel, Nick Nolte. I didn't sleep a wink that night of the new moon with the usual symptoms. I chewed my nails ragged.

I was delirious with bad faith resentments and real (or imagined) losses to cope with. When I got out of bed in the morning, my throat was as bloody and raw as the ends of my nerves. Not wanting to be where I was.

There were no classes for me to teach at West Hill Collegiate on Monday, but I had admin errands and needed to tick off all the boxes. There was a staff meeting at ten o'clock. Teachers called it "the Zoo." Just as well, I kept to myself and nursed my sore throat by sucking on an orange. I'd laced it up with two fluid ounces of Smirnoff Vodka I had injected with a 3-ml syringe and a heavy-gauge needle.

In addition to culture and media studies, I had two senior classes of English lit to teach every day of the week. *Othello* until March break; *Romeo and Juliet* until June. During my "spares," I hung out with some relatively new people I'd met in the staff room. The first person I made friends with was another first-year English teacher named Nadine Segal. Nadine was about my age, only much smarter and the popular center of our crowd.

I'd grown impatient waiting for Leslie's letters, which I missed and depended on. We'd taken to calling each other two and sometimes three times a week for our mutual solace. Usually, she'd call collect from Linda's or from wherever else she was staying.

Leslie usually called after midnight her time. That's when long-distance rates were the cheapest. I preferred letters to late-night phone calls interrupting my sleep. First-year teaching required lots of preparation in place of what I lacked in experience.

After my birthday in January, Leslie's letters began appearing once again in my mom's mailbox. The return address on the envelopes was no longer from L. Van Houten, Booking No. 4186-613, but rather from an entirely new person calling herself L. Chiaramonte, c/o 22246 Victory Boulevard. Her new address and secret identity seemed a nice way of starting over. The first letter, stamped from Woodland Hills instead of the LA county jail, read in part:

Dearest Peter—

I miss you so deeply. And as always, the words are shallow in tryin' to tell you my heart. Being near you is the most natural, right thing I have ever felt in my life. Believe me. I want so much for us to be together forever and always. The way it's so obvious we are meant to be. Boy, did we ever luck out! I look at my ring constantly. Thursday I will get it sized. Then I'll ask Linda to take a picture of my hand and send it to you with all my love.

This evening Mom and I will have our first real chance to be alone and I'm going to tell her the wonderful news. But I want to do it when I'm alone with her, keeping in mind all the things that we spoke of. That talk you had with her really did wonders. Ever since then she has been so mellow about us making definite plans for the future. I think it's something she and I should share alone as mother and daughter.

I'll close this now so it can get on its way from me to you. I'll write again tomorrow after I've finished work. Please know I love you and don't you forget.

Yours always—Leslie-Lou

p.s. Your birthday present may be late. I had it made by a silversmith. But I know that you'll love it. It represents your mercurial personality. That's a hint...

* * *

Leslie made her first public appearance as a free woman on Wednesday the 25th of January 1978. She and Max Keith had a hearing in court before Judge Ringer. Max had requested a further postponement of Leslie's trial, and the judge moved the trial date from February 2nd to the 21st but said it was the last delay he would grant.

When reporters asked her what had been the most difficult thing to adjust to since she had been set free on bail, Leslie explained, "Planning my own time. After all this time in prison or jail, it seems strange to be able to decide for myself what I can do each day."

She said she'd been so busy "catching up on lost time" with her family and friends and that "No," she had not taken time to go to the movies or other social entertainments.

Writing for the *Los Angeles Times*, Bill Farr reported: "One of those friends she had seen in the past month is a 'boyfriend who lives out of state. We have been able to spend a few days together,' she said with a shy smile. She steadfastly refused to say anything that might identify the man. 'I don't want to embarrass the people around me,' she added.

"When asked about reports that she raised the bail money by receiving a large advance on a book she plans to write? 'It just isn't true,' she replied. 'My friends and family got that money together.' But she conceded she might write a book in the future.

"To the apparent amazement of the newsmen who swarmed around her, she said that the book will not be about her life with the Manson family. 'That would not contribute anything to anything or anybody,' she said, even though a reporter noted, 'It could be very lucrative.'

"She hopes to further her education, whether she does it in prison, if she is again convicted of first-degree murder, or as a regular coed, should there be some other verdict. 'It's hard to focus on the future because of it,' she said. 'I yearn for it to be over and for society to let me be the person I am today, not that person who was with the Manson Family, who was a stranger even to me.'"

* * *

Jury selection finally got underway in February. For Leslie, the process wasn't as meticulous as it was agonizing. Some citizens begged off jury duty for perfectly understandable reasons. Financial hardship is always a fair one to choose since it almost always applies. Few working people can afford to serve on such a lengthy case for months at a time away from their jobs.

Besides a lot of romantic odds and ends, here's how Leslie described her time seated in court during this phase of the process.

Hi Hon!

So now it's just three more weeks and you'll be here. It's harder to write decent letters. I know you think the phone is a drag. But I think we both need to hear 'I love you' more often. I know I do. It's important to me. Don't you still love me?

It's such a drag that I'm back here in this scene again. What a waste of everyone's time. I feel my life draining away while lawyers argue about nothing but nothing. Tonight, I go to the ballet. I need a good stretch. I missed last week because I was at the Malones'. This is good exercise in preparation for natural childbirth. I need to keep it up and not miss too many more chances to go.

I dig my judge. So far, I dig him a lot. The more I watch and listen to him the more I do. I'm feeling positive right now. I just hope my instincts are true. I know I've been wrong before. I hope what I'm feeling is some sort of momentum, and not the Earth about to break loose and swallow me up.

I'm in court and it's dragging on. Losing more jurors all the time...already on the second batch and I've lost two and got lots more to go. It always makes me feel so weird to hear complete strangers say how much they hate me. I sure will be glad when it's over. Sitting here and listening to lawyers nose around in the worst parts of people's lives. Their game is about determining if other people's prejudices match their own. It's such a pathetic process. One thing I would never want to be is a lawyer!

Lunch is over now and we're back to the same ol' stuff. I lost five jurors out of this batch. A lot of them just said straight out they wanted a conviction. No ifs, ands, or buts. It's a reflex reaction. Sometimes I think these people are as programmed as I was. I'm really anxious for you to come soon so we can talk and discuss things. There's a lot of pressure here, believe me. It's not easy. It's still a lot like being in prison. Just getting to court is a chore. I'm anxious to stop all this running back and forth. I hope we can spend some laidback time—you know—just the two of us talking and hanging out. Being alone in each other's arms.

They must have looked at a hundred people today. Just about all of them had to be excused. I don't think any of them wanted to be here anymore than I do. I'm not looking forward to this ordeal. Aren't you glad you don't have to be here to witness this yourself...? This whole thing is making me grumpy. I'll be talking to you about it tonight.

Come hold me tight tonight in my dreams...? I want to kiss you!

* * *

All throughout February, either Les or I would telephone the other on a Friday or Saturday night. I often tape-recorded our calls with a Radio Shack pick-up wired into my Sanyo cassette.

One Saturday night, Leslie called from Santa Barbara, where she and Linda Grippi had gone for a break from their various trials and tribulations in the city.

"What are you up to, mister?" Leslie asked.

"Reading the final act of *Othello*," I said. "What about you?"

"Talkin' to Linda...reading brochures about UCSB and the City of Santa Barbara. Would you rather live in the city or near the campus in Isla Vista? I think we should check out both scenes. Which do you think would be the most likely to have room enough for the garden I want?"

"I'm sure you'll know when you see it. Take your time and keep looking 'til *it* finds *you*. It's kinda like falling in love. How long are you guys planning to stay before heading back to LA?"

"Leaving here tomorrow. I'm coming back this way again soon with the Malones. Oh, oh! I just noticed something. It says here that married student housing is separate from everything else. Nope. No room for a garden there. There's a place to get lumber for bookcases and stuff. And a needlework place where I can get all the things that I'll need.

"It says, non-resident tuition is 635 dollars per credit. Does that mean you too? Doesn't that change when we're married?"

"Everything changes when we're married," I said, pausing to think that one over. Before something else popped into my head.

"Hey, Les, did I hear you say something last time—right at the end? Maybe I didn't hear it right. Did you say Manson's been sending you letters?"

"I got two letters, yeah. He knows that I'm out, which is why he probably sent them. Oh, God, I'll type them up and send you copies. Maybe you can make better sense of it than me or Max. Manson's mind is a creepy jumble. You'll see. Tell me if you think he's threatening to kill me or somethin'?"

"Can you have them Xeroxed?"

"Can't. They're in pencil...and messy. Max needs the originals to stay here in the office. But I'll even type in some of the things he misspells. Sometimes he does that on purpose."

"I'd love to see how his mind works. That tiny scat of a man. What threats?"

"I wasn't upset. But then Pat sent me one that sounded just like his. You know, what ticked me off was the way he misspells my name on the envelope, 'L-E-S-S,' right? Well, I can accept that coming from him...knowing his game now as I do. So, he saying I'm less of a person does not bother me. Nothing he says even matters to me. But when Pat did it, that hurt. Because I know damn good and well that her name isn't 'P-A-T-T,' ya know? So, I got kinda pissed off at that."

"Maybe this was all Charlie's doing? You can't blame her if he's deluding himself into believing he's still in control."

"I just wrote her a real nice letter and told her, 'Do what you do, Pat. Just remember, I know you. And I'm just fearful that you'll forget that I know you and that you've known me.' I told her I had a funny feeling that 'you're going to start seeing me through other people's eyes.' Just like the strangers I see looking at me at the courthouse."

* * *

After Valentine's Day, I'd started teaching Shakespeare's *Othello* to two senior classes. When students read through the scene, their characters all sounded like discarnate answering machines. I don't know what I expected. Probably something more akin to poor players strutting and fretting on a Venice Street at night. Rather than stuttering and shivering mechanical voices echoing in a cold and dark portable classroom. Of all the terrible jobs I've ever had, this was the absolute worst ever.

A twelve-by-nine-inch envelope from Max Keith's office arrived in my mail. In it were two typewritten copies of the letters Charles Manson sent to Leslie from prison. On the cover page, Leslie wrote: "Lots of bad typing. I'm still pretty rusty. There are some words he kept misspelling, so I retyped them the way that he wrote them.

"It all sounds so shallow and voodoo-ie now. Notice how he tries to play off so many angles. Laying on guilt. It's the same kinds of junk he used all the time. It's hard to believe his words once meant everything to me."

What follows is an abridged version of Manson's letters to Leslie. The originals are twice as long, but mostly repetitive gibberish.

Manson called Leslie "Green" on account of her love for flowers and gardens. The rest of Charlie's Crayola rainbow-pack legend of nicknames refer to "Red" for Lynette "Squeaky" Fromme (Manson's acting head of the Family in his absence, who was eventually sentenced to life imprisonment for attempting to assassinate President Gerald Ford in 1975); Susan Atkins, who was often called "Violet"; Patricia Krenwinkel, who was sometimes referred to as "Yellow"; and Sandra Good (who Prosecutor Stephen Kay once dated in high school), who was called "Blue" for reasons I never heard or read about.

Green
   ...You gave yourself to something and gave faith beyond your earth brain understanding. That is something still. As each one has fell down, become divided, lost faith etc. and Love understands the falling down and loss of faith,

but a love that's bigger for other things sees beyond life, death or in and out games. Yes you got a life to live but its not your own... You wanted to stop the war etc. and you did and got what you wanted. But I was in a bigger circle than you seen...

Much more than I didn't have time to explain to you... Did you believe Linda Kasabian's story... Each that breaks their own circle with me broke their own circle because I was only a servant to the truth and in others thoughts I had less will in it than a child. Only people I cut or shot or beat were for the circle I seen as my own. Had you been for your circle...

I was and am so far out in space universe that I was already borned in the thought you Pat and sue brought to the court room. Judge older was about 2 years old and I let him set up on the bench because I loved the world. Don't be surprised if you see me setting in the court room on your 3rd or 4th trial if you can get off by then or if on the day you get out the dead woman comes to meet you...The change will come one way or the other...

What happened to all your hippie friends who wanted you to stop the war. How far did they go with you. Jane Folda etc. and the likes...As you have pulled and let others pull form the real reasons why things came down the way they did... I wanted to save the damn thing. We did it. We saved a world we can't live in but don't worry no one else will ever be that crzy again.

So the earth's water will be red mud and air not fit for your dogs and don't come to me for no front game...I won't ever do nothing for none of you ever-----Red and Blue will never give up and I will never give up we are locked into forever life it or not...I don't see how you can get off on me when its me who been with each one will always be... Red and Blue, Yellow, Tex, and Bob, Bruce etc. All who been in worse cells and did harder time than you...

Your tiral has been a joke up and down the hall ways. I get the news days behind for I'm so deep in the hole no T.V. or radio and the papr I do get is a Hearst S.F. papr and it is pure B.S. I get a few clippings days behind and you didn't bother to see where your Red and Blue was at. Huh you gave all to a thought and after death decided to change your mind. What about the struggles the rest of us been going through that you haven't even seen in your rest home. Bobby's face ain't good looking no more from base ball bats and Steve been downed and Mary's lies fell on us hard and the side of my face has been pushed in. Did you want world fixed over night. Weren't we moving fast enough for you. Girl you gave your life to all of us and we haven't fell down on that. And what of the 100's of kids in prisons all over the country that came in behind yous. They haven't stopped and won't stop until the job is done.

I've been 30 years on a job and the little time you've done is a little gift to a big world...Are you gonna dupit off on someone else to get out or keep on wht the rest of us... Keep yur faith woman.

LETTER #2:

Before you came to the ranch did anyone ever tell you the turht, or care for you and your Green etc...Your lawyer comes to court drunk and phonie Christians work for phonie jews selling the bloods sacrifices of their children. What happens to all your Jerry Rubins, Abbie Hoffman's Jane Fondas...wanting to stop wars but only if it could make them some money. Your sould and brains were sold to the dollar bill brain before you were born. I showed you how to redeem your sould and how to save your world and al it did was cost me mine... You seen my good side and you seen my under will—now look at the other side of yourself. I stand right outside your courtroom in your thought...

Any for you to play me off as a fool is only your own concern and know you this—as all water goes to the ocean (sea) rain drops in millions there is still only one water—I am that water and without me there is no Green...

I won't push you. Red's ka chamber will do that for you are locked in your own circle for as a woman locked what she thought was man, she locked herself in the money madness. You were neo-woman and should of kept up on our own thought...

In my own thought I'm the smartest person in the world for I am now your water and time for survival on earth is short. We didn't blow earth up but what good is it without water. Water is life and as all water is one so is water.....Also when you open up the gas chamber again that gives everyone a gaschamber for everyone... Does your lawyer still hate me because he didn't understand his daughter. Are you playing me as the willian they would be in their sex hang ups. If you play in likes they play in you must as much in the night of your cell you can't hide from me for I'm your alone and you are alone...

...I think you should look at your family again before Red's ka chamber gets to Green's re chamber 'cause if you don't you may not see any green left for it to rain on. Once

a thought is set and locked to the universe only I can reset it for I never told you all I was doing because I trust myself only. your brain would not of understood it nor could you cope with it... I wish you get your wish and you could get out in Red's ka chamber. I see not break in the circle and your corss boss is in the middle.

P.S. The world you left in 1969 went on to somewhere else and its gone. The world Red left is running in her now ducks snakes snitches rat on and other hells that others have created with their lack of faith. I still hold faith in you alive or dead but look at what you are doing to Green and how nice lady bird took your tree and gave it to her fears. Why didn't you wrote? Did you think there was an end to giving yourself for a cause—all is forever always—there ain't no divorce in death life or in between...

What do you think that mark is on your head for?

Les was right. It wasn't just a narcissistic put-down. It was in part just as much a comic put-on. Who did he think he was fooling now? Was he threatening to have Squeaky Fromm assassinate her in her cell? He's going to turn the Earth's water to blood and acid? I wrote to Leslie to say it amazed me to see how seriously he took himself and how little he had to go on. "In retrospect, all things are obvious."

All that winter of my discontent, each time Les would call or pick up, I felt there were always a thousand more things to say that we never got to. I couldn't rest, so I stayed awake late almost every night when I knew she would call. Then I'd waste half the time complaining to her about how much I hated my job.

Rather than have them study the play in the order it was written, during my lesson plans for everything after Act I, we deliberately hopscotched our way forward and backward throughout scenes but never at random. We moved in and out of some scenes as if we were shooting a film out of sequence, then openly discussed which scenes to include and which to leave out.

I encouraged them to read the play as written for themselves. But I was too much of a dunce to verify the results with due diligence. So, it caught me off guard when I heard gossip coming from a few students anxious about how sorting through this havoc would affect their department-set exams. I hadn't considered that. Only, they had.

Prior to the exam, I made sure to spend at least one session acting out an entire synopsis of the play from my point of view, which we all seemed to enjoy. Me, especially.

* * *

Martin Bijaux was in town for one night on his way back to Montreal. Family business. His brother Guy was in trouble with the law. Martin picked Yorkville Village to meet since it was near the Park Plaza Hotel, where he was staying. I picked a spot for us to meet near the corner of Yorkville and Hazelton Ave. The name of the place, which has changed a dozen times since, is absent from my diary.

I arrived first at six and chose a quiet table with a view of the Cumberland walkway. A public runway where all the fashion models and showy shoppers strut, look for more stuff, and hang out with the rest of us. I was indulging my rare thirst for a shot of Seagram's Five Star to have with my Canada Dry when Martin came in from the cold, where a light snowfall was just beginning to taper off.

"Well, Peter. This part of town sure has changed since the sixties."

"I miss Neil Young at The Mynah Bird," I said, pointing across the street to the site on the corner where that club once was. "Don't miss the bikers, though."

"When is your piece on all the fuss about Mexican resorts coming out?"

"Jean told you? Yeah, I still have to write it. That story was secondary. I desperately needed a break."

"On a warm sunny beach with lots of good food and friendly people—I get that," I laughed. "That took priority."

"How about you? How goes tryin' to teach Shakespeare to teenie-boppers?"

"Oh, so you heard? You hear everything, don't you? It's only for four more months, until June. Then I'm heading back to LA and Leslie. From there to Santa Barbara…maybe forever." He didn't blink.

"Heard her new trial starts very soon? When exactly are you going to see her again?"

"March break. We're planning a quick trip up the coast to Isla Vista. Then Laguna Nigel for a couple of nights, staying with friends. First, I have an interview at UCSB to take care of. I've applied for the doctoral program in higher education; concentrating on institutional leadership, and particularly, I think I'll specialize in the governance of universities. We'll see."

Martin's eyebrows pointed north like a jagged furry monument.

"Good luck with that. Whatever 'that' is," he said, refilling his water glass from the cold, sweating carafe.

Before our drinks and snacks came, Martin reconvened, "About Van Houten's new trial, Peter. I wish I could be there to cover some of it, at least. But I won't be. This whole mess with Guy, you know."

"Maybe just as well then," I said, raising my water glass in a toast. "Say 'hi' to Guy for me when you see him."

Martin nodded, seeming to smile at me, or so I thought at first. When I turned around, I could see he'd meant it for the waitress who was bringing shots of Canadian rye and ice in fresh glasses.

"Marty, what *would* you ask me if you were covering the trial that you haven't asked me already?"

"Well, for one thing—since you ask—you've often alluded to the whole drugs and cult angle as one frame of reference, in which you argued for a reduction in bail and/or plea to a lesser charge. You did say last time how she was a victim of 'groupthink' and 'brainwashing'? I thought then and still believe now that she was. But then, isn't everyone?" Martin smiled, enjoying the fact that I didn't answer back right away.

"Come on, Peter. You know I've seen the hard work it's taken her, working with those in psych and corrections to help her get a sense of herself back."

"Considering the source and severity of such madness—let alone Leslie's rehabilitation in prison—if the department of corrections actually embodies its espoused beliefs in redemption, it might serve some purpose," I stated, making it sound like a question.

"Maybe. I don't think she would ever have been convicted of murder if this had happened in Canada," he admitted. "I can't see what purpose her spending any more time in prison will serve."

"Maybe you can write a decent piece about that," I suggested.

"Interesting… Do you know Americans imprison more of their own people than any other country in the world? Makes it hard to say, 'Let's forgive and forget,' doesn't it?" Martin seemed to conclude, and we left it at that for the time being.

Martin finished his drink, and we both sat quiet and still for a moment. He was staring outside, and I thought I noticed a change of mood come over him.

"Pete. Let me ask you something. When she gets up in the night to pee, does it ever occur to you, she might come back with a cleaver and chop your nuts off?" He kept a straight face the whole time he said it.

Before I finally cracked and laughed out loud. Loud enough for even the invisible wait staff who served our table to take notice.

"To be honest, for your sake and hers, I hope she does come away with a plea to a lesser charge. From what I've read, she's been a model prisoner. There's no dispute about that. Not even the prosecution can accuse her of misbehavior inside of prison."

"Which doesn't mean they'll let her out right away, regardless," I said.

"No one has all the answers. Not me, not you. Oh, I don't know… Now I forget what I was going to say. I'm feeling jet-lagged and still have a train to take first thing in the morning. One more drink, and you can walk me to my hotel?" he asked.

Martin looked as though he'd said his peace for now. Yet, I could sense he was hiding something he hadn't let go for some reason. Before we settled up and left for his hotel, I felt compelled to add one thing more to our friendly debates. I don't know why I thought it would help if I told him what I was thinking. It only seemed right that I try.

"Did you know, after the first trial and during the sentencing cerebration—while the jurors deliberated sending Charlie and the girls to the gas chamber—one of the male jurors withheld his final judgment 'til the end? Somehow Max Keith found this out but couldn't use it.

"One juror, out of those twelve like-minded people, pointed to Leslie's lesser involvement as mitigating circumstances to weigh in her favor. Then, as you know, in August, nearly half the jury followed their conscience in the second trial and voted for 'manslaughter' on the last ballot," I said, and he nodded.

Somewhere deep down, Martin understood there was *no* proof to suggest Leslie would have—or could have—maturely and meaningfully reflected upon the gravity of the intent she had stuffed into her mind that night in August 1969. Her mind wasn't her own. All she did or could do was obey Manson's orders. Martin could see what Leslie Van Houten did was horrible, but it was *not* first-degree murder.

I was feeling pretty lashed from drinking and talking too much. While we waited quietly for the girl serving us to come back with the check, looking somewhat disquieted, Martin jutted his chin out and said, "Listen, I'm not sure how to say this or whether I even should..."

"Say what?" I could sense some tidal wave coming.

"Ah, well, a guy I know who works at the *Times* in LA says he knows your friend, Mister Peters. I've told him about your relationship with Leslie. Thing is, this guy said he heard something innocuous about her being seen with some guy at the paper. He thought the guy looked like he could be a reporter."

"When was this?" I asked, trying to take another sip from my empty glass and feeling the certain onslaught of anguish.

"I don't know. Maybe less than a month. I don't know."

The blushed look on my face might have led him to add, "I take it, it wasn't you he was talking about."

19

O, DESDEMONA!

The week before her third trial for the same crime was to start, Leslie called me while she was still on a road trip with our friends Michael and Jane Malone. They took their motorhome.

Regrettably, that was a week after I'd sent Leslie a caustic letter recounting my meeting with Martin. Much of it, I conjured out of self-doubt and envy. Imagining the worst of what I might do if I were in her shoes and projecting that onto her instead of owning it myself. Thankfully, she hadn't received my letter yet when she called. I might have warned her, only I was too ashamed by then, so I didn't.

"I'm still sold on our living close by the campus in Isla Vista, aren't you?" Leslie asked, phoning from her own room at the Big Sur Lodge.

"What week in March are you coming back to me?"

"I'll call Air Canada tomorrow to reconfirm the flight," I said. "I've asked my brother for a ride out to the airport on Thursday the sixteenth. There's a direct flight arriving after nine at night. Will you be there, or will you be busy?"

Those poorly chosen words were bad enough, but it was the tone of my voice that I most regretted.

"Don't start picking a fight," Leslie said.

"If you're seeing somebody else," the worst in me rushed to say, "then maybe I should cancel completely."

Coolly, she said, "Peter, I understand you getting jealous, but I think it's a waste of time and energy. It's childish, honey. You're a better man than that. Yes, I do attract attention, and I don't think you should be alarmed about it, because I'm not. If I fed off it—or phony-assed to get it—that would be one thing.

"You know you can trust me."

"Is that what I know? That's not what I'm saying."

"What *are* you saying?"

"I'm saying it makes me look like a fool, which I am, let's face it," I ranted on pitifully. "Friends hear rumors that I can't defend..." and so on and on. Awful.

"Rumors are just that," Leslie said. "*Rumors*. There's nothing to defend. Don't blame me for that too. It's you that always listens to rumors. Why not trust me instead?"

Trying to shift the blame to someone else, I said, "I'm sure Judy has been just aching to set you up with some friends of hers. That way, she can be rid of me and start catching your overflow."

"What does Judy have to do with anything? I thought you wanted a truce on that. So, what if that sort of thing happens? Means nothing to me. You think I'm so easily impressed with... whomever...?"

"Forget it."

"Honey, I'm feeling like—rather than freaking out—you should be more proud than uptight. If I encouraged it, that would be different. I am not a cheap tramp, and you know that. We have so many things to talk about and to share. Please don't make this into something it isn't."

"What's there for me to feel *proud* about?"

"That I love *you*. Don't be a bonehead."

"I'll let you know about the sixteenth when I've decided for sure if I'm coming," my strange, threatened ego responded. "Bye for now, Leslie," I said and ended our call like a big baby.

After all the cruel BS I gave her over the phone and in a letter, Leslie was gracious as always and sure to forgive me. I imprudently assumed this reprieve would last forever, or at least until the next time I made a similar gaffe and cracked under pressure.

The next week, Leslie telephoned to warn me of a change of plans in terms of where we would be staying when I arrived there in March.

"I had it together that you and I were going to stay at Linda's in March. She was going to be gone on vacation, right? Now, that's been canceled."

"Is this just your way of letting me down? Is there more you aren't telling me?" I ascribed. Not having learned my lesson.

"Stop it. Don't even start, Mr. Snide Remark. I thought we were past all of that nonsense?" She was right.

"I'm sorry, Les. I have no defense. I'm making excuses for being such a mess. I swear I'm just a horribly defenseless, irrationally jealous, jealous guy who, once again, has crumbled under pressure."

Leslie paused, and I could hear her take a breath and sigh before speaking again. When she did, she spoke serenely.

"One option we have is that we're invited to stay at the Malones' in Laguna. I love it there, don't you? Their place makes me yearn for us having a space of our own to call 'home.'

"I like the collections of things they have gathered. Simple things. Vases, seashells, photos, and prisms. Slowly we will accumulate our own history the same way. I'd love for us to stay there the whole time; only it's a bit far to go during the week if court is in session."

"Okay. Whatever you say, boss," I said, letting her gentle, even tone of voice calm my anxieties. "I ache just thinking about how far away you and I are *again*. I'm sorry. That makes me jealous over all the time lost."

"Peter, I haven't dared to say much about it. I know it's hard to consider but, win or lose, they can't keep me locked up forever. Still, you're worried I might not get out right away, and think of this time apart as time lost. But we shouldn't see things that way. I see this as time spent building our future."

Busy reflecting on what she just said, I couldn't respond.

"Naturally, I wish you were here," she continued. "We've discussed all of this over and over. This trial scene sucks. But we have no choice right now but to see this stage through to the end as it's given to us."

"I'll wait for as long as you want me to."

To myself, another voice only whispered...*but I will not pine any longer.*

* * *

Air Canada flight no. 793 arrived in Los Angeles on time, just after nine at night. Leslie was waiting for me in the arrivals' lounge when I stepped off the gangplank. She was lovely and beaming, just like, yet unlike, any other pretty girl at the airport waiting to meet her boyfriend.

I spotted her right away through the crowd's chaos and clutter. She was wearing a pretty white blouse under a new, faded-blue denim jacket and a pair of my boots and jeans.

She seemed never to stop talking or smiling the two hours it took us to make our destination in the MGB, one hundred miles up the road toward midnight in Santa Barbara. Nor did I. We drove the whole way without stopping. Having the top down tousled her chestnut-brown hair, and some long, fine strands occasionally broke free from under her scarf.

It was just before twelve o'clock when we checked in at the Holiday Inn in Goleta. We had the pool to ourselves and took a quick, quiet swim under the starlight. The water wasn't terribly warm, so we didn't stay in long.

Leslie kept both arms wrapped around me under a blanket as we hurried back to our room. Underneath, she had on a bright-colored caftan over her swimsuit. I thought it was exciting the way she let them fall tangled inside out on the floor with the towels.

Still on Toronto time, I woke up early and went for a run along Cathedral Oaks Road. Leslie was just getting dressed when I got back to the room. Before changing out of my sweats and into a damp swimsuit, I spotted a small gift box propped on my pillow.

"For me?" I asked and waited for Leslie to say it was all right before I dared to slip off the tiny blue ribbon and opened it up.

"It's months late, I know, but it's taken this long to have made. It was supposed to be for your birthday. Happy late birthday, Peter," she frowned.

Then, still sweating from my first warm-weather run in a while, I followed up with a big smacking kiss on her lips.

Inside the box was a shiny medallion hung on a box-linked silver chain.

"How perfect," I said, taking it out of its cradle. "Here, help me to clasp it on." I turned around and felt the tips of Leslie's fingers on the nape of my neck. "I promise I'll never take this off. Not so long as I'm breathing." I crossed my heart with her hand in mine.

She draped both arms around me and kissed me ever so gently that, for a moment, I couldn't tell where my body ended and hers began. I'd never been kissed like that before, nor ever since that I can remember.

"Liberty dimes are 90 percent pure silver. Did you know that?" she asked.

"Same as you and me? Ninety-percent pure but imperfect."

Leslie was told the reason these coins are commonly referred to as "Mercury dimes" is based on a mistaken assumption. The face on the coin represents Lady Liberty, not the swift-footed messenger of the gods. I liked them *both,* and I said so.

"I had a silversmith cut out the face of one coin and weld it on top of the other. See the relief? So, there are two faces and not just one. Do you like it?"

"One face is hidden. I love it," I said, propping the coin on my thumb for a closer look in the mirror. "Les, this will always remind me of you. Unconditionally forever and always."

I kissed her again on the lips and then pushed her back on the bed with her knees pinned under my shoulders. She pushed me off, saying, "You need a swim or a shower." There was a delicate firmness to her voice, so I did as I was told.

Sitting outside on a restaurant patio close by the corner of Pardall and Embarcadero del Mar, we held hands all throughout breakfast. Rather than hunt for rental places with overgrown gardens needing attending, we shopped in a few funky shops where there was great music playing. Everything seemed scented with hashish and sandalwood wherever we went. Except the Bank of America.

After that, I took Les for a tour of the UCSB campus.

The University of California at Santa Barbara is bordered on three sides by the Pacific Ocean. Much of its early architecture was based on sixties-style tinted concrete blocks with Spanish tile rooftops among odd leftover army barracks. All the buildings were surrounded by lush, tended gardens with plenty of tall palms and aromatic eucalyptus trees planted around.

Leslie was inclined toward the azure lagoon, so we walked down the sandy path that led past sea cliffs to the beachfront. All the while talking about her trial and my prospects for getting into this graduate school. On both counts, we still had the jitters.

Our first appointment was at 3:00 p.m. with Isabelle Reilly in the registrar's office. This meeting with the assistant registrar was mainly to sign ourselves up in case we opted for married student housing. We'd need a backup in case I failed in my bid for a scholarship. The real tests lay ahead.

When it was time for Ms. Reilly to lead me upstairs to meet the Confluent Education and Institutional Leadership faculty, Leslie was free to wander around on her own. She said she'd meet me downstairs in the Phelps Hall courtyard around five-thirty. Then, gave me a sweet kiss for good luck. Everything seemed to hinge on a few precious moments.

Ms. Reilly ushered me into a conference room where professors George Brown (Harvard), Stewart Shapiro (USC), and Mark Phillips (U. Mass.) were seated around a long table. The only one missing that day was Professor Laurence Iannaccone (Columbia).

"How was your trip from Toronto?" Mark Phillips asked.

He was the youngest and junior member in the department—a frail-looking guy with wild, curly red hair in a style that harkened to Harpo Marx. Mark held an EdD from the University of Massachusetts at Amherst. I've forgotten specifics, but what I instantly liked best of all about Mark was his quick-witted energy and keen regard for his colleagues. He put me at ease.

"It's great to be away from the cold and damp for a couple of weeks," I said in response to impatient though requisite small talk about such things as the weather and what I read on the flight. I could see Professor Brown was still looking over my file when Professor Stewart Shapiro began to ask more increasingly pertinent questions.

"George tells us you have quite a background in amateur sports but little experience teaching. Is that right?"

It took me a second to refocus, deliberately trying not to appear too defensive.

"Well...yes and no. I've competed in varsity football, hockey, and track. I'm coaching track right now. And teaching English lit and media studies to teens until June.

"I've also done some teacher training before. Quite a lot of that, in fact, these past two years with the University of Toronto Track Team. I've been involved in at least a dozen clinics for schoolteachers and coaches. Does that count?"

"Could be," Stew Shapiro smiled. "To be honest, what impressed us most were your letters of reference. Very impressive...."

Then, as I recall, the more heavy-set George Brown seemed to cut in as a way of speeding things up.

"I liked what you wrote about skipping two years of high school and living with your principal and his family," he said, laughing and smiling broadly at me and the others. We all had a chuckle over my explaining some of those circumstances.

George asked me, "What do you know about our program in terms of Gestalt psychology and confluent education?"

"Only what I've read so far in two of your books on the subject. I'm familiar with some of the source work you reference."

"Such as?" Mark interrupted. I responded by namedropping scholars like Rollo May, A.S. Neill, R.D. Lang, Alan Watts, Aldous Huxley, and a half dozen more before he waved the yellow flag to slow me down. Just as well. I was a tad nervous.

Eventually, we got around to more in-depth discussions about institutional leadership and higher education in its latest conceptions. They each took turns explaining their research and methods of teaching. *Confluent education*, as they put it, sought to renew one of the soundest traditions in Western education. That is, education for the *whole person*—mind, spirit, body, and emotions. Not just the mind by its lonesome.

That started a congenial riff on the performance of sport as a branch of aesthetics. I thought that maybe I'd just found a home for what I'd been working on for so long.

"As coaches, at the U of T, we were taught to recognize it's not the performance itself that's the focus. Nobody dedicates the best years of their lives to just running around in circles for nothing," I said at one point. Feeling less and less nervous but also noticeably revved up with enthusiasm for the topic.

"The focus is on the whole person, *not* just hers or his performance. And our success at anything we do as a team has a lot to do with the development of strong interpersonal relationships.

Vital for achieving dramatic improvements in human performance of any kind.

"No individual, no group or organization can ever really be the best they can be without coaching. And coaching is all about setting expectations. *Great* expectations."

When it came time to wrap things up, Mark and Stew said they had somewhere to be right away. George asked me what my immediate plans were. I told them my fiancé was waiting downstairs and that we were due back in LA later that evening.

"Would you like to meet her?" I asked automatically.

"We'll walk you out then, shall we?" George said.

Only, as we got nearer the courtyard, my mind jumped in the way of my body. The others looked back seeming puzzled when I stopped walking. Looking past them, I saw Leslie sitting on a bench all alone smoking a cigarette and reading a book.

The line from *Love's Labour Lost* still comes to mind: "What fool is not so wise to lose an oath to win a paradise?"

There was no choice left but to risk it. So, I swallowed hard.

"Ah, gentlemen," I said without warning, "it's been a pleasure meeting you. This was fun. I hope you will give my application serious consideration."

"You'll be sure to hear from us soon," said George, looking puzzled.

After a pause to take another breath, I went on to say, "If you don't mind, I'd like to introduce my girlfriend, Leslie." I pointed before I continued. "But, first, I think I should explain who she is."

That got their attention. I made the rest up as I went along.

"I'm here with Leslie Van Houten," I said.

Each of the others took turns looking at me, then at each other. I could see they knew who she was, but it still must have come as a shock in the moment. Stew Shapiro spoke first.

"Well, I'd certainly like to meet her," he smiled. Then, each of them stepped forward to greet her.

Leslie kept smiling as I introduced everyone. After which, I smiled back at Les and sheepishly shrugged.

As Stew and George held out their arms for a handshake, Mark turned toward me to say, "You realize, of course, Ms. Van Houten is a very controversial figure here in this state at the moment?"

I tightened my jaw and wondered aloud, "Would that count for or against us?"

Mark laughed with me. All the same, I knew there would always be other graduate schools, but only one Leslie.

Les was charming as always just by being herself. We stood there shooting the breeze for ten minutes or so before I sensed it was time for us to be leaving. There was a lot for us all to take in and process. By the time we skipped clear out of sight, I'd already begun cheering. Even that understated my feelings. We were ecstatic! Quite a rush!

"That went very well! Don't you think?" I practically shouted.

Leslie agreed wholeheartedly. Things looked to be going as well, or better, than we had expected. We vowed to keep our hearts tangled and our fingers crossed.

After a snack on our way out of town, we split a fajita and drove straight on to Highway 101 bearing south-by-southeast down the coastline. We each had that eerie in-sync sense you get by being in the flow of things coming together.

With immaculate timing, Leslie found station KTYD FM 99.9 on the dial and wound herself up singing along with Jim Morrison of The Doors' "Love Her Madly." An easy-listening, lonely song of a deep-blue obsession I knew by heart. A "seven horses dream" that sounded like a huge gamble to me.

Once the music stopped, the sky overhead had grown quite a bit darker. I switched on the headlamps as we passed Paradise Cove. When I did, some of the car's electrics gave out—as anyone who has ever owned an MGB could have predicted. We'd blown a fuse. The circuit lights were dead. I could have stuck a piece of aluminum foil into the breaker, but together, we decided to spend the night in a quirky motel alongside Highway 1. A simple motel majestically named the Malibu Riviera.

We had my mother's 8-mm Kodak movie camera, and (somewhere) there exists a three-minute film of us horsing around in the spirit of youthful exuberance. The best scenes between us were the ones that occurred after the film had run out.

There was something irresistible about having Leslie all to myself. For so long, I had wondered if it could ever be possible. And yet here it *actually* was, as I'd imagined: the prolonged lovers' tête-à-têtes, our laughter over creaky bedsprings, and the noisy, coin-operated gismo called Magic Fingers we couldn't resist.

We nearly cried from laughing so hard.

Afterward, we each imparted a wholesome night's sleep with a pleasant wake-up call to attention at dawn between showers. I tried to mix up my humming like the hairless monkey that I was. *I'm a believer...I couldn't leave her, if I tried.* Crazy, but happy—if unwisely in love.

We had pancakes at daybreak for breakfast at the first family restaurant we found. Purchased an electrical fuse when we fueled up the MGB and soon after were back to making good time on the open road. Only to be stalled for nearly two hours getting through sixty miles of so-called Los Angeles "freeways." We played tapes by the Plastic Ono Band, Bob Dylan, and The Beach Boys. And of course, we talked and talked. Mostly, I did.

We finally arrived at our destination mid-day. A small coastal town near the southern end of the San Joaquin Hills in Orange County called Laguna Niguel. As mentioned before, our friends Jane and Michael Malone lived on Grand Canyon Drive, less than a mile from the coast off Crown Valley Parkway.

After all the usual smiles, cries, hugs, and kisses—the gals wandered into the wilds of Jane's garden to catch up alone. Michael and I snuck off to the garage, where he tossed me the keys to his convertible Mercedes SL. We went for a spin down the canyon to Dana Point and parked in a lot alongside the Marina.

"So how do you like teaching?" Michael asked, sitting down on a lonely rock twenty feet from the shoreline. I remember standing in the surf cooling my toes.

"It's not really teaching. It's more like theater than teaching. It's selfish of me, I know. But it isn't an entirely unpleasant opportunity to read and reflect on all that radiates from an acquaintance with Shakespeare.

"And you, Michael? Now that you're back from Mykonos, what are your plans? Go back to teaching?"

"Just living. Jane has her art and her garden. I thought I'd have a look around for part-time work in some local college. Maybe write a new edition to my last textbook. Speaking of teaching and writing, how did things go for you in Santa Barbara?"

Holding myself back from exuding too much unwarranted optimism, I told him things went as well as expected. I mentioned how well-received Leslie was.

"Do you think they were able to see Leslie for who she is and not hold the public view of her against her?" he asked.

"I've thought about that. Remember, when you and I each got to meet Leslie, she was already rehabilitated. It may be wishful thinking on my part, but I'm pretty sure that's how these guys also responded.

"It's not hard for sensitive, intelligent people to intuit sincere humanity in another's character, is it?"

When Michael asked more about the faculty's reaction to meeting Leslie and me as a couple, I told him the truth. Which was: There's no telling for sure. When he asked, candidly, how things were going between Les and me, I told him the truth, but not all of it.

"I wouldn't trade her for another girl. Here, did I show you the Liberty medallion she gave me?" I asked, lifting it away from my chest so he could see it.

"We did see the ring on her finger. She seems very happy indeed, Peter. Congratulations.

"What's wrong? You had an odd look on your face for a moment." Michael was keen in picking that up. I hadn't realized it myself until he mentioned it.

"Her being out of reach to me so much of the time distresses me. It's like she's not really mine. If you know what I mean."

"I know she's *not* 'yours,'" he said, with a smile.

Pinching my chin to my chest to look at my medal, and lifting it with my thumb, I said, "This may become a symbol of my demise. Even though I've only worn it a few days; already, I feel unsecured without it."

* * *

Sunday morning, we four went shopping for pastries and books and browsed for sets of Mexican glass and ceramics. Before lunch, Les and I snuck away to be alone in their oversized indoor jacuzzi adjoining the guest room. A luxury Les said she loved to afford in the attempt to shed the last of the jailhouse from her body and soul.

Les would almost always rather we talked about something else besides her case. So, whenever anything remotely political came up, we all made attempts to segway to something more cheerful. Still, there was no way of escaping the fact, she had no control over whether she would remain free to enjoy such simple pleasures.

Soon it was time for Les and me to pack our gear and head back to Jane's place in Monterey Park. Michael was kind in helping me fit the MGB with better circuit breakers and fuses before we set off for LA.

Leslie had to be in court early each day of that week. The rest of the time we were not out and about, we camped out in the guest room at Jane Van Houten's house. Leslie was shy about sleeping in the room next to her mom's. But the last night we were there, Jane and her next-door neighbor Georgie were away in Port Hueneme.

Since I was visiting, Leslie asked Max Keith and Glen Peters for evenings off from her two part-time jobs. She had secretarial training after high school and was able to split her time between their two offices.

Most days during court, I sat with Linda. Or with Betsy, David, Shannon, or someone else from the family entourage who could make it on any given day. On the last day I made it to court on that visit, Judy Frutig and I sat together a row back from the front. I preferred to hang back and watch from the corner. But Judy said she needed to hand messages to Max. Although that rarely happened that I ever saw.

Once court was adjourned, Leslie whispered something to Max, and I thought (or imagined) I saw her hand him a letter she had stashed in her notepad. She may have glanced over her shoulder at me, though; in any case, I pretended not to notice.

Later, while Judy and I waited on West Third Street in front of Max's office for him and Leslie to run up after some document, I asked Judy straight up if she'd ever noticed Leslie passing letters to Max in the courtroom. She said "No," she hadn't.

"Probably just another admirer or something," Judy seemed pleased to inform me. "Letters get sent to her care of Max all the time."

"Does she ever write back?"

"She wrote back to you, didn't she?"

Leslie and Max dropped me off at LAX early on Monday morning. Les and I knew this would be our last embrace for another three months. Right as I turned to make my way inside the terminal, Leslie tugged on my shoulder strap, swung me around, and looked me straight in the eye.

"I know you don't believe it...and I never could stand on my head—so there's not much more I can do to convince you. I hope we won't have to keep going over this again and again.

"Peter, there's absolutely nothing goin' on. Please stop this suspicion, because there's no need. Let's start fresh, okay?"

Awkwardly, I said, "I know when this stretch of the ordeal is over, we'll both be on firmer ground. I'll try not to blow it."

"I'll call you tonight after midnight. What time is that in Toronto?"

"Three a.m.," I moaned and she giggled.

"Until then. I promise I'll make it worth your time," she said and blew me a kiss.

* * *

Air Canada flight no. 792 left at 1:20 p.m. and landed in Toronto at a quarter-to-nine. I wish I could say it was good to be home. Only somewhere, deep down inside, I felt that it wasn't.

* * *

A few weeks later, on April 3rd, 1978, Leslie Van Houten attended the 50th Academy Awards ceremony at the Dorothy Chandler Pavilion. It was, among other things, the occasion of Bob Hope's final appearance as master of ceremonies. Leslie was there with a mysterious escort. (Don't ask; I didn't.) Woody Allen skipped off, so, for sure, it wasn't him that brought her along.

I've often wondered what Mr. Hope's monologue might have been like if he'd known a former Charles Manson co-defendant was seated among the crowd.

It was still a great big world, all right, but also a rather small club. I never asked Leslie who she was with that night at the Oscars, and she never told me.

I was trying my best to act more grown up about such things from then on.

20

JURORS DEBATE FATE

The next day, April 4th, nearly seven years after her first conviction for the murder of Leno and Rosemary LaBianca, Leslie was back in court to hear Deputy District Attorney Stephen Kay present the prosecution's case against her for an unprecedented third time. Here's what Mr. Kay had to say in his opening statement:

"Neither drugs nor sex forced her, and she always did just what she wanted to do," he told the judge and jury of seven women and five men. "Even when it came to murder, she had to weigh and consider at least two days before she could decide if she could kill anyone... She knew there were two guns and two knives in the car, and she knew what they were to be used for. She knew exactly what had happened the night before and knew exactly what was going to happen. They were out to commit murder."

In Leslie's defense, Max Keith told the jurors that the woman who stood before them now was not the same woman who took part in that tragic nightmare eight years before.

"For her to have done what she did...to have believed what she believed...there must have been something horribly wrong. At the time of the murders, she was not aware of her obligation to obey the law. Therefore, she could have had no malice aforethought. Mr. Kay makes her sound like a tramp. That is not so. Evidence will show that she suffered from a type of mental illness that has been called 'group psychoses' by some doctors, and 'phobia famille' by others."

Max's defense was the same as the one that had won him a hung jury the last time. He meant to prove that Leslie could not be held entirely responsible for her actions—not while acting as a member of the Charles Manson cult. For instance, who in their right mind would ignore a deal for immunity from the death chamber to protect some self-proclaimed guru faux-Jesus Christ? Instead of the truth, Leslie lied to save Manson and Watson. Whose idea was that? Certainly not a perfectly sane Leslie Van Houten. Now she admitted lying during the first trial. But either way, Stephen Kay used this against her.

Max Keith said he hoped to show how, at the time of the killings, Leslie's psyche had been so severely damaged by Manson's mind control methods that she could not have meaningfully premeditated murder.

Max argued that Leslie admitted her part in the killing of Rosemary LaBianca, but her psyche was too badly impaired by the cult's use of psychoactive drugs for her to have meaningfully formed the intent. Without a will of her own, Leslie found herself at Waverly Drive that night for no other reason than to obey Charles Manson's commands.

Manson was the only one with a clear motive for planning these torturous crimes. And it was Charles Manson and Tex Watson who brought the knives and guns, not Leslie Van Houten.

Max's defense was that Leslie had paid the price of her youth behind bars for what awful madness she let herself in for. She has expressed sincere remorse for what happened and her android-esque role in going along. Her prison record was flawless. What more could she do to prove she deserved a chance at redemption?

Because Leslie's second trial (the first retrial after her original conviction had been overturned) ended in a hung jury, the prosecutors saw to it that the jury in the subsequent third trial was *not* required to decide that she premeditated and deliberated the murder herself. The felony-murder instructions were given to the jury by the court—which allows a defendant to be charged with murder for a killing that happened during a dangerous felony—even when the defendant is not the killer.

The fix was in.

* * *

Leslie called after midnight on Saturday the 8th of April. She and Linda Grippi had returned to Santa Barbara to look at more places we might want to live, if she got to stay out with another hung jury. *Assuming* I was accepted into UCSB graduate studies. A couple of big "maybes," but not seeming so far out of reach as before. I taped the phone call on my tape deck.

"Will you accept a collect call from Leslie?" the long-distance operator asked me.

"Yes, of course," I said, yawning into the mic.

"God, I didn't even hear it ring... I just picked it up to see if there was a dial tone. What were you doing?" she asked.

"Reading the last act of *Othello*. How about you?"

"Daydreaming about livin' in Isla Vista. Aren't you glad that I called?"

"Where are you exactly?"

"We're at the motel. Linda and me drove all around IV today. Oh, there are some fine places, Peter. There were some that had these overgrown yards I could fix up so neat. I could plant the *neatest* gardens in them. Oh, and this one...this one had this sunroom. And there'd be room enough for an office where it's quiet and private.

"It's real old and rundown, but you know... It's just the kind of place that I want. I'm sure we can have it real soon. Should I go talk to the agent tomorrow?"

"Did you cash the check I put in the letter? Is that enough, or maybe I should send another in case you need more?"

"No. Not yet. Maybe it will be waiting at Mom's when I get back to LA tomorrow. We've got to be back by seven. Karlene Faith is going to be in town and wants me to go to a concert with her at the Roxy.

Remember? I told you I was going to go to a concert with her and some friends?"

Just as well that I didn't recall. Besides, I wasn't a fan of one-hit-wonder Warren Zevon at all. Had it been another Rick Danko reprise instead, I might have envied those who went tagging along.

"Just be careful," I warned. "Do you think Karlene's friends can protect you?"

"Oh, never mind that now," she said, practically reading my mind full of sorrows. "I'll call you back when I find out what's what. You hang up first. Here's a kiss... Smack! My darling, don't ever doubt my love for you...not for an instant. Not ever. Please know that I love you. Say you believe me."

"You believe me."

When I looked down, there was a line that leaped off the page I'd been reading before falling asleep, I read it aloud in response: "'I'll see before I doubt...away at once with love or jealousy!'"

"Can you guess which character in the play says that?"

"Now I'm confused. Tell me later what that's supposed to mean?" Leslie had every right asking. I didn't know myself.

Before we hung up, I suggested, "I think it means it's hard to be wise and in love at the same time, *Desdemona*."

Didn't I know it?

* * *

The first week back at West Hill Collegiate, and I was feeling displaced and all out of sorts. Just counting the days and punching the clock. Word was out among the teachers that anyone hired in the last two years was going to be put on "surplus" status come the end of the school year. That had a lot of people uptight.

Someone said they'd seen the principal, Mr. Budd, leaving "Notice of Surplus" memos in everyone's mailbox. Certainly, this caused a bit of a stir among all the rookies but one. I felt badly for my friends on the bubble, but as far as my own future in the Scarborough Board of Education was concerned, I would have paid them to let me off early. I wished I'd thought of it sooner.

We were into the second week of *Romeo and Juliet* when Mr. Vice Principal George Peck came into my sixth-period class to conduct an impromptu "teaching inspection." In keeping with the methods I'd tested when teaching *Othello*, we approached the play back to front. I neglected to explain this to my "superior." Why we were into the final act of the play in week two instead of week ten must have thrown him. I introduced the day's lesson as follows:

"Romeo thinks Juliet is dead from the poison. So, broken-hearted, he drinks the poison himself. Then, Juliet wakes up and finds Romeo dead, so she commits *seppuku* with his dagger."

To confuse our uninvited guest even further, I directed alternate endings. "First, let's try to read our parts as a comedy of errors," I said, "not as a tragedy. And then see where that leads us."

That really took Mr. Peck over the edge. He soon left in one heck of a huff. I wasn't worried. Though the kids seemed to think that I should be.

"Oh, boo-hoo," I trembled. "What if *Mister* Peck leaves a nasty note in my mailbox?" I froze with mock horror, bringing my hands up to cover my mouth. Not every kid in the room was laughing. But I was. I just wanted out of there. Sooner than later was not soon enough.

* * *

Les moved out of Linda Grippi's tiny apartment and into my old room at Judy Frutig's significantly larger condo on Micheltorena Street. One Friday night in May, when Les and I had prearranged a time for me to call her, Judy's sister Jennifer picked up the phone to say that Leslie and Judy had gone out on a date to the movies.

Leslie called the next night to tell me that the Sly Stallone blockbuster she'd gone to with friends had really sucked. I didn't ask whom, besides Judy, she went with. I tried to act nonchalant. Inside my jealous heart, phantoms of dread were still stirring. I worried all the time that I might lose her to someone who treated her better than I did. Which wouldn't be hard.

"Anything new and exciting happening in court these days?" I asked her, grinding my molars.

"Max and Kay are still getting into it. Hey! Know what cool thing the judge said today?"

"I'm too tired to guess. Was it a good or a bad thing?"

"He said, 'Hold ho! Gentlemen, have you forgot all sense of place and duty?' Isn't that great?"

"That is good," I laughed. "Did either Max or Kay signal a recognition of where that quote was from?"

"No. They both kinda looked puzzled. Ringer just rolled his eyes and assumed he was the only one who got the joke."

"You know which play that line comes from?"

"It's *Othello*, right?" she said.

"Right. It's Iago, who's pretending he's for peace when it's really him who started the fight." (I hoped this wasn't an omen.) "What were Max and Kay fighting about anyway?"

"You remember Snake. Diane Lake? She was going on about how tired *she is* of being dragged back in again to testify about things she's been trying to forget. The fighting was about something she said I said. Who can remember?"

"Here's something else, though. I plan on writing an opinion piece for the *Times* that has to do with teachers who bring very young children into the courtroom. I think twelve- and thirteen-year-olds are too young to hear all the heavy gore in the coroner's reports. That's irresponsible. I'm going to ask Max to speak to the judge."

"Let me see when you have a draft. How is old Max holding up to the tag team of Steve Kay and Dino Fulgoni?"

"I think he's been able to put some important things more out front. Things that show there were different planes of involvement. Like the fingerprint man. He said that *definitely* the prints in the bedroom were wiped with something different than with what was used in the living room and kitchen. Kay has been trying to put me in places I never was.

"And Harold True. The guy Charlie and Linda Kasabian met who used to live next door to the LaBiancas. Turns out—even though he testified as to how illiterate Charlie was and every-thing—when he met him, he was interviewing Charlie for his master's thesis. Know what on? On people who had seen visions of Christ.

"An' guess what? It was the *judge* who brought all of that out! That's a good sign, I thought."

"What kind of influence do you think this judge will have with the jury? What's their impression of him so far?"

"It's hard to know what the jury thinks about anything. Ringer keeps asking something extra of every witness to help them out. Maybe the jury can see what he's tryin' to figure out. Like he said to Linda Kasabian: 'You mean to tell me that *you* went with a gun and knives, and you didn't know anything was going to happen? You mean to tell me you didn't see the bolt cutters, and you mean to tell me that you went the second night knowing full well what was going to happen?'

"He isn't treating her like a saint and me as a tramp. Which is what Kay always does.

"He reads from a bad script. He's such a faker. Today, he got lost repeating himself and going in circles. The judge had to step in and clarify what was going on for the jury.

"Then, the judge asked Linda, 'Did Charlie ever talk about philosophers or people he might have read?' and she said, 'No.' Which is a lie. She's such a sad little lady.

"This guy, Judge Ringer, he is really getting into it. I'm *really* feeling positive about him. I'm sorry we had to have a jury in front of him."

"Why do you say that?" I was surprised.

"Because I'm sure I'd get manslaughter with him as my only judge," Leslie said matter-of-factly. "He sees what's true and fair."

"Then, why didn't Max counsel that option?" I asked, still startled by the idea.

"Because that's too much pressure to put on someone in his position. That's what I've been told. It's like... I talked to a couple of the attorneys that hang out in his court. They said: 'as fine a judge as he is, *everybody* in this business has selfish goals.'"

"You think there might be too much political pressure? He's used to high-profile scrutiny. I doubt it's because of all the publicity."

"Even if he wanted to let me go, he'd probably have to cave in at the end," she said. "But he seems to be doing the best he can. Man, it's clear to me that what he's sayin' is that, by law, I might be guilty of manslaughter, not murder. I feel like that anyway.

"And there's something else. It kind of creeps me out, though."

"What's that?" I wondered how much creepier things could get.

"Both Stephen Kay and Dino Fulgoni are *deliberately* trying not to question one single witness about the effects of the drugs and Charlie's mind-pounding 'Helter Skelter' into our heads. It's something they've gone out of their way to avoid. I can't quite figure that out. Everyone knows the story."

"Not necessarily everyone on the jury, though."

"Hey, honey, did you get any of my letters? I started writing again," she said, changing the subject. "Though some of it will sound moody 'cause I was upset when I wrote them. I wish we could just lie in bed and talk about things in private. I always feel there may be someone else listening in.

"You know I can't wait to feel your arms around me and have your lips kissing mine. You want to know something else? Nothing has ever seemed so right or more natural to me than being with you. I want you to know that. It's the truth. I'm yours, and that's all there is to it."

On the one hand, I longed to hear her say it. But at the same time, I was suspicious that *the lady doth protest too much.* Why couldn't I shake the unfounded suspicion that was she hiding something from me?

When Leslie's letters did come, they came two at a time and all out of sequence. I invented all sorts of sinister reasons for why her tempers might vary. But for the most part, she seemed happier day to day than I was. I was more gently up and down.

One thing was certain. We both hated being so far apart physically. Although we each dealt with it differently. One card she sent contained a poem about having so many feelings, ideas, and moments to share, "that would have made you smile and frown, sigh and wonder." Along with a caption where she added, "Why must you be so far from me when I need you so?"

Hello My Love—

I feel so bad about my lack of letters to you lately. But writing is very difficult at this moment. Doin' hard time. I move from the stress of the courtroom to more and more tension wherever I go. I try to relax and then when I do complete exhaustion takes over. It's clear something's missing—it's you! I long for the summer and starting life over in Isla Vista. It's time to get on.

I've counted the months and now I'm relieved to know it will be only weeks until you hold me close and not let me go. I got some more houseplants this weekend that we can take with us. I also found some string-of-hearts. Remember we saw them in that window in Santa Barbara? I can hardly wait to fix our place up. I think it's going to be wonderful. We'll have fun doin' it together!! Did I tell you that mom is giving us the desk that's in her garage? It's pretty big and strong. We sure can use it.

I'm in court right now. Mr. Kay is trying to break Paul Watkins' testimony. Kay's upset with Paul admitting the thought-control methods Charlie used and how it affected him also. Now little Paul is into saying he wasn't able to kill for Charlie. It's hard to go on hearing this. One moment it looks like the jury sees through it, then the next time it doesn't. I wish I could write you sunshine-filled rose-hued letters, but we have to face what's going on and be completely honest about it.

It's very upsetting. Now it's a word game between Kay and Paul. But it's my life that hangs in the balance. Kay, as usual, is pulling a lot of dirty tricks and the jury seem more amused than disgusted. This is why I haven't written you much about it. It's so knotted up and depressing. I'm super uptight. The only thing getting me through this are thoughts of us moving to Santa Barbara.

Any word yet from the U of C?

Kay is really getting raw jaw now—trying to make me into the ultimate bad guy. For heaven's sake now he's implying that Max and I stayed together when we had to go to Tecopa. He's so sick! I've got to contain myself before I hurt that man with angry words. He even looks like a rat—all nervous and gnawing.

I'm pretty much able to scope everyone's scene out. I see how Fulgoni plays off of Kay when he trips over himself, and which Max reacts to. They both take the bait. And then Dino comes back in as the knight in shining armor. (Tho' Judy thinks he looks more like a character from the

Dick Tracy comics.) Dino is also really into bringing out the "N" words and Charlie's "Nazi" junk. What on Earth has this to do with me!? I think it's just to anger the black juror and the judge who I guess is Jewish. God, honey—the vibes in this courtroom are as vile as can be. See, this is why I haven't written. This is what you're missin'. Glad you don't have to see what it's doin' to me.

It goes without saying I wish you were here! It won't be long...

Man—I'm all Mansoned out. Can't you see?

I miss you honey—Your girl—Leslie-Lou

What was I doing so far away from her when she needed me? Why was I just as afraid of not giving her space as I was about losing her when I had to let go? There was nothing predictable about being in love in such circumstances.

I certainly wasn't the least bit afraid of what the school board might do if I skipped town and ran straight back to LA a couple of months early. I asked fellow teachers Greg and Dave what they thought VP Peck and Principal Budd might do. The consensus was that they would probably celebrate by getting drunk and then calling Customs.

The last Friday in May, there were piles of mail waiting for me when I got back to my mom's after teaching school. None were from Leslie. Under a stack of bank statements and a postcard Tricia sent from her vacation in Berkeley, there were two letters from the University of California, Santa Barbara. One was from Dr. G.I. Brown, and the other was from the dean of the Graduate School of Education. I opened the one from George first.

His letter said he was pleased to offer me admission into the master of arts with a view to entering the PhD program beginning with the New Year. The dean's letter further informed me that I had been granted a waiver of tuition and out-of-state fees, plus awarded a half-decent stipend for instructing undergrad candidates in pursuit of their California state teacher's credentials.

Registration was to begin September 18th. I was ecstatic! Felt inside the same way it feels when you let go of the javelin and watch as it catches an upward draft. The nose rises up at exactly the right space and time to make a great distance seem relatively effortless. A rare treat.

Unsurprisingly, I was excited to tell Leslie the news so we could update our plans ASAP. Maybe she was right about things coming together. I called Judy Frutig's place right away. It was mid-afternoon in LA, but there was no answer. I called Andy Higgins at the U of T and told him about UCSB and what my immediate plans were.

When I got home, I tried calling Leslie again. This time Judy picked up. She said she didn't know where Leslie was but expected her home any minute. I said I'd ring again later and to please tell her I called. When Leslie called me back hours later, she was no less excited than I was.

She said, "Things are finally going our way! Didn't I tell you?"

* * *

With less than a month to go before leaving to rejoin her in California, I found myself doing less and less preparation for classes and spending more time readying myself for what lay ahead later that fall. In particular, I read all the F.S. Perls I could find in the campus bookroom. I ordered Roberto Assagioli's *Psychosynthesis* techniques for the "imaginative evocation of interpersonal relationships." When it came into Britnell's Book Store, I took it home and read it all in one go.

No matter whatever else I used for distractions, at least I was obsessing less about what Leslie might be up to.

On Wednesday, June 14th, I was eager to hear how Max Keith's closing argument to the jury had gone. He said the evidence showed Leslie's ordinary thought processes had been profoundly disordered by the combined effects of acute domination by Manson and the prolonged use of psychedelic drugs among his cult. Furthermore, Max wasn't asking the jury to acquit Leslie of any wrongdoing.

According to the law on diminished capacity, the appropriate charge in this case, he conceded, would be manslaughter, not first-degree murder.

On the contrary, prosecutors Stephen Kay and Dino Fulgoni argued that Leslie knew what she was doing and willfully took part in what she knew was going to happen. They offered the same tired and predictable slogans, saying a verdict of any lesser degree than first-degree murder would be "a travesty of justice."

In the *Los Angeles Times* article titled "Jurors Debate Fate of Manson Follower: Leslie Van Houten's Third Trial Focuses on Mental Capacity," dated June 23, 1978, Bill Farr quoted Judge Ringer's final instructions to the jury before their deliberations.

"If you find that the defendant's mental capacity was diminished to the extent that you have a reasonable doubt whether she did, maturely and meaningfully, premeditate, deliberate, and reflect upon the gravity of the contemplated act or form the intent to kill, you cannot find her guilty of murder in the first degree."

Manslaughter, the verdict asked for by the defense, was explained as "an unlawful killing without malice aforethought."

Furthermore, Judge Ringer informed the jury that second-degree murder is defined as "the killing of a human being with malice aforethought, but where the evidence is insufficient to establish deliberation and premeditation."

Reading this in the *Times* made me think back to what Leslie said about the judge trying her case instead of a jury.

One still had to wonder whether a jury of everyday people would be up to the task. The justice system charged them with deciding whether the accused was capable of knowing that society would consider the acts she engaged in to be both *morally* and *legally* wrong at the time.

To my way of thinking, all Leslie could have known at the time was what Manson had deluded her and others into believing. Indoctrination wasn't free will after all.

21

HEAVEN CAN WAIT

My last ever week of teaching high school began with my submission of grades and ended with student complaints about final marks. And what a joke that was. I was already as gone as the wind. I skipped all the stifling staff meetings, tired speeches, and phony end-of-year celebrations. Instead, I opted out by counting the stores of textbooks returned to my classroom instead. One hundred and forty *Othello*s and that sort of thing.

By Wednesday, I was feeling bored stiff and rebellious. I left school early on Thursday and skipped out on Friday completely. Instead, I rode my brother Mike's Ducati downtown to the university and sat in on a summer session at Innis College. I stayed to see Jean Renoir's *La Grande Illusion*.

I wanted time itself to pick up its petty pace, so I stayed up the whole night and slept on the plane the next day on my way to Los Angeles. I recorded dreaming my escape from von Rauffenstein's fortress just before waking. *Just in time to return my seat back to its upright position...*

* * *

Air Canada flight no. 791 arrived July 1st, 1978 at LAX at noon on the button. The plane got in ten minutes early, and Leslie was ten minutes late. Perfect timing, just as predicted. We had no delays other than a quick stop north of Ventura for fuel, oranges, and coffee.

Two hours later, we checked into the Holiday Inn in Goleta again, unpacked, and backtracked to have dinner at the Head of the Wolf on State Street in downtown Santa Barbara.

"Even onions taste better on this side of the fence," Leslie said, splitting her Mexican salad with me.

The rest of the evening, we walked around downtown, stopping to look in on a series of interesting, one-of-a-kind stores and bookshops. My favorite was a place called The Earthling.

Before the evening was out, we drifted down by the pier snacking on shrimp dipped in beer and sea salt. After a quick dip in the pool and a shower, we moved the bed in our room to give us a clear view of the mountains.

First thing in the morning, we headed straight to Isla Vista to look at two places advertised as available for a short-term rental. It had been Leslie's idea all along that we temporarily set ourselves up close to the campus. That way, we'd save ourselves time looking around town at longer-term options.

It didn't take long for us to settle on a first-floor, one-bedroom apartment at 895 Camino Del Sur. We handed Mr. Bob Emery, the landlord, a check for four hundred and ten dollars. That would carry us through to September 15th, when Mr.

Emery's regular tenants returned for the school year. By then, we imagined we would find a more suitable space to settle into.

With that business out of the way, we drove up the San Marcos Pass to have a late afternoon snack and beer at the Cold Spring Tavern. Judging from the Arizona and Alabama license plates on so many cars and trailers parked outside, we weren't the only tourists in town.

Besides there being a family of four quietly saying grace in the corner, the only other thing I can recall about the place was something Leslie said just as we were leaving: "Look, honey. See? I have a purse now. Did I show you? It's been such a long time, I still can't recall all the things I need to put in it."

There were so many things about Leslie I still took for granted.

In no real hurry to head back to LA right away, we parked a few miles away on a dusty old Stagecoach Road that led to the site of the Charlotte Lotte Lehmann ruins. "Lotte" Lehmann was a German diva of the Vienna Court Opera who emigrated to the US in the thirties. She fell in love with the magnificent views from her mountain lodge. With the Pacific Ocean below on one side and the San Rafael Mountain Range and valleys on the other.

Unfortunately, she only had a month to enjoy her exurban retreat; a forest fire burned it to the ground. Lotte Lehmann barely escaped as the blaze swept through the mountainside.

We stayed up on that ridge overlooking Santa Barbara, until it grew dark enough for the city lights below to take on the sparkle of lighted pearls laced together by the side of the ocean. Seated in the MGB, I put the top up and started the engine to warm the cockpit. With her head resting on my shoulder, we drove back along Ridge Road to catch the 101 south to LA.

We arrived back at Judy's well after two in the morning. She was still up entertaining a date she had over. A shy-looking guy whom Judy introduced as a photojournalist. Les and I had a couple of polite sips of wine from the same glass and excused ourselves to be alone in her room.

We slept in Monday morning until Leslie's brother David came over with coffee and donuts. He and I had a date to go check out a few bikes at an Italian motorcycle shop in Glendale. I was hoping to test-ride a couple of new café racers that day. When we got to the shop, we discovered it was closed for the Fourth of July weekend. I planned to come back on Wednesday when they were sure to be open.

That evening, Les and I went out to Westwood to see Warren Beatty's new picture *Heaven Can Wait*. A decent retelling of the forties' classic *Here Comes Mr. Jordan*. Afterward, we went for pizza and beer. I can still vividly recall walking right past Liza Minnelli and some guy she was seated with in some upscale restaurant window.

"If she only knew who I am, how do you think she might have reacted?"

"She'd probably call the cops for protection," I said. "We're lucky it's her and not Clint Eastwood and Steve McQueen armed to the teeth."

Come to think of it, other than outside the courthouse, I can't recall anyone recognizing Leslie in public when we were together. Neighbors at both Linda's and Judy's knew her for who she actually was. The pretty young woman in the apartment next door. Not the counterfeit image of an evil monster that some vested interests were so single-minded to go on perpetuating.

* * *

The Fourth of July, Independence Day, 1978. How ironic. The average annual cost of depriving someone like Leslie her liberty in prison was equivalent to what out-of-state residents paid for the best state college tuition.

Leslie and I had been invited to spend the day at a barbecue picnic in Monrovia, complete with a local fireworks display put on that evening by friends and neighbors of David and Shannon Van Houten. It was late when the modest but earnest fireworks ended.

Les and I decided to spend the night back in Monterey Park at Jane's instead of Judy's. Jane was spending the night at Georgie's, so we had the place all to ourselves. Our plan the next day was to stop by the condo again and pack up some more things for our upcoming move to the outskirts of Santa Barbara.

Leslie suggested we hurry to bed once we got there. We had other things planned for tomorrow, including test-riding Ducatis and Moto Guzzis in Glendale. So, we headed upstairs straight away. Somewhere nearby, someone was still setting off fireworks.

I'd already turned out all the lights. To me, it always seemed better that way—closer somehow. Leslie pulled her top up over her head, tossed it toward the wicker chair, and missed. When she slipped in between the sheets beside me, I heard the crackle and felt the spark when we made contact.

"Have I told you yet just how much I've missed you all these months?" Leslie asked.

"Have you really? Care to prove it?"

Laughing, she said, "You always say that."

Leaning back to take a close look into her eyes, I felt, even then, like a drowning man released from the depths at the last possible moment. "You know I love you, my jealous heart," she said, in a somewhat serious tone.

"It's not that I don't want to believe it; it just feels like that's asking too much. The truth is, I love you more than I ever expected I would when we started. I never imagined anyone could make me feel as connected as you do. I don't deserve it."

"Yes, you do. But why all the senseless, jealous episodes, Peter? You have no reason to feel insecure. I've never done anything I'd be ashamed to tell you. Yet you try and shame me for something you made up on your own."

"When you say it like that, it bites right to the heart of the matter, doesn't it?" I admitted. "I hear my old man's raging voice in my head, saying things directed at making you feel guilty about something you never did. I'm insane."

"That's another kind of violence. Women do it too. We don't need to play games with each other. At least try not to get so lost in it. There needs to be deeper understanding, honey. It's not going to work if you threaten me with leaving on account of some fantasy scenario you come up with."

"Each time I imagine you're with someone else, I feel I'm losing you. Like an angry child, I pretend I'm not coming back for more abuse. When it's me that's doing the abusing. Once I do stop to think: What if I did turn and walk away from you? I'm too scared to move."

"Despite all of the head games and insecurity," Leslie said, "we're a very stable scene, you and me. It does my heart good to believe this can last if we want it to. Right here, right now, what I'm feeling is hard to describe."

That night, at that moment, I confess I felt it too. I wanted those feelings to last a lifetime—raised as they were with the "scent of shadows and sighs."

The next morning, on the 5th of July 1978, I recorded a nightmare in my journal describing an airplane ride where the pilot jumped out of the plane and carried me with her. We parachuted safely to land.

Mysteriously, I wasn't the least bit startled or bothered to notice that another woman was left strapped in the plane alone, soaring straight up to the vanishing point. While the pilot and I watched from the ground, the plane crash-landed in an open field of pink and blue clover.

The woman inside the wreckage had changed into somebody else. She didn't appear the least alarmed by the fire in the cockpit. She simply climbed out, dusted herself off, and skipped away over and out of sight. When I turned around, both women had vanished.

This was going to be big day for me and Leslie. My original plan was to make a return visit to the motorcycle shop in Glendale first, so we could test-drive one or two Italian-bred café racers. After that, make a choice, settle on a price, and buy one.

If all went according to plan, we'd spend the afternoon touring LA beaches and canyons in outfits of denim and leather.

"I can see you're excited," Leslie giggled. "Is it me or on account of something else?"

"Nothin' compares with you, my darling young one."

"Care to prove it?" she asked, and I laughed out of a puzzling nervous exhaustion. It wasn't as though I'd never bought a motorcycle before.

Leslie got dressed in a bright summer print dress. I told her if we brought the bike home later that day, she'd have to change into something sturdier. I zipped up the back of her dress, wrapped both arms around her, and besieged the bridge of her shoulders with kisses. Leslie said she'd make us tea and toast while I shaved.

When I was done washing up and came out to the patio, she was casually smoking a cigarette and reading the paper. I rolled a joint and smoked it alone. I could tell she had other things on her mind besides motorcycles.

Once we got to the shop and parked the MGB, Leslie put her hand on my forearm and told me, "We don't need a lot of things, Peter. You know that. Do we really need this machine more than we need to save for something more lasting?"

"One step at a time."

They had only one Ducati 900 Super Sport on the floor, but it was priced way out of our league. However, there were at least ten new and used Guzzis all spiffed up and polished.

Leslie asked the salesman if she could use the telephone. Meanwhile, I climbed on a fire-engine red V2 Moto Guzzi Le Mans. It was a tad exotic—with a five-speed shaft drive and some relatively new appliance they called "integral braking." I couldn't wait to turn her on and twist open the throttle.

"Get off the phone Leslie, will ya?" I called out impatiently.

It was routine during the jury's deliberations for Leslie to check in every couple of hours. She'd usually call either Max or Dante, her bondsman. Since she was still out of reach on the phone, I guessed she might be talking to her mother.

The salesman kept smiling and helped me to push the bike out to the curb where I could start her. I was just about to switch on the engine when, looking ashen and pale, Leslie came walking toward us.

"We gotta go" was all she needed to say. I knew what this meant. The verdict was finally decided.

The jury informed the judge they had reached a unanimous decision. Now, the court was waiting on Leslie and Max to show up.

Max was en route back from his ranch in Paso Robles, which is two hundred miles north of Los Angeles. Depending on traffic, it would take him hours to get into Superior Court for the County of Los Angeles.

Leslie and I arrived at the courthouse before him. When Max arrived, we made our way past the swarm of reporters beginning to buzz around the corridor in front of Judge Ringer's court.

Max ushered Les and me into a conference room off to one side of the courtroom. For almost an hour, or so it seemed, Leslie and I held hands while bailiffs set the stage next door. When the time came for Leslie to be led into the courtroom, I gave her one last kiss for good luck. Then, I walked to a spot among the gallery of friends and reporters.

I was certain there were people I knew all around me, but Les was the only point on which I affixed any awareness.

After all the preliminary rituals had been dispensed with, the jury foreman read out the verdict: "We the jury, in the above-entitled action, find the defendant, Leslie Van Houten, guilty of murder. And we further find it to be murder in the first degree."

Leslie flinched a split-second and gripped the arms of her chair. There were some gasps in the courtroom. Someone somewhere was crying. There may even have been some shouting like you see in the movies. I stood still. Turning my head around, I searched for Jane but didn't notice her right away. Leslie turned around quickly, then looked straight ahead once again. Stoic as ever.

During that slenderest glimpse, I thought I could see a startled look in her eyes. Her lips were parted, and her cheeks were pale.

After hearing the verdict, the judge announced he was revoking Leslie's bond. According to protocol, he remanded her into the custody of the sheriff until formal sentencing, which he immediately scheduled for July 21st.

Sheriff's deputies put Leslie in handcuffs and led her away out of the courtroom. The door closed. The walls of the courtroom pinched inward. The air in my lungs left me feeling like a pocket pulled inside out. I was among the last to leave the room, except for the hurried bailiffs who led me and some journalists out.

Outside, in the hard marble hallway, I passed goodfellas Stephen Kay and Dino Fulgoni in the corridor outside the courtroom. I heard Kay tell his colleague, "The battle is over. We won."

All I could muster was a pathetic taunt of no consequence. First, admitting to myself how easy it is to be brave from a distance, I said, "It's just a game to you, Mr. Kay, isn't it?"

"Huh?" was his unphased response.

He started walking away and then turned around and squeezed out a familiar cliché, "No," he said with a shrug. "It's the law."

So much for the philosophical banality and tyranny of modern conservatism, I thought.

Then, for the first time, I became aware of Jane and the rest of the family and friends who had gathered away from the gaggles and chaos of reporters as best they could. The next thing I recalled I was making my way outside. The fresh tears on my cheek dried to a crust in the hot glare of desert sunlight.

* * *

District Attorney John Van de Kamp told the press he felt this verdict vindicated him for the decision to prosecute Leslie a third time on three counts of first-degree murder. One each for Leno and Rosemary LaBianca, plus an additional count of conspiracy to commit murder—which included the five victims at 10050 Cielo Drive.

Even though that carnage was something Leslie didn't know about until the day after it happened. The DA needed the conspiracy charge to justify his claims about premeditation. It's all about score columns with them, in my view. "Justice" be cursed. It's mostly a slogan.

Prosecutors Stephen Kay and Dino Fulgoni upheld that Leslie's involvement in these terrible crimes was the result of malice aforethought on her part. Even though she didn't actually kill anyone herself, she was found guilty of aiding and abetting a crime where co-conspirators murdered their victims.

The DA's office was like a Russian chess team. They'd stay up nights hoping they'd get away with changing the charge to felony murder. On the bogus claim of it having been committed in the act of a robbery. When, indeed, all that they took—aside from Manson running off with Rosemary's purse and credit cards and with Leno's wallet and cash—were a pair of shorts and a small bag of coins.

Clearly, robbery *was not* a motive. "The truth, the whole truth, and nothing but" be damned.

What a stroke of immoral genius Van de Kamp and his den of devotees came up with. Whereby, by tying the murder indictment to include felony robbery, meant that the jury could be directed to disregard Leslie's state of mind at the time.

This despite the fact that *anyone's* actual state of mind at the time of the crime is exactly what distinguishes first- and second-degree murder from manslaughter. That's the difference between a life sentence with, or without, the possibility of ever being paroled.

Part of this tragic irony is that, in the first trial in 1970–71, deputy DAs Vincent Bugliosi and Stephen Kay insisted, "there was no evidence of ransacking or robbery."

After Kay lost the second trial to a hung jury, Van de Kamp installed Fulgoni to challenge the psychiatric testimony presented in the third trial. Asking the jury to "follow the law instead of emotions."

It occurred to me that we talk about laws, ideas, and emotions as if they were separate. Indeed, we can talk about them abstractly for the sake of analysis. But, in reality, they occur together. And that's the whole point of justice, isn't it? To get to the truth, the whole truth, and nothing but.

After the verdict was read, Jury Foreman John L. Crigler told the press that he and his fellow jurors "felt Ms. Van Houten had suffered some diminished capacity. But we just couldn't determine that it was diminished to the extent that was required to relieve her of responsibility for what she had done." I couldn't help wondering why no one bothered to ask Mr. Crigler for his understanding of the phrase, *beyond a reasonable doubt*.

I spent the next days and weeks camped out at Jane Van Houten's house. David and Betsy were also there with me off and on much of the time. Linda Grippi stopped by the most. Max Keith was looking the worst for wear I would say. Thankfully, Judy Frutig was there to look after him.

For me, the overall mood was one of shock. Numb disbelief and a feeling of absolute emptiness. As always, the person who held it together best was Leslie's mom—with the likely exception of Leslie herself.

First thing in the morning the day after the verdict, Jane and I went to see Leslie at Sybil Brand. We wished we'd seen the last of that place already.

This was the worst visit that I can remember. I acted a coward. Pacing the visitors' room, glaring at Leslie. I wasn't the poised, compassionate man I hoped I would be at this moment.

When the time came to stand tall, I shrank into ugliness. I was childish. Crazed with utter senselessness. Leslie was next to crying. I could hear devils inside my head chattering behind every wall. To make matters worse, I behaved horribly in front of her mother. I said some things I'm sure must have been terribly hurtful, stupid, and small.

"Maybe if you hadn't had Max parade your dates as 'character witnesses' during the trial, he may not have turned off the jury."

If words of comfort skillfully chosen were summoned for, I did far worse than miss the call to chivalry. Shame has mercifully scoured the surface of those recollections.

"Please don't pick on Max like that," Jane softly asked.

"He is working to get Paul Fitzgerald, another lawyer, to help him with further motions from now on," Leslie added.

"Max looks exhausted," I said.

"We may still have some options. The first step will be to ask the judge for a delay in the sentencing. Maybe reach a deal to be given the date of my expected release.

"What? You don't think there's a chance? I know it still sounds like a long shot."

Before I could say what I'd thought about long shots, like a matador masterfully cutting short a bull's charge, Jane tapped my shoulder to signal it was time to wrap up and move on. I told Leslie I'd be back the next day.

Jane and I sat in the car in the parking lot. Speaking with my chin pressed down against my medallion gave my voice a faint echo. "I'm sorry, Jane. I behaved despicably."

"I know you are, honey. You're feeling lost. It's painful for both of you, I know."

When Leslie called a few days after that, she told me, "It's hard to say this to you, Peter, but I've made the decision... So, here goes. I think it would be too hard for me to see you right now. That's all. I hope you can accept this without going into any full-blown explanations."

"At least you might try," I whispered sheepishly.

"Okay. Maybe I'll write more when I'm feeling better. You know, Peter, it's important to me that you are free. You have a way of locking yourself up just like I am. I haven't the choices you have anymore."

"What are you saying?" I asked, feeling dazed and confused.

"I don't want you to ever *not* do something you wanted to do. Not because of me, or some thought of me getting in the way. You know what I'm saying. I don't want you to wait for me any longer."

Every word she delivered felt like a body blow. Therefore, I tightened my gut. All I could think to say was, "I can't think of anything to say."

She said, "It's just super-important that you understand the way things are different now. Some things we wished for will never be. Okay? There's no use pretending. I want you to be free. It's important."

"That wasn't the plan, Leslie. If not for you, I wouldn't be here. Living in one of the most splendid garden spots in North America, going to a world-class university."

"It's still a 'plan,' Peter. Your plan. There's no role in it for me anymore. That was the *dream*. The plan would have come later. Now, we must make other plans."

I was crushed.

"I'm tryin' to explain as best...," Leslie restarted.

"What's to explain?" I spoke. "It's clear to me." Clearly, it wasn't. Leslie repeated her stance.

"I'm not very good at this, but I have to put down the phone now. I think by now it is obvious things *aren't* the same, nor will they ever be. You need to find somebody else."

"Okay then," I said. I could see there was no choice but to respect her decision.

Once I had time to think things over, I felt she was letting me off for bad behavior, for my own good as much as her own. If I were ever to stand a chance of remaining a close friend and correspondent, I'd have to prove to her and myself that I really wanted to accept her new terms.

22

UCSB OR NOT TO BE

The Moto Guzzi Le Mans was now out of the question. But Leslie's MGB still had to go on the block. It was burning a quart of oil with every fill-up. So, David Van Houten and I prowled around several car auctions that week—hoping to trade in the MG for something modestly better.

I swapped my 1973 MGB, plus some cash, for a mocha-brown 1977 Fiat 124 Spider. Disc brakes on all fours. What she lacked in appearance and horsepower, she made up for in lightweight control. My kind of go-cart. If I'd gotten the bike as planned, this car would have been our family car.

David was helping me wax the Fiat in the laneway in the back of his mom's house. I was just starting to fasten my new blue and gold California license plates (no. 442-VGC) to the bumper when I spotted Judy Frutig's 240-Z parked at the end of the alley. It looked to me like she had somebody with her, but I couldn't make out who it was.

"She here for you?" I asked David, loud enough so that Judy could hear me.

"No," Judy said. "It's you I wanted to talk to, Peter. If you don't mind?"

Davy pondered his cue, dried his hands off on his jeans, and went through the garage and inside the house.

"I'm not sure you fully appreciate what a *private* person Jane is," Judy announced. "As a friend of the family, Glen asked me to remind you of this in case you missed it. She's been through plenty and needs this time to herself. And given the change in circumstances with Leslie, there's no need for you to be here any longer."

"This is a message from who exactly, Judy? You or Glen? No matter. What you say about Jane is true enough. She's asked me to stay until I've found a new place to stay in Santa Barbara.

"But you're just telling me what I already know. Is that in case I missed it?"

"It's not always about you, Peter. It's what's best for Jane and Leslie that we should be talking about. Don't you have somewhere else to go?" I didn't say it was.

"What's it to you where or when I'm going? And why are you and Glen always so concerned with my whereabouts?"

I'd already told Jane I planned to leave that week to find a place to live for the fall and winter semesters.

The next day, I drove to Laguna Nigel to visit with Michael and Jane Malone. I wanted them to see my new car. We left the Spider parked in the driveway and took their white Mercedes saloon-class sedan to Tijuana for lunch.

After another quick stop on the Baja for something, we continued as far south as the Rosarito Beach Hotel. Just like we'd planned once before as a foursome. Inscribed over the entranceway were painted these words: *Poresta Puerta Pasan Las Mujeres Mas Hermosas Del Mundo.* Which Michael translated as *Through These Doors Have Passed the Most Beautiful Women of the World.*

We talked about Leslie the whole way and back. Rosarito didn't know all it was missing. And thinking about what Leslie might be going through was really breaking my heart.

A couple of days later, Martin Bijaux called again, checking in. I can't honestly say that I'd missed him. And he was a good companion to take with me to cancel the interim rental Leslie and I had left for the apartment on Camino Del Sur.

What I needed now was a dark cabin in a thorn brush somewhere to match my ragged disposition.

Looking for the student housing office on campus, we passed by Phelps Hall. As luck would have it, we ran into Professor Mark Phillips straight away. His office door was wide open.

"Doctor Phillips, I presume," I said, leaning my body inside without knocking.

"Peter Chiaramonte! Good to see you."

"It's good to see you too, professor. Mark, I'd like to introduce my friend Martin."

"Martin, a pleasure. Please come in and sit down.

"I must say I was sorry to hear the news about Leslie. Tell me, how is she holding up?"

I answered quickly, hoping we might change the subject. "We only stopped by for a moment. I'm looking for somewhere to live. We were just searching for the housing office—"

"There's not much time left. Most places are already taken." Then he sat up straight from his casual slump and added, "As a matter of fact, it just so happens my current housemate is returning to Germany at the end of the month.

"I'll be looking for someone to take over his end of the house. I'll be home in an hour if you'd care to see it? It's a pretty big ranch house built on a cliff overlooking the ocean."

Listening to this, I giggled nervously, thinking he might be making the part about the ocean view up. Then I could see he was serious.

Mark drew us a map when I asked for directions.

Martin and I left straight away. We drove south on Las Palmas Drive through one of the wealthiest suburbs in all of southern California—the incorporated exurbia of Santa Barbara known as Hope Ranch. Even in those days, there wasn't a home priced below millions of dollars.

We passed out of the eastern gates and into the more reasonably bourgeois neighborhoods off Cliff Drive. Mark's house was just off Yankee Farm Road at the cul-de-sac of Braemar Drive. The shelf of land on which it stood was hundreds of feet above Hendry's Beach, with a clear view of the ocean.

"Leslie should see this," I kept repeating to myself.

There was an overgrown vegetable garden beside the garage that needed attention. Facing north, you could see mountains climbing above Rattlesnake Canyon. Looking the other way around—about an eighth of a mile from the shoreline—there appeared to be four or five surfers in wet suits straddling their boards.

Only one was riding a rather tame wave while some others were just paddling out. Or else floating in blue-green swells and waiting their turn for the big one.

"What do you think?" I turned to Martin and asked. Assuming he was in the same state of awe that I was.

"What do I think? I think it's ironic. In some bloody strange way, you've stumbled into a Xanadu, you lucky sod."

"Do you think Leslie would like it?" I asked, ever hopeful. Martin said nothing but shrugged.

Just then, Mark turned into the long narrow driveway. Before he had time to come to a complete stop and turn off the engine, I asked him, "When can I move in all of my stuff?"

* * *

On Friday, July 21st, 1978, Leslie appeared in court with her lawyers. Judge Ringer granted her lawyers' request for a three-week delay in the sentencing. That way, the defense would have time to prepare the new series of motions that Leslie had spoken about.

The first motion would ask the judge to grant Leslie a new trial and/or grant a reduction in charges. To our way of thinking, this only seemed fair. Given the incessant levels of reasonable doubt.

If Judge Ringer were to agree to such a reduction, a further motion would ask that Leslie be granted immediate release on probation. That didn't just seem like wishful thinking/black magic either. It was fair to say we still felt there was reason to believe in the possibility.

* * *

Friday, August 11th—nine years after the crime for which she originally stood convicted—Leslie Van Houten was sentenced to two life terms for the August 10th, 1969 murder of Leno and Rosemary LaBianca. Plus, an additional life term for conspiring to murder, including those killed at 10050 Cielo Drive the night before.

As I keep repeating: The Tate-Polanski residence was somewhere she never was and something she didn't know the first thing about until after it happened. The law always seemed a curious contraption to someone as naïve as I was.

During my next visit with Leslie, I could see despite all that had happened that she remained hopeful in spite of the odds. We were sure she'd be at least given a firm date for her release in as little as six to nine months. Even I could wait that much longer.

"I can't seem to sleep much," she said. "I'm too tired to read or write either. Please don't expect too many letters from me right away. I'm feeling pretty beat up. Maybe I'll write more when I'm feeling better.

Leslie repeated her stance. "I'm not very good at this, but it's inevitable so I want to do it now and get it over with. I think by now it's obvious things *aren't* the same, nor will they ever be."

"Whatever you say, Leslie." I stood up but continued to talk on the headset. "If you want it this way, then that's the way it must be. You say when it's okay for me to come see you."

"Okay then," she said.

Leslie put down her headset, stood up, turned around, and was taken away to her cell. Weeks later, she was taken under armed guard back to the California Institution for Women at Frontera. Which made it sound more like a college campus than what it was.

AFTERMATH

Once I arrived at Mark Phillip's house overlooking the Pacific beaches, there was more than one sense in which my situation appeared to get better in proportion to how Leslie's grew worse. Less than a week later—on the 23rd of August, for her twenty-ninth birthday—I sent Leslie a card with a long letter enclosed.

On September 7th, I paid my first month's rent. I went out and bought paint for my bedroom, hallways, and bathroom—mostly Mediterranean white—with pastel blues and green trim.

I lay awake on the couch the whole first night while the paint dried, listening to ocean waves crashing. The next morning, I felt more at home when the first mail addressed to my new address arrived in the mailbox.

The letter was from Leslie Van Houten, CIW 13378, 16756 Chino-Corona Road, Psychiatric Treatment Unit 67, Frontera.

My dearest Peter—

It's very late at night. I can't seem to sleep. My legs have recovered a bit from a week of throwing pots around—lifting heavy pans of excess food and running clean dishes to their proper locations. It's a job that eats up a large part of the day. Not what you would call intellectually stimulating.

It was good to hear from you and even better to hear you're as anxious as I am to get started with school. I know it will make you feel better once you find peace and order in your life again. You couldn't be living in a more beautiful place or going to a better university. It's really fine there. I wish I could be there to join you.

I'm holding up OK. Thanks. It's hard. But slowly I'm creating a mellow scene for myself. I'm spending a lot of my time alone. I would rather be alone than get into the jail talk—all the games—and so on and so forth. Old faces I can't relate to. It's rough writing because I must probe my own thoughts, rather than just entertain them. You know what I'm talking about. It's no journey's end and I mean it.

I'm anxious to start receiving the information from Antioch College. I think I'll start with English literature. Then move into film studies from there. What do you think? We can discuss it when you visit. It shouldn't be much longer before your forms are approved. Please give my "hello's" to your friends and all the wild horses tied to the fences...

Love—Leslie

When she telephoned the house the next weekend, she said, "Your report came in and it's on the superintendent's desk. I'll call you when I hear their determination, which should be some-time later this week. I sure hope so.

"I have no one to talk to. Sometimes I miss a good conversation more than I miss eating good food."

The annual Confluent Education Retreat was held that fall in a venue out by the edge of the Devereux Lagoon at the University of California facility known as Cliff House. This small conference center was built on a fine point of land that overlooked the spectacular view of the Channel Islands.

Inside at one end of the hall, there was a wood fireplace made of fieldstone. At the opposite end, the kitchen was all laid out for the potluck. I brought two bottles of wine, two loaves of fresh bread, and four jars of white sturgeon caviar. I'd picked up the wine and caviar that same afternoon from my new neighbor's Portuguese cook.

I was the last to arrive. A few minutes late and probably stoned when I got there. (That's why I kept a bottle of Scope in the glove box.) George and Stew were just coming to the end of their introductory remarks when I was putting the wine in the freezer. I could hear individual members of the new cohort introducing him or herself. I was last to say who I was, where I was from, and what led me to Santa Barbara. I didn't exactly make up the last part, only I left out any reference to Leslie.

Later on in the evening, I found myself working in either one-on-one or slightly larger ensembles of colleagues, mostly from Europe. (Only half the class that year was from the United States.) I was especially drawn to working with a trio of fast friends I met that were from Norway—Otto, Annamarit, and a beautiful woman named Audhild Brændsrød.

I don't know what I was trying to prove by taking her with me to Laguna Nigel and Rosarito. But that's what began to happen on a regular basis.

My first semester in graduate school involved basic training in Gestalt therapy, psychosynthesis, body-mind conditioning, and dreamwork. It was kind of a cult, come to think of it. I also read antecedent philosophy and existential psychology on my own. In addition to insightfully encouraging me with my studies, my professor and housemate, Mark, was an excellent stickball player. He grew up in New York after all.

* * *

During the aftermath of what had happened with Leslie, Stewart Shapiro got involved with my personal affairs. He and I had a meeting with George and Mark, after which George recommended—and Stew insisted—that I undergo special counseling with a Jungian psychiatrist, Samuel Correnti. Dr. C. was a colleague of theirs who worked in private practice.

Since Stew wanted to make this a condition of my being admitted into doctoral studies, I agreed to see Correnti twice a week for an hour.

When Leslie called me over the phone, I asked how her own psyche work was going.

"It's been kinda rough in here lately.

"Today was a real bummer. We had our weekly group. All that means is that everyone sits in a room and complains. It's stifling. Everyone takes advantage of the fact that if anyone leaves before it's over, they get a write-up. So childish. So boring. Nothing positive. Only gutter talk.

"I told you I'm seeing the Malones when they visit. It helps to have friends on the outside."

"Isn't there anyone inside you can count on for friendship?"

"Only some. I need to protect myself from all the ugliness inside of this place, that's for sure. It beats down on your soul. See, in here, even the *word* 'positive' is something you never hear used.

"I need to protect myself from that sort of thing. I need to have my guard up to maintain my own sense of who I am as a person."

What could I say? Nothing. I hoped she'd say more without prompting.

"I'm sorry I haven't responded much to your letters. I feel there's a lot I want to say, but it's hard to write about nothing but sadness. It will be better when you visit me here in Frontera. Then we can talk and at least search into each other's eyes.

"This evening I turned on the radio to listen to whatever was on. It was 'Here Comes the Sun'—I certainly hope so.

"I know you must be wondering where the visiting forms are at. Well, they are stuck at the Bureau of Identification. I think it's taken longer than we expected on account of your being Canadian."

"Well, that's the first time I've ever felt sorry for being Canadian," I confessed.

"By the end of the week, I'll follow up to see what the hang up is. It's a drag, I know.

"Looks like my time's up. Please take good care of yourself and write when you can. Even if I don't write you back right away. Let that be okay, okay? I hope that you understand."

* * *

Several weeks passed without any word from Leslie. I thought she had promised to call me on November 27th, but for some reason, that call never happened. Although, that same afternoon, I received the following letter from Kathleen M. Anderson, the superintendent at CIW in Frontera.

CALIFORNIA INSTITUTION FOR WOMEN
16756 CHINO-CORONA ROAD, FRONTERA,
CALIFORNIA 91720

November 24, 1978

Dear Mr. Chiaramonte:
Thank you for your interest and letter of inquiry, dated 11-18-78, in which you ask about your visiting privileges status regarding Leslie Van Houten, housed in PTU (W13378).
I approved this request on 11-6-78. The Psychiatric Treatment Unit Program Administrator, Mr. Nelson, informs me that Leslie intended to advise you of this approval before now.

Sincerely yours,
Kathleen M. Anderson, Superintendent

When Leslie called a few days after that, I asked her to please explain the meaning of Anderson's letter.

"Why the delay in my finding this out? I thought this was what we both really wanted?" Then it hit me. I felt the impact before she even let go of all the words.

Though I tried not to dwell on being too broken up over the way things were falling apart. As fate would have it, I had the good fortune of a highly capable psychonaut to help me work through the blind spots.

The next morning, I had my first appointment with Dr. Samuel Correnti at his office.

NO JOURNEY'S END

My first appointment with Dr. Samuel Correnti was at his office on State Street near the mission in Santa Barbara. Dr. C. was a dark-haired, good-looking man I guessed to be in his forties. The first time we met, he wore a brown and black wool and suede sweater.

I remember admiring the way he carried himself, and I noted how bright and bristling with self-confidence he was. Like a tennis pro.

We talked very little about the whole business with Leslie at first, even though that was what I had been thinking about. Instead, we spent most of the first week's sessions discussing my family upbringing and where I grew up. School years in the city; summers on the farm. Moving to the suburbs with all the other reasonably affluent baby boomers in the sixties.

Just before leaving, he asked me to come prepared the next time with a written account of my dreams.

He wasn't precise about how much time would be required for my ongoing "treatment" or for whatever, exactly, he intended. Something about how "a weak ego cannot, by will and faith alone, surmount the profoundest yearning, nor end the deepest sorrows." I found that unexpectedly poetic and pleasing.

At our next meeting later that week, we talked some more about my family history. I rather enjoyed making fun of my horrific father at first. But something happened to change the humor of it. Still in the midst of his preliminary analysis, Dr. C. asked me, "What is the earliest childhood memory that you can recall?"

It took me some time to appreciate just how much each of our lives can be influenced or determined by so few early childhood experiences. The one subject you really need to study is your own experiences during those formidable years.

It dawned on me that whatever the source of my current conflicts with Leslie, my inability to cope at this crucial time may have cost me the love of my life. Then again, some of our friends thought that Les' and my time together was an ill-fated, lost voyage from the start.

"After the trial, there must have been a lot of confusion." Correnti asked me, "Was there something or someone you blamed?"

"No. Well, what I mean is—I acted as though I did. But deep inside, a large part of me knew it wasn't justified. It was easy, somehow, for me to take out, or project, my jealousy and neuroticism onto her."

"Where do you think your jealousy sprang from? Was it entirely unjustified? Was she flirtatious?"

"No. But I felt inferior somehow and tried keeping my eyes closed to what I imagined I'd be doing in her place. Taking advantage of all the attention for no special reason at all. Just because…"

"Because?"

"I'm not sure. Because of the disappointment I felt in the system that engulfed us. For misreading the tide of the times," I shrugged.

"Because I failed, in that trying moment, to endure the hardship of convincing others it's not Leslie Van Houten who is a danger to society.

"Leslie, in a sense, captured my heart as a victim of injustice, not an instigator. I will always believe that, for a time at least, we made each other stronger. I hope so."

* * *

Living in Santa Barbara soon brought about many interests for me to pursue. There were plenty of intellectual challenges, romantic chances, and other distractions to deal with. Besides schoolwork, teaching, training a bit, and soaking in hot tubs—not to mention the hours I spent on the couch in Correnti's office—I met a group of some very good hockey players at the Ice Patch that winter.

That's where I was first introduced to Monte Schulz, son of *Peanuts* cartoonist Charles M. Schulz, the only player in town I thought might be better than I was. Monte and I quickly became friends both on and off the ice. His understated yet innate, competitive spirit reminded me of the late Buck Buchanan.

During that first season playing in California, Monte and I put together a decent "all-star" team I liked to call "The Santa Barbarians." We boasted veterans like Don Swann (another ex-pat from Toronto who worked at Delco), a few former Junior-A players from Flin Flon, Manitoba, and "Boston" Dave Barlow.

When Monte and I played away on the road, the guys in the vans would carry our sticks and equipment—on account of the fact we couldn't fit our bags into Monte's Dino 246 GTS Ferrari.

It was during this time of rising dissimilarity between us that Leslie and I steadily lost touch with each other. She was already redeemed when I met her. Then she steadily outgrew me in the sense that our spirits grew apart.

On February 1st, 1979, the *Los Angeles Times* reported that Leslie Van Houten would have to wait another year before the community release board would reconsider her request for parole. Board Chairperson Ruth Rushen was quoted as saying to Leslie, "We feel we must observe you longer before we can project your parole date."

Despite excellent reports from prison psychologists and prison staff, the board's justification for denying her petition was that: "Society has no defense...in this type of crime, except to isolate the offender."

Another issue Leslie's parole board raised as an objection had to do with the types of men she's been attracted to in the past.

In response to that, Leslie was quoted as saying, "In thinking back, I almost think I had too much going for me. I started dating guys that weren't equal to me. Guys who were into their cars and not their books."

Upon hearing the panel's decision, Stephen Kay remarked out of glee, "Miss Van Houten appeared visibly shaken." And when asked about his personal feelings toward the board's ruling, he added, "This is beyond my wildest dreams. I'm ecstatic! If she gets out by the turn of the century, she'll be lucky."

Even while conceding that Leslie has been a model prisoner, during her entire incarceration, he insisted, "Society is happy she's doing well in prison. That's a good place for her to stay." What a clear-cut incredible creep.

When Leslie called on the phone a few weeks later, I asked her how she felt about the parole board's decision. "Naturally, I'm disappointed," she said, "but I feel good about the overall tone of the hearing.

"Did I tell you that I'll be moving soon? When I do, perhaps you'd like to come visit? The hours are better over in the other visiting room. Let me know, and I'll tell you the hours when I move."

I changed the subject. I didn't want to discuss anything more about visiting her. I doubted either one of us wanted to open old wounds. However rationally or irrationally we might have associated these wounds with one another. Parts of me hoped—and felt anxious about—that Leslie might need and want me in her life as much as I still needed and wanted her.

"I'm doing okay, I suppose," she said. "School was delayed on account of the moving. One cool thing is that I'm taking a philosophy course *and* a psychology course both at the same time. I keep trying to put them together. That's natural, right? I've also started a writing course through correspondence with Antioch College. I'm really excited about that one. It's going to be great.

"In the philosophy class, I'm doing a presentation on behaviorism. Can you point me in the right direction? You know, give me the names of authors and references I can look up."

"Sure, Les, of course. Aside from that..."

"I know what you're going to say. If you want to know the truth: Once in a while, I do get terribly lonely. It's great to see Mama, of course. She always has something nice to say or to ask about you. She really enjoys seeing you when you stay overnight in LA.

"I was happy to hear that you got that part-time job on the UCLA campus that you wanted."

"I don't get the chance to see your mom as often as I'd like to when I'm there. How about you? What else is new?"

"I have to be honest. At times, my spirit sinks very low. I know this sounds stupid and sulky, but in my lowest moments, I wish I *wasn't* so tough and determined. It only adds weight."

I lied and said, "I know what you mean."

"Did I tell you I work in the hospital clinic now? It's a new experience for me. It's nothing too heavy. I doubt I'd ever work for a hospital on the streets. I mean, when I get home. I don't like using the phrase 'on the streets' and I'm trying to break myself of the habit."

"What's it like being back with the main population?" I wondered aloud.

"Pretty awful. The people on this side of the compound are not nearly as kind and flowery as those in the psych unit. Here, they feed off each other like vultures. Pretty 'tough cookies'...as they say. Speaking of which...it's getting crazy right here in the hallway.

I've got to go deal with this now. I'm having a rough time putting my attention to this. Sorry. I really enjoyed reading your letter. Write again when it suits you. And let me know when you feel that you'd like to visit."

* * *

In late 1979, Leslie sent me a brief update on the courses she was taking through Antioch College. There was no real mention of anything personal. I believe the last time we actually spoke was on January 17th, 1980. That was the same day Leslie had her hearing with the state board of prison terms. Once again, they denied her release. It was also my twenty-ninth birthday.

After an afternoon game at the Ice Patch, friends and teammates threw me a surprise party. Even Tricia Woodbridge and Martin Bijaux drove up from LA together with Martin's latest girlfriend. Naturally, I invited them to spend a few nights as my houseguests.

There was this big barbeque with over twenty people. Plus, a memorable six-a-side ball hockey game on my driveway. My side was losing when we ran out of daylight. But it was great to see my hockey buddies having such a good time rapping with friends from UCSB and the confluent program.

Another two solitudes that were destined to meet.

The good ol' boys from Flin Flon got a huge bonfire blazing out in the fire pit we built near the Coulter pines and white fir trees that lined our neighbor's fence. My friends from Amsterdam, Fried and Yvonne, led the gang 'round the inferno in a medley of songs by The Beatles and The Mamas & The Papas. Others were dancing and casting their shadows onto the stones, bushes, tree trunks, and branches.

Inside, a dozen people were drinking cheap wine and talking. Tricia and I wandered off outside together by some rocks near a picnic bench on the cliff's edge.

The planets above were all whirling in orbit, and to me, the ocean looked like a sea of molten iron and lava.

"You know, Peter," Tricia said, "this whole time I've been meaning to ask you if you're still in touch with Leslie Van Houten."

"Not much anymore. Sometimes, I think I've forgotten about her completely. Then, all of a sudden, there she is again in my thoughts. And dreams."

"What does that tell you?"

"Maybe something about how irresistible love can become absolutely impossible at times. But no less irrepressible. Confirmation that nothing ever works out, lawyers are mostly awful, unlawful cutthroats and thieves, and nobody gets me but me. How does that sound for being hard-done-by?" I asked, fumbling for comfort.

I didn't dare mention the guilt I felt for having treated someone I loved so much so badly.

"Peter, I know you must have heard this question a lot, but do you think she'll ever be released from prison?"

"For one thing, there are different roots of the term 'release.' One is 'to redeem,' did you know that?"

"No, professor. I do now," she said.

"'Rehabilitation'…'redemption'—they're all great *words.*"

"Maybe you forgot one, 'retribution.'"

"*Vengeance,* you mean. Rehabilitation can mean clearing someone of suspicion."

"Of course. Such as?"

"To clear someone of suspicion," I finished, preceding a rather long pause while we walked along a path near the cliff's edge.

"This all sounds very sad and abstract," she said, and I kissed her gently for saying that, out of instinct.

"What's so amazing about Leslie is she's never entirely what you would expect. She always has lots more to offer, no matter the subject or what we were planning to do about it.

"Romance never goes unpunished, does it?" I concluded.

It wasn't late yet when we went back inside to the party. I'd already had one or two cups of the magic mushroom tea that Annamarit and Dulcie had brewed with honey and almonds. Everyone, including Trish and myself, had started to get off. It felt to me as if the whole building was charged with an underlying magnetic force.

I saw Tricia's hair turn to fire and her skin looked and felt like some electric-orange silken fabric. Her entire body was aglow, burning a hole in the room. I closed my eyes and the fires continued. I asked her to please play David Bowie's song "Heroes" a second time while I sat on the floor watching the panorama of flames passing in view.

The next thing I recall was Mark calling my name from the kitchen.

Over all the music and chatter, I thought I heard him say there was a collect call from Leslie as he passed the receiver.

"Sounds like a pretty nice party," she said, over all the noise in the background.

"Yes. Leslie! What a wonderful surprise."

There was a quiet break and then the crackle of static. A bad connection?

"It's been a long time, Peter. How are you?"

"I wanted to wish you a 'Happy Birthday.' I'm glad I got through. It's good to hear your voice. Though, maybe I should let you go and have a good time if you're busy..."

"No, wait. I'll ask them to turn down the music," I started to say. Seconds later, our connection was lost completely.

Dead silence at the other end. This wasn't the first time something like this had happened. No reason to panic. I don't know how long I went on waiting for her to call back, but she never did. Not then or ever again.

After hanging the receiver back on its cradle, I stepped outside to have another look 'round at the bonfire. Ostensibly, to make sure we weren't burning the place down to ruins. It seemed to me as if I were staring the wrong way through a pair of trippy binoculars. From the corner of my eye, I caught a flash of firelight reflecting off some shimmering object that lay beside the rocks on the ground.

When I approached it, I saw it was the silver chain and medallion that Leslie had given me. I didn't realize it had come undone or that I had dropped it. When I picked it up, I saw that the top face of the coin must have sheared off from its base. Although I searched for it all through the night and again when the sun was up, I never found it. Not then or ever again.

EPILOGUE

At Leslie's parole hearing in 1980, then-prosecutor Stephen Kay told the board: "I'd feel better releasing a middle-aged, forty-year-old Leslie Van Houten than a thirty-year-old Leslie Van Houten." Kay further admitted, "I've always said Leslie was the smartest and maybe the most normal of them all." He told the *Los Angeles Times* in 1980 that he didn't think Leslie should be locked up forever, but added it was "too soon to release her now."

Only later, perhaps frightened by the prospect of growing public support for her release, Mr. Kay enlisted members of the families of the victims to petition for keeping Leslie and the other convicts—whose identities have been permanently wedded with Manson's—imprisoned forever. The campaign was eagerly led by the sister of murdered actress Sharon Tate, Debra.

Although Deputy District Attorney Stephen Kay was quoted in 1980 as saying, "She's [Leslie] the only one I could ever see getting parole," later in 2002, he testified that parole for Leslie Van Houten at any time "would be an error in judgment."

A typical flip-flop from what I'd seen of him firsthand in court during the 1977 and 1978 retrials.

Los Angeles Times staff writer Kathleen Hendrix once described Kay in her column as "bandbox neat," with a "wearing nasal voice" and an expression that seldom changes.

After the initial convictions and sentencing in 1971, then-lead prosecutor Vincent Bugliosi originally predicted—based on his sense of the legal norms at the time—that being "the least committed to Manson," Leslie would serve "fifteen to twenty" years tops.

He hadn't a clue yet himself how long and lasting the mythos of Helter Skelter he'd perpetrated would be culturally sustained and assimilated.

Bugliosi admitted to radio/TV host Larry King, "I was impressed by her [Leslie]... She seems to be a model prisoner, and everyone seems to say she is very remorseful for the murders."

Then, without any known bad behavior or further misconduct on her part, years later, he told *The National Enquirer*, "I want Leslie Van Houten to remain in prison for the rest of her life."

Bugliosi subsequently failed with his political ambitions. Twice he ran for Los Angeles County district attorney and twice he failed to win the voters' confidence.

Vincent Bugliosi passed away in June 2015 at the age of eighty from cancer, but his *Helter Skelter* legacy persists. Parole boards and governors have continued to insist—regardless of the laws they espouse to obey and protect—that one reason they cannot give Leslie Van Houten a firm date for release is because of "the enormity of the crime itself."

As Leslie's good friend, Hollywood filmmaker and author John Waters, has said, "It's the only thing she can never change." Waters, who met Leslie while writing a piece for *Rolling Stone* magazine, pointed out that, "No matter how much progress she's made, or how good the psychiatric and conduct reports are, there's nothing she can do to change things." The monstrous fable persists.

In 1982, I received a letter from Martin Bijaux telling me that "Leslie had fallen in love with an ex-convict named Bill Syvin," who had begun corresponding with her while he was in jail. (Martin always was the bearer of such glad tidings, wasn't he?)

Evidently, Mr. Syvin was serving time on a grand theft auto rap and drug-related charges when he started writing to Leslie. Frank Andrews had done the same while he was serving time for armed robbery, starting a romantic pen pal relationship with Leslie a couple of years before I entered the scene.

Once he was released from prison, Leslie arranged for Syvin to visit her at the penitentiary in Frontera. She and Bill were married in a private ceremony at the prison chapel and were permitted conjugal visits. When we were still together, Leslie once described the "married arrangements" at CIW Frontera to me as "kind of like hanging out alone together in a crowded trailer park."

Syvin was later arrested and charged with possession of a stolen Chevy Corvette. A search of his residence also uncovered a set of stolen California Department of Corrections women's uniforms—like those worn by the female guards at Frontera. When Leslie found out about Syvin's apparently wild scheme to arrange her escape, she immediately filed for divorce and never heard from him again.

I earned my Doctor of Philosophy degree in institutional leadership from the University of California at Santa Barbara in

1987. A privilege for which I remain fervently obliged and a vital and lasting experience for which I am forever grateful.

Leslie has also earned her bachelor's and master's degrees from Antioch College while in prison.

Since the late eighties, I've worked as a full-time professor at universities such as the University of Western Ontario in London, Canada; the Kenan-Flagler School of Business at the University of North Carolina at Chapel Hill; Chapman University San Diego; Dalhousie University, Halifax; and Mansfield University of Pennsylvania.

Prior to the Russian invasion of the Republic of Georgia in 2008, I was also full professor and vice president for academic affairs at the Georgian American University in Tbilisi.

On June 4th, 2002, Superior Court Judge Bob Krug issued an order requiring the California parole board to provide evidence to show why Leslie Van Houten should not be paroled. Judge Krug directed the board to explain specifically what she must do to secure her release sooner than later.

The judge stated that *a sentence of life without parole was unauthorized by law.*

"I cannot find any indication where Ms. Van Houten has done anything wrong in prison," Krug decided. "They can't keep using the crime forever and ever. That turns her sentence into life without parole." Therefore, he ordered that, according to the California Penal Code, the parole board had a legal obligation to sanction her release unless a *firm case* could be made that public safety remained in jeopardy.

Subsequently, the Fourth District Court of Appeal reversed Krug's decision in 2004, ruling that he'd applied the "wrong standard."

Krug had claimed the parole board denied Leslie freedom based solely on the nature of the crimes themselves, without weighing her exemplary record of rehabilitation while in prison. But Governor Gray Davis announced he would not sign the release papers, *regardless* of whether the parole board (under pressure from the court), so determined or not.

In 2005, I was very sorry to hear from Martin again. As it ended up being the first in a series of Leslie Van Houten-related news and obituaries.

I learned from Marty that Leslie's mother, Jane, had died in her sleep. Similarly, I was saddened to read sometime after the fact that Leslie's former attorney, Maxwell S. Keith, died in 2012, the same year as Leslie's father, Paul.

Largely unmoved—but not entirely unsympathetic—Martin had also been the one with the news that Manson Family co-conspirator Susan Atkins had died in prison in 2009 from brain cancer. She'd been denied the right to die at home only weeks after she appeared at her final parole hearing.

Steve "Clem" Grogan was the first, and so far (in 2023), the *only* Manson Family member convicted of murder to be released from prison.

Originally found guilty and sentenced to death for first-degree murder, Grogan served fifteen years for his role in the killing of Donald Shea. Judge James Kolts had decided Grogan was "too stupid and too hopped on drugs to decide anything on his own," and that it was really "Manson who decided who lived or died." Steve Grogan eventually drew authorities a map to where Shea's body was buried, and that's the reason he was let go in 1985.

Patrick Sequira—the assistant deputy DA who took over the prosecution against Leslie's parole after Stephen Kay's retirement—argued in one hearing that there was "something suspicious" about Leslie going back to college behind bars to get her master's degree "in philosophy." Sequira raged without shame against the courses Leslie was taking: democracy in education, origins of intelligence in children, and the theory of justice.

"Clearly," Mr. Sequira protested, "the inmate has a fascination with philosophy just as she had a fascination with the concepts that the Manson Family embraced. If there was true educational intent in changing oneself, you'd think it would be beyond studying philosophy."

How she could withstand having someone so clearly at the shallow end of the gene pool determining her fate still astonishes me.

* * *

As early as April 14th, 2016, the California parole board, for the first time, determined that Leslie Van Houten was fit for release. But Governor Jerry Brown twice declined to ratify the board's decision. First in 2016 and again two years later.

Brown wrote in his ruling that, although Ms. Van Houten had demonstrated model behavior during her incarceration, "She failed to explain how she transformed from an upstanding teen to a killer." In other words, she's not being kept in prison for bad behavior but for a bad explanation? What nonsense.

Associated Press reporter Linda Deutsch had quoted Leslie as saying: "I know I did something that is unforgivable, but I can create a world where I make amends. I'm trying to be someone who lives a life for healing rather than destruction."

In her statement to the California parole board in January 2019, Leslie responded to the customary accusation, by some, that she blamed Charles Manson for her actions.

In contrast to the governors who were reading from prepared notes, Leslie responded to the question succinctly and without any concealment, pointing out the plain facts of the matter:

I didn't think up the revolution. It's enmeshed, but I in no way minimize what I did. I went. I participated. I have done what I can to make right on what I did.

There is nothing in that night of murder that I don't take the responsibility for, or all that came before. I was a willing kid that jumped in that truck with Robert Beausoleil. I sat and listened to Catherine Share. I went to the ranch. I became a participant in the group at the ranch. I wanted to be part of the revolution, and the murders that were going to happen to spark it.

There's no part of me that says it was his [Manson's] fault that I did all that. I willingly sat and listened. I let myself go of who I had been, and became the whole one thought, one group, one mind. Just like the other people.

* * *

In 2019, Governor Gavin Newsom issued his decision not to accept the parole board's June 3rd recommendation. He simply restated Governor Brown's presumptive "potential for future violence" clause, which was, in my view, *hearsay.* (Technically, reports of another person's words presumed to account for one's own views without cause are usually disallowed as evidence and termed "hearsay" in a court of law.

A lower court in December declined to review a petition arguing that the California governor violated Van Houten's due process when he reversed the parole board's recommendation again in 2020.

*　*　*

After an unblemished, unfathomable-to-imagine prison incarceration of more than fifty years—and counting—Leslie has already served substantially longer in prison than any Nazi war criminal not sentenced to death at the Nuremberg Tribunals. In fact, Deputy Führer Rudolf Hess spent forty-six years in prison, before he hanged himself in West Berlin's Spandau Prison. And yet, for the fifth time in as many years, the California Supreme Court rejected Leslie's bid for freedom yet again.

Governor Newsom's indifferent rejection was made despite the California state commissioners of the Department of Corrections and Rehabilitation's repeated recommendation that Leslie Van Houten be paroled from prison.

*　*　*

On Wednesday, Feb. 9th, 2022, the court refused to hear Van Houten's appeal of a lower court ruling last December that had denied her petition for a review.

Leslie's opponents keep using the severity and shocking nature of the crimes themselves against her. Gavin Newsom—whose ambition to be catapulted into higher office someday has been publicly noted—continues to parrot his predecessor, Jerry Brown, in denying Leslie's eligibility for parole this way: "While I commend Ms. Van Houten for her efforts at rehabilitation and acknowledge her youth at the time of the crimes, I am concerned about her role in these killings and her potential for future violence. Ms. Van Houten was an eager participant in the killing of the LaBiancas and played a significant role."

Clearly one of those most vehemently opposed to Leslie Van Houten's release at any time is Debra Tate, sister of the murdered actress, Sharon Tate Polanski.

Judging by Ms. Tate's media and parole hearing appearances, it seems of no matter to her that Leslie wasn't involved whatsoever with the planning or killing of her sister.

Naturally, I have sympathy for Debra Tate, her family, and all the other victims' families. I don't believe their suffering should ever be undervalued. These were horrific crimes. But I can't help but suspect there might be some impoverished degree of moral imagination behind the thinking of those who continue to petition for keeping anyone locked away for their entire adult lifetime. Especially someone as young as Leslie Van Houten was at the time of her crime and imprisonment.

Without citing proof, Ms. Tate has, at various times, made these misleading claims in the media:

> *These are serial killers. These would be domestic terrorists if it was today. So, these are very dangerous people.*
> *We just can't give them a chance.*

* * *

Leslie's going back to the penitentiary that pivotal day after Independence Day, 1978 was perhaps in the hands of the fates and the broken justice system of the United States of America all along. For some time, I'd convinced myself that—given the strength of our bond and commitment to one another during those heartening, undaunted times—we could have gotten it right in the end.

Perhaps our mistaken sense that some shifting counterculture tide of social justice had turned in our favor was, in retrospect, a dream based on naïve assumptions as we saw things from our star-crossed perspective. Still, without a doubt, Leslie's involvement in my life and my involvement in hers altered my destiny.

The final verdict determined by others may have decided our fate for us. And yet, meeting Leslie when I did—becoming a significant part of each other's lives before our romance and the trust we once had between us crumbled—significantly changed my life for the better.

Leslie remained, for me, the most credulous, adoring woman I had ever known, and I will always miss her.

AUTHOR'S NOTE

Authorship is far more of a team sport than is often recognized. To this point, I want to express my sincerest thanks to Mia Anna, Dylan Chiaramonte, Cameron Ogden, Joseph White, Nicolas Sinn-White, Donald Levin, Gerry Van Rossum, Albert J. Mills, Robert Timko, George Root, Jean-Christian Knaff, Claude Miceli, Michael Losco, Andy Higgins, Mike Flynn, Vera Dolan, Karri Verno, Cathy Vassallo, Marian Chiaramonte, Mark Federman, Bobby Hebert, Darren Pereira, Clemente Pitoscia, Walter Hrynewich, Korrie Smith, Jerome Cleary, Maggie Morrison, Michelle Kam, Wesley Weber, and Century Stone Book Club founders: Lisa, Samantha, Dena, Alana, Tania, Tehya, Jane, and Mallory.

Much of my story stems from personal diaries, original voice recordings, and letters from Leslie to me and a couple from Charles Manson to Leslie. For the background concerning events—during which time, I was not present—I relied on referred books, journals, newspaper accounts, videos, and other databases for additional information/confirmation.

In matters where my diaries were intangibly incomplete, I've reconstructed certain dialogue and described settings based mostly on my own memory. The aim was to capture the essence of each conversation rather than lose pace transcribing notes verbatim.

My primary aim was to provide a glimpse into a woman who the world has misperceived as some kind of monster when nothing could be further from the truth. I would also like to thank Leslie and her family and friends for accepting me into their homes when they did. Although I recognize that their recollections of the events described in this book may differ from my own records, I have relayed these events to the best of my knowledge.

Peter Chiaramonte, PhD
Toronto, Canada, January 2023

SOURCES

Vincent Bugliosi and Curt Gentry, *Helter Skelter: The True Story of the Manson Murders* (W.W. Norton, 1974).

Ivor Davis, "Will California Ever Release Manson 'Family' Member Leslie Van Houton?" Los Angeles Magazine, August 6th, 2019. lamag.com/citythinkblog/ leslie-van-houten-manson-family.

James Buddy Day, *Hippie Cult Leader: The Last Words of Charles Manson* (Optimum Publishing International, 2019).

Rose Duncan, *Manson's Girl: The True Story of Leslie Van Houten* (Trellis Publishing, Incorporated, 2016).

Karlene Faith, *The Long Prison Journey of Leslie Van Houten: Life Beyond the Cult* (Northeastern u. Press, 2001).

Federal Bureau of Investigation Files. Freedom of Information.

Steven Gaines, *Heroes & Villains: The True Story of the Beach Boys* (Da Capo Press,1995).

John Gilmore and Ron Kenner, *Manson: The Unholy Trail of Charlie and the Family*, (originally published as *The Garbage People*, 1971; Amok Books, 2nd edition, 2000).

Jeff Guinn, *Manson: The Life and Times of Charles Manson* (Simon & Schuster, 2013).

H. Allegra Lansing, *The Manson Family: More to the Story* (Independently Published, 2019).

Tom O'Neill, with Dan Piepenbring, *CHAOS: Charles Manson, the CIA, and the Secret History of the Sixties* (Back Bay Books, 2020).

Caitlin Rother and Lis Wiehl, *Hunting Charles Manson: The Quest for Justice in the Days of Helter Skelter* (Thomas Nelson, 2018).

Ed Sanders, *The Family* (Da Capo Press, 2002).

Christopher Sandford, *Polanski* (Arrow, 2009).

Alisa Statman and Brie Tate, *Restless Souls: The Sharon Tate Family's Account of Stardom, the Manson Murders, and a Crusade for Justice* (HarperCollins, 2012).

Jon Stebbins, *Dennis Wilson: The Real Beach Boy* (ECW Press, 2000).

John Waters, *Role Models* (Farrar, Straus, Giroux, 2010).

Tex Watson (as told to Chaplain Ray), *Will You Die for Me?* (Cross Roads Publications, 1978).

Nigel Poor and Earlonne Woods: *Podcast with Leslie Van Houten: Ear Hustle Episode 60*: "Home for Me is Really a Memory." Air Date: June 9, 2021

LOS ANGELES TIMES ARTICLES
December 1976–February 1979

"New Trial for Manson 'Family Member' Assured," December 10, 1976; January 20, 1977.

"Jury Told of Manson Hold on 'Family'; Programmed Members into 'Zombies,'" April 27, 1977; May 6, 1977.

"Miss Van Houten Tells Role in Slaying," May 13, 1977; May 24, 1977; May 26, 1977; May 27, 1977; June 9, 1977.

"Change in Clan's Mood Described—turned 'Murderous,'" June 10, 1977; June 28, 1977; June 29, 1977; July 8, 1977; July 25, 1977; Aug 5, 1977; Sept 1, 1977; Oct 20, 1977.

"Leslie Van Houten Freed on $200,000 Bail," Dec 28, 1977; "Third Trial Gets Underway," Feb. 22, 1978.

"Prosecutor Calls Her a 'Bright Girl,' Defense Says She Was 'Not Aware,'" April 4, 1978.

"'Don't Be Gullible,' Van Houten Jurors Told," June 13, 1978; June 23, 1978; July 5, 1978.

"Miss Van Houten Convicted Again for Two Slayings," July 6, 1978; July 22, 1978.

"Leslie Van Houten Refused Parole for Year at Least," February 1, 1979.

www.ingramcontent.com/pod-product-compliance
Lightning Source LLC
Chambersburg PA
CBHW051938090426
42741CB00008B/1186